Learning beyond Fifteen

TEN YEARS AFTER PISA

OECD

This work is published on the responsibility of the Secretary-General of the OECD. The opinions expressed and arguments employed herein do not necessarily reflect the official views of the Organisation or of the governments of its member countries.

This document and any map included herein are without prejudice to the status of or sovereignty over any territory, to the delimitation of international frontiers and boundaries and to the name of any territory, city or area.

Please cite this publication as:
OECD (2012), *Learning beyond Fifteen: Ten Years after PISA*, OECD Publishing.
http://dx.doi.org/10.1787/9789264172104-en

ISBN 978-92-64-17204-3 (print)
ISBN 978-92-64-17210-4 (PDF)

Photo credits:
Getty Images © Ariel Skelley
Getty Images © Geostock
Getty Images © Jack Hollingsworth
Stocklib Image Bank © Yuri Arcurs

Corrigenda to OECD publications may be found on line at: *www.oecd.org/publishing/corrigenda*.
© OECD 2012

You can copy, download or print OECD content for your own use, and you can include excerpts from OECD publications, databases and multimedia products in your own documents, presentations, blogs, websites and teaching materials, provided that suitable acknowledgement of OECD as source and copyright owner is given. All requests for public or commercial use and translation rights should be submitted to *rights@oecd.org*. Requests for permission to photocopy portions of this material for public or commercial use shall be addressed directly to the Copyright Clearance Center (CCC) at *info@copyright.com* or the Centre français d'exploitation du droit de copie (CFC) at *contact@cfcopies.com*.

Foreword

With the increasing importance of skills for economic and social prosperity, direct measures of human capital are necessary to understand how various skills develop over time, and how they contribute to social and economic growth. Thus, PISA (the Programme for International Student Assessment) and PIAAC (the Programme for the International Assessment of Adult Competencies), two of the most comprehensive OECD international assessments of skills, along with other national and regional assessments, are crucial for taking stock of a nation's human capital and for aligning policy goals to the needs of society. International comparisons provide a good indication of progress achieved and the challenges ahead.

While national and regional evidence continues to be important for management and accountability, it has become increasingly critical for countries to be able to benchmark their measures of human capital internationally for competitiveness and productivity. This evidence helps to identify strengths and weaknesses and to set standards and targets, so that policy makers can make strategic investments to match the pace of progress with that of the rest of the world. Furthermore, in an environment of fiscal restraint, it is more important than ever to ensure that investments in education and training are productive and efficient. Such investments will have greater success if decisions are based on evidence that identifies the policy-sensitive factors that promote skills development over the stages of a life. The demands on data and research to fill these needs are not likely to diminish in the future.

The focus of this report is on the development of reading proficiency during the transition from adolescence to early adulthood. The span of time between the ages of 15 and 24 is a critical period of development for young people. Once compulsory education is completed, individual decisions about post-secondary education, employment and other life choices have to be made, with major consequences for future learning and employment outcomes. A good foundation in reading proficiency facilitates success in specialised education during higher education or during job-related training. Since reading proficiency is not the goal of such specialised or professional learning, reading skills may begin to atrophy. So both learning gains and losses need to be considered as human capital is developed.

The cumulative model of reading development, which is widely used, assumes that once something has been learned it will be retained and applied throughout life. However, evidence now suggests that a more dynamic model of learning, which takes into account both gains and losses, more accurately reflects reality. To broaden knowledge about the acquisition of skills, factors that affect both gains and losses at each stage of life needs to be gathered from longitudinal data and analyses.

Moving forward, new and better measures of human capital will be needed to chart the role of skills in economic growth and social well-being at both the individual and national levels. Countries that have invested in PISA are exploring ways to improve the performance of their education systems to prepare their citizens for adult roles in society. Canada's investments in PISA, as well as in longitudinal data and reassessment of reading proficiency, provide insights into the importance of individual reading proficiency and later outcomes, such as educational attainment, further learning, employment and earnings. This report is thus a vital contribution to the understanding of learning gains between the ages of 15 and 24 and their impact on such outcomes, and provides a basis for evidence-based policy and strategic investments by the community of countries participating in PISA.

The report is the product of a collaborative effort between the countries participating in PISA, the experts and institutions working within the framework of the PISA Consortium, the OECD, and Human Resources and Skills Development Canada (HRSDC). The production of the report was funded by a contribution from the government of Canada. The report was drafted by Fernando Cartwright, Darren King, Satya Brink, and Pablo Zoido. Tamara Knighton, from Statistics Canada, provided analytical support, while Patrick Bussière and Tomasz Gluszynski provided guidance and input for the report from HRSDC and Pablo Zoido from the OECD Secretariat. Marilyn Achiron edited the report.

FOREWORD

Elizabeth Del Bourgo, Juliet Evans, Giannina Rech and Elisabeth Villoutreix provided editorial and administrative input for the report. Fung Kwan Tam designed the publication. The development of the report was steered by the PISA Governing Board, which is chaired by Lorna Bertrand (United Kingdom). The report is published on the responsibility of the Secretary-General of the OECD.

Lorna Bertrand
Chair of the PISA Governing Board

Barbara Ischinger
Director for Education, OECD

David McGovern
Senior Assistant Deputy Minister
Strategic Policy and Research,
Human Resources and
Skills Development Canada

Table of Contents

EXECUTIVE SUMMARY 9

CHAPTER 1 INTRODUCTION 13
PISA and the PISA re-assessment 14
A dynamic view of learning 14
Patterns of skills development 15
Measurement of learning gains and losses 15
The importance of good reading proficiency 16
Value of longitudinal analysis for decision making 16
International policy lessons 17

CHAPTER 2 PISA-15, YITS, PISA-24, AND THE CANADIAN CONTEXT 19
The Programme for International Student Assessment (PISA): An overview 20
 ▪ Reading proficiency in PISA-15 20
 ▪ Canada's administration of PISA-15 22
Youth in Transition (YITS): An overview 22
 ▪ Content in the six cycles 22
The PISA re-assessment (PISA-24) 23
 ▪ Test design 23
 ▪ Data quality and analytical power 24
 ▪ Regression toward the mean 25
 ▪ Overview of Canada and its education systems 26
Chapter summary and conclusions 28

CHAPTER 3 READING PROFICIENCY OF CANADIAN YOUTH AT AGES 15 AND 24 29
An assessment of reading skills among 24-year-olds and how they relate to skills acquired by the age of 15 30
Reading proficiency at ages 15 and 24 30
Demographic characteristics and reading proficiency gains between the ages of 15 and 24 31
 ▪ Gender 31
 ▪ Immigrant background 32
 ▪ Family socio-economic background 33
 ▪ Language 35
 ▪ Urban and rural schools 36
Differences in reading proficiency by education and labour-market pathways, ages 15 and 24 37
 ▪ Educational attainment at age 24 37
 ▪ Education pathways 38
 ▪ Professional experience at age 24 39
Chapter summary and conclusions 39

TABLE OF CONTENTS

CHAPTER 4 GROWTH IN READING PROFICIENCY OVER TIME 43
How do young people's reading skills evolve after compulsory education? 44
Grade progression and growth in reading skills 44
Dynamic learning in the context of the PISA reading framework 46
- Improvements in performance across question types in the PISA reading framework 47
- Question difficulty and improvements in performance 48

Chapter summary and conclusions 49
Examples of PISA reading units 50

CHAPTER 5 PROFICIENCY GROWTH BEFORE AND AFTER AGE 15 73
Skills growth in PISA-24 74
Skills growth and initial reading proficiency at age 15 74
- The observed relationship between skills at age 15 and skills growth 74
- Adjusting for initial skills with school marks 76

A conceptual model of improvement in reading proficiency 76
Positive learning environments before and after age 15 77
- Supportive family characteristics and individual approaches to learning 78
- Supportive school learning environments 80

Proficiency growth outside the classroom 84
What is the net effect of positive early environments? 84
Chapter summary and conclusions 85

CHAPTER 6 THE EFFECT OF EDUCATION AND WORK PATHWAYS ON READING PROFICIENCY 87
Life choices and the acquisition of skills 88
Improvements in reading proficiency, educational attainment and pathways 88
- Educational attainment and growth in reading skills 88
- Educational pathways and growth in reading skills 88

Educational attainment, work experience, and improvements in reading proficiency 90
Educational attainment, time spent in education and the acquisition of skills 91
Learning gains and demographic transitions 92
- Geographic mobility and growth in reading skills 92
- Relationship choices and growth in reading skills 93

Chapter summary and conclusions 93

CONCLUSION 97

References 99

ANNEX A TECHNICAL ANNEX 101

ANNEX B TABLES OF RESULTS 109

TABLE OF CONTENTS

BOXES

Box 2.1   Key features of PISA-15 in Canada..22
Box 2.2   Highlights of Canada's education systems...28

Box 4.1   Perceived and actual reading loss..49

Box 5.1   Dichotomy between phase one and phase two growth..83

Box A.1   The consequences of higher measurement error..105

FIGURES

Figure 2.1   PISA-15: What the proficiency levels measure..21
Figure 2.2   Overview of data collection in Canada: PISA-15, YITS and PISA-24..22
Figure 2.3   PISA-24 questions in the PISA reading framework..23
Figure 2.4   Statistical properties of PISA-24 test questions..24
Figure 2.5   Overview of Canada's education systems...27

Figure 3.1   Comparison of distribution of reading skills, PISA-15 and PISA-24..31
Figure 3.2   Reading performance in PISA-15 and PISA-24, by gender..32
Figure 3.3   Comparison of the distribution of young men's and women's reading skills, PISA-15 and PISA-24...33
Figure 3.4   Reading performance in PISA-15 and PISA-24, by country of birth..34
Figure 3.5   Reading performance in PISA-15 and PISA-24, by socio-economic background................................34
Figure 3.6   Comparison of the distribution of reading skills in PISA-15 and PISA-24, by test language..............36
Figure 3.7   Comparison of reading performance in PISA-15 and PISA-24, by educational attainment at age 24...37
Figure 3.8   Comparison of reading performance in PISA-15 and PISA-24, by educational pathways..................38
Figure 3.9   Comparison of reading performance in PISA-15 and PISA-24, by professional experience at age 24...39

Figure 4.1   Relative grade level and average reading proficiency at age 15..45
Figure 4.2   Comparison of reading performance in PISA-15 and PISA-24, by relative grade at age 15...............45
Figure 4.3   Improvements between PISA-15 and PISA-24, by question type within the PISA reading framework...47
Figure 4.4   BRUSHING YOUR TEETH..51
Figure 4.5   MOBILE PHONE SAFETY...54
Figure 4.6   BALLOON..58
Figure 4.7   BLOOD DONATION...62
Figure 4.8   MISER..64
Figure 4.9   THE PLAY'S THE THING...67
Figure 4.10 TELECOMMUTING..70

Figure 5.1   Observed relationship between reading skills at age 15 and growth in reading skills between the ages of 15 and 24.....74
Figure 5.2   Development of reading skills by PISA proficiency levels and school marks at age 15......................75
Figure 5.3   Growth phases in reading proficiency and their determinants...77
Figure 5.4   Relationship between supportive family characteristics and individual approaches to learning, reading performance at age 15, and improvement in reading skills between the ages of 15 and 24...78
Figure 5.5   Relationship between supportive school learning environments, reading performance at age 15, and improvement in reading skills between the ages of 15 and 24...80
Figure 5.6   Relationship between correlations with PISA questionnaire indices and reading performance at age 15 and at age 24....83
Figure 5.7   Improvements in reading skills between the ages of 15 and 24, by individual and family-related factors associated with skills at age 15..85
Figure 5.8   Improvements in reading skills between the ages of 15 and 24, by school-related factors associated with skills at age 15...85

Figure 6.1   Growth in reading skills between the ages of 15 and 24, by educational attainment at age 24.........89
Figure 6.2   Growth in reading skills between the ages of 15 and 24, by educational pathway............................89
Figure 6.3   Growth in reading skills between the ages of 15 and 24, by educational attainment and professional pathways at age 24...90

TABLE OF CONTENTS

Figure 6.4	Improvements in reading proficiency, by educational attainment and years spent in formal education	91
Figure 6.5	Growth in reading skills between the ages of 15 and 24, by school location at age 15 and location at age 24	92
Figure A.1	Measurement variance, total variance, and scale reliability for reading outcomes based on PISA-15	104
Figure A.2	Illustration of attenuation of correlation due to measurement error using simulated data based on perfectly correlated variables and reliabiltiies of reading outcomes	105
Figure A.3	Expected regression to the mean for PISA proficiency levels for Canadian PISA-15 participants based on retest reliability of 0.67	106
Figure A.4	Expected regression to the mean for PISA proficiency levels under uniform change assumptions compared to observed differences for Canadian PISA-15 participants	106

TABLES

Table 2.1	Item classification in the PISA reading framework, PISA-24 assessment questions and PISA-15 link items	110
Table 3.1	Distribution of reading skills, PISA-15 and PISA-24, Canadian participants age 15 in 2000	110
Table 3.2	Comparison of reading performance at age 15 and age 24 by various demographic groups, Canadian participants age 15 in 2000	111
Table 3.3	Distribution of reading skills by gender, PISA-15 and PISA-24, Canadian participants age 15 in 2000	111
Table 3.4	Distribution of reading skills by assessment language, PISA-15 and PISA-24, Canadian participants age 15 in 2000	112
Table 3.5	Comparison of reading performance at age 15 and age 24 by educational attainment, pathways and work experience at age 24, Canadian participants age 15 in 2000	112
Table 4.1	School grade and reading proficiency, Canadian participants age 15 in 2000	113
Table 4.2	Item difficulty and average differences in item-correct scores between PISA-15 and PISA-24 by item type in the PISA reading framework, and individual characteristics at age 24, Canadian participants age 15 in 2000	113
Table 5.1	Growth in reading skills by alternate measures of initial status, PISA-15 and PISA-24, Canadian participants age 15 in 2000	114
Table 5.2	Relationship between correlations with PISA questionnaire indices and reading performance at ages 15 and 24, Canadian participants age 15 in 2000	114
Table 5.3	Standardised multiple regression coefficients of factors associated with reading performance at ages 15 and 24, Canadian participants age 15 in 2000	115
Table 5.4	Reading skills at ages 15 and 24 and skills growth, by individual factors at age 15, Canadian participants age 15 in 2000	116
Table 6.1	Development of reading skills by educational attainment and education-to-work pathways at ages 15 and 24, Canadian participants age 15 in 2000	116
Table 6.2	Development of reading skills by educational attainment and time spent in formal education, PISA-15 and PISA-24, Canadian participants age 15 in 2000	117
Table 6.3	Skills growth regressions, joint model	117
Table 6.4	Development of reading skills by rural/urban mobility status, PISA-15 and PISA-24, Canadian participants age 15 in 2000	117
Table 6.5	Development of reading skills by initial language proficiency and later living arrangements, PISA-15 and PISA-24, Canadian participants age 15 in 2000	118
Table 6.6	Development of reading skills by living arrangements and educational attainment, PISA-15 and PISA-24, Canadian participants age 15 in 2000	118

This book has... StatLinks
A service that delivers Excel® files from the printed page!

Look for the *StatLinks* at the bottom left-hand corner of the tables or graphs in this book.
To download the matching Excel® spreadsheet, just type the link into your Internet browser, starting with the *http://dx.doi.org* prefix.
If you're reading the PDF e-book edition, and your PC is connected to the Internet, simply click on the link. You'll find *StatLinks* appearing in more OECD books.

Executive Summary

The growing need for internationally comparable evidence on student performance in compulsory education prompted over 70 governments to invest in the PISA assessment in 2009. In addition, six countries–Australia, Canada, the Czech Republic, Denmark, Switzerland and Uruguay–have chosen to use the PISA assessment as a starting point for a longitudinal survey of youth.

Using the results from longitudinal data provides a dynamic view of learning gains and losses. This report is based on a wealth of data that Canada collected through a PISA assessment of 15-year-olds in the year 2000 (hereafter PISA-15), a longitudinal survey (YITS), and a re-assessment of skills at age 24 (hereafter PISA-24) in 2009. It offers valuable insights on how reading skills are developed, maintained and lost between the ages of 15 and 24.

Reading proficiency among Canadian youth improved substantially between the ages of 15 and 24.

Data obtained from PISA-15 and the follow-up assessment PISA-24 show significant improvements in reading skills across the entire population of young people. On average, Canadian youth gained 57 score points in the PISA reading scale between the ages of 15 and 24 - the equivalent of roughly one school year in Canada - improving from 541 to 598 score points, on average. The variation in reading proficiency narrowed from 92 score points in 2000 to 78 score points in 2009.

As a result, the proportion of young people with a score above proficiency Level 3 in PISA increased from 79% at age 15 to 93% at age 24. Level 3 is a key measure of success in PISA. Individuals proficient at this level are adept at "locating multiple pieces of information, making links between different parts of a text, and relating it to familiar everyday knowledge". Since the odds of enrolling in higher education is highest among individuals at these levels, learning gains between the ages of 15 and 24 increased the pool of students who could succeed at post-secondary education to over 90%.

The number of young people with poor reading proficiency dropped significantly between the ages of 15 and 24, which suggests impressive learning gains, particularly among the lowest performing students. Nevertheless, 7% of Canadian 24-year-olds still fail to attain Level 3, and for these adults general literacy remains a priority. These findings highlight the need for policy makers to continue focusing on reading skills beyond compulsory education and into adulthood.

Widespread gains in reading proficiency resulted in reading skills convergence.

PISA-24 shows that the strongest predictor of reading proficiency at age 24 is, in fact, reading proficiency at age 15. While not surprising, this is an important result. Clearly individual characteristics, such as innate ability, play a role. Beyond these factors, this result provides evidence of the importance of the investments governments make in compulsory education, and the efforts parents and teachers make in helping their children and students learn. It also strengthens the rational for PISA's focus on measuring skills at age 15.

However, reading proficiency at age 15 is negatively related to the rate of improvement in reading proficiency. The nature of PISA-24 is such that those who score exceptionally well in PISA-15 are likely to score lower in PISA-24 than they did in PISA-15. The opposite is true among those who scored exceptionally low in PISA-15; they are likely to score higher

EXECUTIVE SUMMARY

in PISA-24 than they did in PISA-15. Therefore, one needs to be cautious about the actual strength of the relationship between reading skills at age 15 and growth in reading skills between age 15 and 24 as measured by PISA-15 and 24. However, the analysis consistently shows a gradual movement towards skills convergence, rather than a "fanning-out" of the distribution of skills across young people. By age 24, those with lower proficiency scores at age 15 had improved substantially, though they had not completely caught up with those who performed well at 15, who improved more slowly. After leaving compulsory education, the group of young people who had performed poorly when they were 15 were later in learning environments that helped narrow the performance gap between the two groups. These findings relate to reading skills only. In fact, it is possible that students who showed strong reading skills at age 15 have been able to build on this by developing other competencies that are not measured here more effectively than students who struggled with basic reading skills at that age.

However, most reading performance gaps evident at age 15 persisted at age 24.

Young men, Francophones, rural students, and those from more socio-economically disadvantaged backgrounds were able to narrow the gap in reading performance that was evident at age 15. While the actual extent of this catching up is hard to measure, the general trend is evident in the data. Even after relatively faster growth in reading skills, however, there remained large differences in scores related to these characteristics at age 24. Where participants do not converge in reading proficiency, the persistent gaps appear to be partly the consequence of explicit student behaviours between the ages of 15 and 24, for example decisions on whether to continue into further education, rather than demographic characteristics.

In general, greater growth in reading skills was observed among those who had performed poorly when they were 15, but they were not able to fully catch up with their peers. For example, girls outscored boys in PISA-15 by an average of 32 points; by 2009, that gap had narrowed to 18 points. Socio-economically advantaged students outscored their disadvantaged peers by more than 65 score points in PISA-15; by 2009 that gap had narrowed to 50 score points. However, by age 24, the average performance of young people who were considered socio-economically disadvantaged at age 15 (568 score points in PISA-24) remained below the average performance of socio-economically advantaged students nine years earlier (572 score points in PISA-15). These groups therefore merit the continued attention of policy makers.

Those with immigrant backgrounds performed as well as native-born youth at age 24.

Students with an immigrant background, though initially disadvantaged, show that it is possible to completely catch up, even in a country with a high percentage of immigrants, such as Canada. By the age of 24, young people with an immigrant background fully bridged the gap in reading performance that separated them from 15-year-olds born in Canada. Students born outside of Canada scored an average of 524 points in PISA-15, while those born in Canada averaged 545 points. In PISA-24, all participants averaged around 600 points, whether they were born in Canada or not. In addition to highlighting the value of integration, these results demonstrate that the right policies for vulnerable populations can return a large benefit to a country's human capital. Canada provides an example of successful education policies towards foreign-born students after completion of compulsory education, and also before. The performance gap in PISA between domestic and foreign-born students is particularly narrow in Canada both as a result of education and immigration policies.

Skills development into early adulthood is shaped by frequent practice and use of skills.

Recent research shows that a key factor in the dynamic process of learning is the use of reading in daily life. Overall, the patterns of improvements in reading proficiency are related to the regular use of reading skills. While improvements in proficiency were widespread between the ages of 15 and 24, the results analysed here suggest that reading proficiency among young adults may already be in decline. For example, PISA-15 and PISA-24 show that approximately 59 score points were gained annually while students remained in formal education, but that the level of reading proficiency at age 24 was lower than that estimated for students at the completion of grade 12. This suggests that the acquisition of skills may not continue at the same annual rate as measured in 2000 when students were 15 and still in compulsory education.

Research, and to some extent the evidence in this report, confirms the importance of reading activities to maintain and ensure high levels of proficiency into adulthood, and supports earlier evidence from the International Adult Literacy Survey that showed that a decline in skills may begin quite early in adult life.

EXECUTIVE SUMMARY

Substantial growth in reading skills is apparent in each of the main dimensions considered in the PISA reading framework (context, text structure and reading process), but the rate of change in proficiency is not uniform across these key dimensions. For example, larger gains were made on reading questions related to personal, rather than educational, contexts, as most people between the ages of 15 and 24 would continue reading more in the former context.

Educational attainment is strongly related to improvements in reading proficiency.

Participation in some form of formal post-secondary education is consistently and substantially related to growth in reading skills between the ages of 15 and 24. For example, educational attainment is closely related to reading skills at age 15 and 24. University graduates at age 24 had an average score of 652 points in PISA-24. In contrast, those with only high school attainment scored, on average, nearly 100 points lower, at 564 points. When those with university-level attainment were 15, they averaged 596 points on PISA, substantially above the scores attained nine years later by those whose highest educational attainment was high school. This underscores the importance of ensuring high reading proficiency by the end of compulsory education.

Completing a post-secondary degree by the age of 24 is also strongly related to skills growth even after accounting for skills at age 15, socio-economic background and other individual characteristics. Those with only a high school diploma at age 24 or those with substantial work experience (more than three years) by age 24 tended to attain lower scores at age 24 than those with higher educational attainment or less substantial work experience. Differences in skills development in a broad sense will ultimately depend on the kinds of skills used and practiced in each field or industry, a topic worth further analysis.

A sense of ownership is key for proficiency improvements, particularly among low-achievers.

Continued improvement in reading proficiency after age 15 is not necessarily associated with the same factors that were associated with reading proficiency at age 15. The degree of control one feels one has over one's life, an individual's sense of mastery, is one of the strongest factors related to improvements in reading skills after the age of 15. In contrast, the sense of mastery was negatively related to skills at age 15. From childhood to age 15, the strongest influences on reading proficiency are from parents and the home learning environment, and from teachers and the school learning environment. As individuals transition into adulthood, however, the emphasis shifts to the choices young people make about post-secondary education and the extent to which they practice their reading skills in employment and leisure.

Greater autonomy and capacity to make individual life choices is generally related to greater improvements in reading performance, particularly when combined with participation in post-secondary education. Those individuals who entered the labour market soon after compulsory education tended to be poor-performing students at age 15 and their reading proficiency at age 24 remained poor; in fact, the rate of their skills growth was relatively modest.

But not all life transitions were associated with improvements in reading skills. Young people who had the advantage of supportive learning environments up to the age of 15 showed relatively slower improvements in reading proficiency as they made the transition to independence. In contrast, those youth who did not thrive in their early learning environments made greater improvements if they changed those environments in some way, for example, if they moved out of their parents' home.

Independence and self-efficacy allow individuals who may be disadvantaged during their younger years to find environments that foster greater reading proficiency later on. For example, young people who performed poorly at age 15, as measured by reading marks in school, showed greater improvements between the ages of 15 and 24 if they made a change in their life circumstances, such as changing the status of a relationship (e.g. from single to married) or moving out of their parents' home.

Second-chance programmes and system flexibility can help young people who have not had the advantages of supportive learning environments earlier in their lives.

While it is unlikely that low-achievers will be able to completely make up for initial disadvantage, this study has identified several mechanisms that mitigate such disadvantage.

Across all levels of educational attainment, improvement in reading proficiency is strongly related to time spent in the education system. For instance, young people who never completed a programme above high school, but who spent

EXECUTIVE SUMMARY

four or more years in school (e.g. on incomplete degrees or diplomas at the post-secondary level) between the ages of 15 and 24, showed improvements in skills that were similar to or greater than (70 score points or more) those observed among young people who spent four or more years in education after high school and completed a university degree (60 score points or more).

High proficiency at early ages prepares young people for further education and creates opportunities for additional studies that may not be as readily available to low-achievers. While the most common and direct path through secondary and university-level education appears to maximise improvements in reading proficiency, not everyone takes that route. The evidence in this report shows that given the opportunity, many low-achievers found ways to improve their proficiency in the years following compulsory education. While not all of them catch up with the top performers, the skills they acquire later help them to fully participate in society.

Introduction

The development of reading proficiency is a dynamic process that involves gains and losses. Whereas gains at early ages depend on initial reading proficiency, gains and losses at later ages are affected by whether or not individuals engage in activities to maintain their skills. The value of such research for addressing internationally shared policy concerns is high. This chapter introduces the key concepts examined in this report.

INTRODUCTION

PISA AND THE PISA RE-ASSESSMENT

The Programme for International Student Assessment (PISA) is a valuable source of information about the skills and competencies of youth. Data from the assessment describe the competencies of 15-year-olds (hereafter PISA-15) and examine how those skills are distributed throughout this population and in various sub-populations.

However, policy makers are also interested in knowing how the competencies developed by the age of 15 will affect students' life trajectories, particularly their educational attainment, transition into the labour market, and the continuation of skills development. PISA, alone, cannot answer these questions.

Thus, when Canada participated in the first implementation of PISA in 2000, it used the assessment as the starting point for a longitudinal study of young people. In addition to the assessment of reading, mathematics and science, the 15-year-old students in Canada and their parents also completed a detailed questionnaire, called the Youth in Transition Survey (YITS). At two-year intervals after the initial assessment and interview, the original PISA-15 respondents were contacted and asked to provide information on their activities related to education and employment, their life choices, and their attitudes. These data have given rise to a rich body of research related to a wide variety of public policy issues.

The direct measures of student skills in PISA helps to explain longitudinal patterns in the YITS data because proficiency in reading, mathematics, and science is associated with the degree of success of many transitions during a young person's life. An analysis of the role of competencies in shaping the trajectories of young people can be found in *Pathways to Success: How Knowledge and Skills at Age 15 Shape Future Lives in Canada* (OECD, 2010a).

This report further explores the transition from adolescent to adult by examining gains in reading competency between the ages of 15 and 24. The analysis uses the PISA-YITS data as well as a PISA re-assessment at the age of 24 (hereafter PISA-24), a selection of PISA questions that were administered in 2009 to a subset of the original PISA-15 students in Canada. The result is a longitudinal survey of youth that begins with a reading assessment at age 15, ends 9 years later with a reading re-assessment at age 24, and contains a detailed accounting of their education and employment pathways in the intervening years.

The purpose of this report is to examine how reading proficiency has progressed in the years following the PISA assessment. These years, from age 15 to 24, contain many key transitions in the lives of young people, including completing compulsory education, progressing to post-secondary programmes, and entering into the labour force. Improvements in reading proficiency measured at age 24 in relations to the students' initial proficiency level at age 15, some of these students' life choices, and other factors were analysed.

The report investigates the magnitude of learning gains or losses following compulsory education, and how these gains and losses vary across gender and immigration status, and other demographic characteristics. It also examines whether competencies and learning habits at age 15 are related to later skills acquisition, and the characteristics or factors associated with proficiency gains between the ages of 15 and 24.

Are early disadvantages persistent? Are there policy interventions that might help low achievers improve more over time? The report also studies the relationship between post-secondary education and improvements in reading proficiency, and how work experience and other life transitions affect learning gains.

A DYNAMIC VIEW OF LEARNING

The notion that knowledge and skills can be gained and lost has long been accepted by educationists, but attempts to measure those gains and losses have been largely unsuccessful. Education experts engaged in curriculum development are keen to determine how learning losses and gains are related to future economic and social outcomes, for both the individual and society. To do so, they need to understand the dynamics of skills acquisition well beyond the period of compulsory education.

The concept of learning gains and losses takes a dynamic view of learning rather than a cumulative view. In other words, it cannot be assumed that once something has been learned it will be retained. While new learning may rely on a foundation of existing skills and abilities, these existing skills must be maintained through continuous use or they may be lost.

Skills development can be characterised by both gains and losses, depending on the age and the experiences of the individuals. Previous research suggests that skills development actually peaks between the ages of 25 and 35 (Desjardin, et al., 2005). A shortcoming of this study and many other similar studies is that they rely on age differences

INTRODUCTION

drawn from a cross-sectional survey. As a result, it is difficult to determine if differences in age-related changes between young adults who had embarked on various educational or life trajectories were the result of variations in initial reading proficiency between groups or of other factors that intervened along these trajectories.

Very little is known about skills development between the end of compulsory education and the early years of a work career. Canada decided to longitudinally follow 15-year-olds who participated in PISA in 2000 and to re-test them at age 24 in an effort to fill this gap in knowledge.

PATTERNS OF SKILLS DEVELOPMENT

Early models examining the development of skills suggest that the rate at which students acquire skills is affected by their existing communications skills, such as vocabulary and verbal reasoning (Dreyfus and Dreyfus, 1986). The hypothesis in these early models is that the higher the level of existing skills, the better students are able to understand new material and draw inferences from texts. According to these models, differences between high- and low-performers as age increases would tend to persist. This is in line with the limited longitudinal evidence that does exist (e.g. Wylie and Hodgen, 2007; 2011; Bynner and Parsons, 2009). Less is known empirically, however, about whether or not the differences diverge or converge over time. Catell's (1987) investment theory, for example, suggests a divergence or "fan spread" pattern, i.e., the stronger get stronger, and the weaker get weaker over time. Substantial research shows that gaps in performance are persistent, but also that a deterministic view of skills development is misguided (Beswick, et al., 2008). It might be possible that convergence is possible in critical skills-formation periods, such as during adolescence. During this period, skills of all kinds are thought to increase up until at least the early 20s. Beyond this period, however, certain types of skills may begin to decline, particularly those relating to cognitive mechanics, such as attention capacity, processing speed, reasoning, working memory and spatial ability (see Catell, 1971). The rate of decline is thought to be subject to levels of mental, physical and social activity which are, among other things, a function of lifestyles and the type of occupations people enter (for a recent review, see Desjardins and Warnke, 2012). Accordingly, convergence seems more likely during critical skills-formation periods, when all kinds of skills are being acquired, but then divergence may be more likely as adults enter different pathways that influence skills formation.

Although skills may be developed through education, they can also decline rapidly through disuse. The "summer slide", whereby students' skills deteriorate over the course of the summer break, first identified by Heyns (1978), provides an example. Moreover, the rate of skills decline varies greatly depending on the number and type of organised activities available to students. Thus the summer period has often led to increasing inequality in competencies between socio-economic groups that are presented with different opportunities for learning during the months when school is not in session (Cooper, et al., 1996). Some evidence suggests that the summer decline has lasting consequences associated with lower educational attainment for socio-economically disadvantaged students (Alexander, et al., 2007).

As gains in skills continue throughout adolescence and into adulthood, a variety of factors confound the relationship between initial reading proficiency and its rate of growth. Evidence about changes in reading skills in the adult population in Canada, taken from the Adult Literacy and Lifeskills survey (ALLS), suggests that reading skills are characterised more by decline than growth after age 25, with greater loss among those with lower initial proficiency (Desjardin, et al., 2005). The transition from reading skills growth to decline suggests a corresponding shift from the importance of initial proficiency to ongoing maintenance through practice.

MEASUREMENT OF LEARNING GAINS AND LOSSES

Many countries have instituted national assessments during compulsory education to monitor progress and to benchmark their progress with other systems. In Canada, the Pan-Canadian Assessment Program reports on the assessment of 13-year-olds in reading, mathematics and science in the ten provinces so that competencies at that age can be compared across provinces (Council of Ministers of Education, Canada (CMEC) 2008). In addition, there are a number of standardised student tests administered by individual provinces. Comparisons of results between students and systems can shed light on policy-sensitive factors that are associated with higher proficiency. However, these assessments are not designed to show how proficiency changes over the course of an individual's life. Data from PISA and the re-assessment are uniquely placed to answer those questions.

Using PISA to measure skills gains and losses has several advantages. First, PISA is an assessment of reading proficiency that is not tied to curricula, but is generally representative of essential life competencies. In addition, the measure of competencies in PISA is internationally comparable. Second, when PISA was implemented in Canada, it was accompanied by a detailed survey of students, parents and school principals, and was linked to a longitudinal survey of the students.

INTRODUCTION

This data record is crucial for explaining the observed proficiency gains over time. Third, PISA assesses proficiency at the age of 15, when students are nearing the end of compulsory education. The nine years between assessments is an extremely important period for skills development.

Measuring learning gains over such a long time period presents a challenge for research design. It requires a sustained investment to pay for longitudinal surveys and expensive individual assessments for a relatively large sample of youth.

Because there are now over 70 countries participating in PISA, the value of sharing investments in PISA-related research among them is multiplied. A key policy question underpinning investments in compulsory education: How do competencies gained during compulsory education relate to future learning gains and losses?

The value of such investments in data will be evident from the analysis in this report and in future research using these data. There are potentially three sets of benefits: The first are the results of the analyses themselves. They enable researchers to address such policy issues as the durability of early learning advantages, the value of skills for preparing youth for transitions through post-secondary education and entry into the labour market, and the factors related to ongoing skills development and maintenance.

The second arises from peer learning among the countries participating in PISA. Currently, only a few countries can undertake a similar investment in data. The integration of PISA data with longitudinal data and an additional assessment that can be analysed in relation to subsequent labour-market and social outcomes could lead to significant new policy insights for countries sharing the same policy concerns.

The third set of benefits arises from adding to the store of knowledge concerning methodology. There are many challenges, ranging from sampling and tracking issues in data collection to analytical difficulties. These challenges are briefly discussed in this report, and a detailed description can be found in Cartwright (2012).

THE IMPORTANCE OF GOOD READING PROFICIENCY

The capacity of education systems to develop human capital is being evaluated in light of the rise in market demand for competencies, and changes in employment requirements that include critical thinking, the use of technology, and innovation. A future-oriented view of education focuses squarely on the importance of foundational skills and lifelong-learning opportunities in order to build and maintain key competencies. This report demonstrates the importance of early reading proficiency, and the benefits of ongoing learning opportunities for continual skills growth.

The report is organised into seven chapters. Chapter 2 describes the three sources of data (PISA-15, YITS, and PISA-24) that were linked to create this database. It also details some of the methodological challenges inherent in this type of data collection and analysis. Chapter 3 provides a descriptive analysis of reading proficiency at age 24 and improvements in proficiency for key population groups. Chapter 4 relates the observed learning gains to expectations for proficiency improvements at age 15 to show how proficiencies may change with age. It also examines learning gains across the various domains of reading proficiency examined in PISA. Chapter 5 considers some of the PISA variables that were key to explaining proficiency at age 15, and considers how these relate to skills gains after the age of 15. It also highlights the critical role of initial reading proficiency in explaining skills gains. Chapter 6 examines education, work and demographic transitions in the lives of young people, and relates these to observed learning gains. The last chapter provides some concluding remarks.

VALUE OF LONGITUDINAL ANALYSIS FOR DECISION MAKING

This report showcases the depth and breadth of data collected in Canada by combining PISA-15 results with those of a longitudinal survey (YITS) and reassessment of competencies (PISA-24), all at the individual level, and provides examples of the types of analysis that can be conducted with such data. The results yield valuable insights to respond to questions about how reading skills are developed, maintained and lost between the ages of 15 and 24. The report also shows how countries participating in PISA can maximise their investments and how such analyses can provide results that assist decision making based on evidence.

While other approaches can confirm these results, the power of this study stems from the wealth of information available at the individual level. The richness of PISA-15 data, which were gathered from the assessment of reading skills at age 15 and from questionnaires addressed to students, parents and school principals, is coupled with nine years' worth of data on individual pathways through education, labour markets and other important life choices and, most important, a re-assessment of reading skills at age 24 conducted through PISA-24 in 2009.

INTRODUCTION

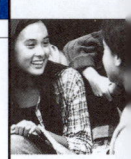

The primary policy lever in developed countries to ensure that all citizens have a good start on lifelong learning is their investment in compulsory education. However, evidence on how reading skills are developed, how they are maintained and how they are lost is scarce. Key policy questions can only be answered by longitudinal analyses related to direct assessments, such as those offered in this study. How do competencies gained during compulsory education relate to future learning gains and losses? Are early advantages and disadvantages persistent? Which policy-relevant factors can increase learning gains for low achievers after the age of 15? Are there patterns of learning gains and losses associated with particular pathways and life choices? Can policies mitigate losses and enhance gains? Results from this study shed light on many of these questions.

INTERNATIONAL POLICY LESSONS

The growing need for internationally comparable evidence on student performance in compulsory education has prompted over 70 governments to invest in the PISA assessment in 2009. In addition, at least six PISA-participating countries – Australia, Canada, the Czech Republic, Denmark, Switzerland and Uruguay – have chosen to use the PISA assessment as a starting point for a longitudinal survey of youth. Using the results from such longitudinal data provides a realistic understanding of a more dynamic view of learning gain and loss. Though there are opportunities and challenges associated with a re-assessment linked to PISA, the Canadian experience will no doubt encourage others to make similar investments.

Key policy lessons can be drawn from this report that can be used by policy makers in other countries. First, quality compulsory education that equips students with strong reading skills provides them a good foundation for further growth and development. Second, all young people continue to improve their skills, which, given the right circumstances, can reduce the gap between high and low achievers that may have been evident when these individuals were younger. Third, better reading skills enable young people to benefit from higher education, which, in turn, is associated with better learning and employment outcomes.

PISA-15, YITS, PISA-24, and the Canadian Context

This chapter describes the three data sources used to explore learning gains and gives an overview of the Programme for International Student Assessment (PISA) in Canada and the linked longitudinal Youth in Transition Survey (YITS). It also provides a detailed description of PISA-24 and related data-quality issues, and a concise review of Canada's education systems.

PISA-15, YITS, PISA-24, AND THE CANADIAN CONTEXT

Canada was one of the 28 OECD member countries that participated in the initial Programme for International Student Assessment (PISA) survey in 2000 (PISA-15). To enhance the value of PISA's internationally comparable data, it developed a longitudinal survey, the Youth in Transition Survey (YITS), which followed the students who participated in PISA-15 through to their young adulthood. Data on education and labour-market outcomes were collected every two years. This allowed for an analysis of how the competencies acquired by the time the students were 15 years old influenced subsequent education and work pathways. The link between cognitive ability at age 15 and educational attainment has been documented in the report, *Pathways to Success* (OECD, 2010a).

While *Pathways to Success* showed that PISA reading scores are closely associated with educational outcomes, it was not possible to directly measure learning gains after the age of 15. Indeed, it was not clear whether reading proficiency continued to improve after compulsory education. Information on reading proficiency collected at age 24 would add to an understanding of the key factors affecting learning gains after compulsory education.

This chapter provides a brief overview of PISA and YITS and offers more detailed information on the PISA re-assessment (PISA-24) conducted at age 24. The chapter ends with a brief overview of the Canadian education systems. Annex A provides more detail on the technical challenges of using the PISA-15 and PISA-24 assessments to study skills development, including ceiling effects, measurement error and regression towards the mean.

THE PROGRAMME FOR INTERNATIONAL STUDENT ASSESSMENT (PISA): AN OVERVIEW

The Programme for International Student Assessment (PISA) assesses the extent to which students near the end of compulsory education have acquired some of the knowledge and skills that are essential for full participation in modern societies, with a focus on reading, mathematics and science. PISA seeks to assess not merely whether 15-year-old students can reproduce knowledge, but also to examine how well they can extrapolate from what they have learned and apply it in unfamiliar settings, both in and outside of school. In addition to data on student achievement in the three key domains of reading, mathematics and science, PISA also collects information on individual, family and school characteristics that may be associated with student performance.

PISA has been conducted every three years since 2000; in 2009, 75 countries and economies participated in the international assessment. Decisions about the scope and nature of the PISA assessments and the background information to be collected are made by leading experts in participating countries. Stringent quality-assurance mechanisms are applied in designing the test, in translation, sampling and data collection. As a result, PISA data have high validity and reliability. Although originally created by OECD countries, PISA has become a major assessment tool in many regions around the world. This study uses data from PISA-15, which focused on student achievement in reading. To supplement the PISA scores, separate questionnaires were also distributed to students, principals and students' parents.

Reading proficiency in PISA-15

In PISA-15, reading literacy is defined as the ability to understand, use and reflect on written texts in order to achieve one's goals, to develop one's knowledge and skills, and to participate effectively in society. This definition goes well beyond the notion of reading as simply decoding or literal comprehension; it includes the value of reading proficiency in the real world.

Some 141 questions were used in the 2000 assessment of reading. Performance on three subscales (retrieving information, interpreting texts, and reflecting on and evaluating texts) was also assessed (OECD, 2001). Scales were developed based on a hierarchy of tasks, from simple retrieval of information to higher-order analytical thinking. In this report, the five proficiency levels developed for PISA-15, based on the hierarchy of tasks, are linked to the tasks demanded of young adults in their daily lives. Figure 2.1 describes in detail what the proficiency levels measure. These proficiency levels were developed to describe skills at age 15, thus they provide an approximation of skills at age 24.

The relevance of the knowledge and skills measured by PISA is confirmed by studies tracking young people in the years after they have been assessed by PISA. Longitudinal studies in Australia, Canada and Switzerland show a strong relationship between performance in reading on the PISA assessment at age 15 and future educational attainment and success in the labour market.[1]

PISA-15, YITS, PISA-24, AND THE CANADIAN CONTEXT

■ Figure 2.1 ■
PISA-15: What the proficiency levels measure

	Retrieving Information	Interpreting texts	Reflecting and evaluating
	What is being assessed on each of the reading performance scales:		
	Retrieving information is defined as locating one or more pieces of information in a text.	Interpreting texts is defined as constructing meaning and drawing inferences from one or more parts of a text.	Reflecting and evaluating is defined as relating a text to one's experience, knowledge and ideas.
	Characteristics of the task associated with increasing difficulty on each of the reading performance scales:		
	Task difficulty depends on the number of pieces of information that need to be located. Difficulty also depends on the number of conditions that must be met to locate the requested information, and on whether what is retrieved needs to be sequenced in a particular way. Difficulty also depends on the prominence of information, and the familiarity of the context. Other relevant characteristics are the complexity of the text, and the presence and strength of competing information.	Task difficulty depends on the type of interpretation required, with the easiest tasks requiring identifying the main idea in a text, more difficult tasks requiring understanding relationships that are part of the text, and the most difficult requiring either an understanding of the meaning of language in context, or analogical reasoning. Difficulty also depends on how explicitly the text provides the ideas or information the reader needs in order to complete the task; on how prominent the required information is; and on how much competing information is present. Finally, the length and complexity of the text and the familiarity of its content affect difficulty.	Task difficulty depends on the type of reflection required, with the easiest tasks requiring simple connections or explanations relating the text to external experience, and the more difficult requiring an hypothesis or evaluation. Difficulty also depends on the familiarity of the knowledge that must be drawn on from outside the text; on the complexity of the text; on the level of textual understanding demanded; and on how explicitly the reader is directed to relevant factors in both the task and the text.
Level			
5	Locate and possibly sequence or combine multiple pieces of deeply embedded information, some of which may be outside the main body of the text. Infer which information in the text in relevant to the task. Deal with highly plausible and/or extensive competing information.	Either construe the meaning of nuanced language or demonstrate a full and detailed understanding of a text.	Critically evaluate or hypothesise, drawing on specialised knowledge. Deal with concepts that are contrary to expectations and draw on a deep understanding of long or complex texts.
4	Locate and possibly sequence or combine multiple pieces of embedded information, each of which may need to meet multiple criteria, in a text with unfamiliar context or form. Infer which information in the text is relevant to the task.	Use a high level of text-based inference to understand and apply categories in an unfamiliar context, and to construe the meaning of a section of text by taking into account the text as a whole. Deal with ambiguities, ideas that are contrary to expectation and ideas that are negatively worded.	Use formal or public knowledge to hypothesise about or critically evaluate a text. Show accurate understanding of long or complex texts.
3	Locate and, in some cases, recognise the relationship between pieces of information, each of which may need to meet multiple criteria. Deal with prominent competing information.	Integrate several parts of a text in order to identify a main idea, understand a relationship or construe the meaning of a word or phrase. Compare, contrast or categorise taking many criteria into account. Deal with competing information.	Make connections or comparisons, give explanations, or evaluate a feature of text. Demonstrate a detailed understanding of the text in relation to familiar, everyday knowledge, or draw on less common knowledge.
2	Locate one or more pieces of information, each of which may be required to meet multiple criteria. Deal with competing information.	Identify the main idea in a text, understand relationships, form or apply simple categories, or construe meaning within a limited part of the text when the information is not prominent and low-level inferences are required.	Make a comparison or connections between the text and outside knowledge, or explain a feature of the text by drawing on personal experience and attitudes.
1	Take account of a single criterion to locate one or more independent pieces of explicitly stated information.	Recognise the main theme or author's purpose in a text about a familiar topic, when the required information in the text is prominent.	Make a simple connection between information in the text and common, everyday knowledge.

Source: OECD (2001).

PISA-15, YITS, PISA-24, AND THE CANADIAN CONTEXT

Canada's administration of PISA-15

Because it is a bilingual country, Canada conducted the PISA-15 assessment in both English and French. In addition, since it would be important to report the performance of students in each of the 10 provincial education systems, the sample size was increased to 30 000 students from the 5 000 that most countries assessed. Such a large sample allowed for more detailed analysis of the performance of subgroups, such as boys, girls, and first- and second-generation immigrants, and provided a sufficient sample for a longitudinal follow-up study. A questionnaire was also addressed to parents to elicit more background information on the family and the student (see Box 2.1).

> #### Box 2.1 Key features of PISA-15 in Canada
>
> Canada tailored the administration of the PISA-15 survey to ensure that the data collected offered a rich source for analysis.
>
> - 29 687 15-year-old students in 1 242 schools participated in PISA-15, in comparison to the 5 000 students surveyed in most participating countries.
> - Assessments were conducted in two languages: English and French.
> - An additional questionnaire, addressed to parents, collected more background information on the family and the student.
> - Information was collected for the Youth in Transition longitudinal survey that would follow the students to age 24.

YOUTH IN TRANSITION (YITS): AN OVERVIEW

The main goal of the Youth in Transition Survey (YITS) was to develop evidence to support policies to improve the education and labour-market outcomes of Canadian youth, and ultimately to help ensure Canada's continued prosperity.

Figure 2.2 shows the data-collection cycles of YITS for students who participated in PISA-15, and highlights the timing of the PISA-24 2009 re-assessment.[2]

■ Figure 2.2 ■
Overview of data collection in Canada: PISA-15, YITS and PISA-24

	PISA cross-sectional sample
	YITS longitudinal sample
	PISA-24, 2009 re-assessment of reading skills at age 24 with PISA reading linked items

	Age	2000	2001	2002	2003	2004	2005	2006	2007	2008	2009	2010
PISA-15	15											
	16											
	17											
	18											
	19											
	20											
	21											
	22											
	23											
PISA-24	24											
	25											

Content in the six cycles

The information gathered in each cycle of YITS varied, depending on policy needs and the age of respondents. The information gathered in 2000 came from four sources:

- data derived from the PISA-15 survey;
- a specially designed student survey that collected information on learning behaviours;
- a questionnaire for parents that collected information on learning environments at home; and
- a specially designed school survey, which was distributed in addition to the PISA school questionnaire, which collected detailed information on the learning environment at the school.

PISA-15, YITS, PISA-24, AND THE CANADIAN CONTEXT

In subsequent cycles, only the student survey was re-administered. Questions were adjusted to account for the youths' current situation and their previous responses. No data were collected from parents or schools. Instead, the survey focused on pathways and contextual information to measure progress and change.

YITS gathered information on four main areas: demographic and family characteristics; high school experience; post-secondary education and labour-market activities; and financial factors related to post-secondary education (Motte, et al., 2008; Statistics Canada, 2007). In some cases, the information was used to check data from previous cycles; in others, it provided an update on the respondent's situation and related decisions. The information collected over the six cycles tracked the students' transition to adult roles in higher education, work and society. Though data was collected only every two years, detailed questions were asked to cover the intervening two years.

THE PISA RE-ASSESSMENT (PISA-24)

The PISA re-assessment (PISA-24) involved a subsample of the PISA-15 cohort that was subsequently re-interviewed through the Youth in Transition Survey (YITS) every two years. The sample was representative of the population of 15-year-old Canadian students in 2000. These respondents were 24 years old in 2009.

Among the respondents who participated in the fifth cycle of data collection for YITS, a subsample of approximately 2 000 were selected to participate in PISA-24. These students were grouped into 12 categories (sample strata) according to gender, PISA reading level and education status. A random sample within each category took the re-assessment. Some 1 297 respondents agreed to take the assessment, which was conducted during May-June 2009 and consisted of a follow-up assessment of readings skills and a background questionnaire.

The PISA-24 survey was scored in conjunction with the PISA assessment in 2009. Since the PISA-24 items were also included in the PISA 2009 assessment, qualified coders who scored the PISA 2009 test booklets also scored the PISA-24 test items. Adjusted weights are included in the final data, ensuring that the sample remains representative. Annex A provides details on weighting adjustments and other issues.

Test design

PISA-24 used a selection of assessment questions known as the PISA link items. This selection of test items was also used for testing reading as a minor domain in PISA 2003 and PISA 2006 and allowed for trend analyses. As Figure 2.3 shows, the PISA-24 survey consisted of 28 questions covering the spectrum of reading competencies, contexts, formats and text types assessed in PISA. For example, 18 out of the 28 questions included continuous texts, typically composed of sentences in paragraphs, and non-continuous texts (Table 2.1). The other 10 questions involved information that was not conveyed in prose, such as figures, maps or forms. PISA questions were set in four different contexts: educational (eight questions), occupational (seven questions), personal (six questions) and public (seven questions).

■ Figure 2.3 ■
PISA-24 questions in the PISA reading framework

Reading process (Aspect)	Item format (Question format)					
	Multiple choice	Complex multiple choice	Short response	Closed constructed response	Open constructed response
Interpreting	8 Questions (3Qs Level 1, 3 Qs Level 2 and 2Qs Level 3)		1 Question (Level 2)	1 Question (Level 4)	3 Questions (1Q Level 2, 1Q Level 3 and 1Q Level 4)
Reflecting and evaluating			1 Question (Level 4)		7 Questions (1Q Level 1, 2Qs Level 3, 1Q Level 3 [Level 2 if partial credit], 1Q Level 4 [Level 2 if partial credit], 1Q Level 4 [Level 3 if partial credit] and 1Q Level 5 [Level 3 if partial credit])
Retrieving information	1 Question (Level 3)	1 Question (Level 4 [Level 2 if partial credit])	2 Questions (1Q Level 2 and 1Q Level 6 [Level 4 if partial credit])	3 Questions (1Q Level 1, 1Q Level 3 and 1Q Level 4)	

Note: Figure 2.1 provides all the details on the PISA reading framework.
Source: Cartwright (2012).

Data quality and analytical power

A repeat assessment presents several challenges. Many of these are discussed in a technical paper (Cartwright, 2012), but this section offers a brief overview of the main challenges. One of these is the suitability of using the assessment tool, which was designed for 15-year-olds, to assess the reading proficiency of 24-year-olds. Does the test suffer from a ceiling effect: that is, do those students who performed well in PISA-15 have any room to improve in PISA-24? Another concerns measurement error in the context of a repeat assessment and the related problem of regression to the mean: those who did relatively well by chance in PISA-15 are likely do relatively less well in PISA-24.

Is the PISA reading instrument suitable for 24-year-olds and is there a ceiling effect?

The years spanning adolescence to age 24 are a dynamic period in the lives of young adults, when they are choosing career paths and making important decisions about place of dwelling, life partnerships and parenthood. During this period, young Canadians, who largely followed similar curricula in reading skills during primary and secondary education, begin to use language differently, based on the specific contexts, jargon, and formats found in their educational and labour-market experiences. A study linking PISA-15 questions to assessments of adult literacy showed that the PISA questions were relevant for a population older than 15 years of age (Yamamoto, 2002). In particular, the study showed that while overall performance had improved, the PISA questions retain their relative difficulty.

The International Adult Literacy and Lifeskills survey (ALL) and the Programme for the International Assessment of Adult Competencies (PIAAC) use the same items to test cohorts of respondents ranging in age from 16 to 65 (OECD, 2009). The results of ALL and the evidence emerging from PIAAC suggest that relatively generic reading tasks remain strong predictors of the performance of individuals in their educational and professional careers as well as in their personal lives.

■ Figure 2.4 ■
Statistical properties of PISA-24 test questions

Item name	Question number	Unit item code	Percent correct in PISA-15 among PISA-24 participants	Estimated question difficulty in PISA-15	Percent correct in PISA-24
Drugged Spiders	Question 1	R055Q01	84	-1.38	93
	Question 2	R055Q02	53	0.50	73
	Question 3	R055Q03	61	0.07	84
	Question 4	R055Q05	77	-0.88	91
Aesop	Question 1	R067Q01	88	-1.73	97
	Question 2	R067Q04	54	0.52	76
	Question 3	R067Q05	62	0.18	85
Shirts	Question 1	R102Q04A	36	1.21	58
	Question 2	R102Q05	42	0.91	66
	Question 3	R102Q07	85	-1.57	98
Telephone	Question 1	R104Q01	83	-1.24	94
	Question 2	R104Q02	41	1.11	54
	Question 3	R104Q05	29	1.88	45
Exchange	Question 1	R111Q01	64	-0.05	87
	Question 2	R111Q02B	34	1.37	60
	Question 3	R111Q06B	44	0.81	72
Employment	Question 1	R219Q01E	70	-0.55	90
	Question 2	R219Q01T	57	0.28	87
	Question 3	R219Q02	76	-0.92	95
South Pole	Question 1	R220Q01	46	0.79	66
	Question 2	R220Q02B	64	-0.14	89
	Question 3	R220Q04	61	0.16	78
	Question 4	R220Q05	85	-1.60	92
	Question 5	R220Q06	66	-0.17	76
Optician	Question 1	R227Q01	58	0.20	68
	Question 2	R227Q02T	60	0.05	73
	Question 3	R227Q03	56	0.30	81
	Question 4	R227Q06	74	-0.92	84

Source: Cartwright (2012).
StatLink http://dx.doi.org/10.1787/888932577289

The difference between the two samples, the test at age 15 and the test at age 24, is most evident in the much greater rate of success on all test items in PISA-24. One concern about the validity of the re-assessment results is that the greater success might lead to a "ceiling effect" where the rate of success is so uniformly high on the test items that variation between respondents is more due to statistical error than individual proficiency. However, an analysis of question-level performance conducted on the PISA-24 sample concluded that despite the higher range of performance, there was still sufficient variation in question-level performance, and that there was no artificial restriction in the range of proficiency due to a "ceiling effect". In other words, the questions used to assess 15-year-olds in PISA remained sufficiently challenging for 24-year-olds that they captured a true range of proficiency, with no indication that the best performers were clustered at the highest proficiency level. Cartwright (2012) provides further details on these analyses.

The nature of PISA-24 is such that the scores produced by the re-assessment are not necessarily the same as those in PISA-15. The re-assessment test is a modification of the PISA-15 assessment test. For example, PISA-24 only focuses in reading, while PISA-15 measured reading, mathematics and science. PISA-24 contains a smaller number of questions than PISA-15. The order of the questions is not necessarily the same in PISA-24 and in PISA-15. Therefore, the scores produced by the PISA-24 re-assessment represent a similar construct of reading performance. The design of PISA-24 is such that it allows for an interpretation of the results in the same numerical scale as PISA-15 reading proficiency. The level of accuracy of PISA-24 results is similar to the level of accuracy of the domains that are not the focus of a particular PISA cycle – the minor domain.

Regression toward the mean

In practice, any measurement is subject to error, and any repeated measurement is subject to regression toward the mean – the tendency of whatever is being measured to be closer to the average when measured for the second time. In a two-stage assessment, and as long as at least some of the error in measurement is random, any extreme measurement in the first stage is likely to be less extreme in the second stage.

Given that performance in both PISA-15 and PISA-24 is measured with a certain degree of uncertainty, the assessment of skills development based on the difference in performance between the two assessments is naturally associated with a greater degree of measurement uncertainty. The wider measurement uncertainty is a consequence of repeat assessments, since random error enters into the measure of skills at both points in time. In other words, the estimate of skills growth includes measurement error from the initial and the follow-up assessments, compounding any inaccuracies.

It is impossible to avoid measurement error in the estimates of reading proficiency; and as long as the error is random, it is not a serious problem. However, in repeat assessments, the error in the estimate of skills growth is correlated with the initial measure of skills.

To see why this is the case, consider one way that error may enter the estimate of initial proficiency. There are many reasons why a student's score on the PISA assessment may differ from that student's true level of ability. For instance, 15-year-old students have good days and bad days, and this will affect their score on the assessment. A student who had a particularly good day when he or she completed the PISA-15 assessment might achieve a higher score than if the same student took the test the day after.

When improvement in reading scores is calculated, students who scored lower than their true level of ability on their first assessment will likely show above-average gains in proficiency. Conversely, a student who performed better than expected on the first assessment will likely show below-average proficiency gains. Thus, when skills growth is examined over the distribution of initial proficiency, one would expect to see larger proficiency gains among students who originally had low scores, and smaller gains, or even a decline in skills, among students who originally had high scores. This would be true whether the tests were completed nine hours or nine years apart.

Regression towards the mean is particularly important in PISA-24 since, as discussed in subsequent chapters, initial proficiency is one of the most significant determinants of skills growth. Because the observed pattern of growth is identical to what one would expect from regression towards the mean, it is important to test if this pattern is a statistical artefact of measurement error or not by cross-validating and contrasting analyses across distinct subpopulations. Moreover, it is often important to try to control for the initial scores of the 15-year-olds when examining the relationship of other variables to skills growth.

To account for regression towards the mean, this analysis has used young people's grades in high school language classes, as reported in PISA-15, as a measure of initial proficiency level. Even if school marks are self-reported measures of proficiency, they are based on a large number of assessments and therefore they are less prone to measurement error, which reduces the risk of regression towards the mean. However, any relationship between skills growth and initial PISA score should be treated with caution. A more detailed discussion of the measurement error in the estimates of skills growth can be found in the Annex A.

Overview of Canada and its education systems

Canada is a federation composed of ten provinces and three territories.[3] The provinces are autonomous in the administration of social programmes, such as health care and education. Indeed, to fund these two public services, provinces collect more revenue combined than the federal government does, which is unusual for a federated structure. While the federal government may initiate national policies, provinces can opt in or out of these, though they rarely opt out.

Canada spends approximately 6.0% of its GDP on all levels of education. This is higher than the OECD average of 5.9% and is the eleventh highest among all OECD countries. Of this, 3.6% is spent on primary, secondary and post-secondary (non-university) education (compared with the OECD average of 3.8%), and 2.5% is spent on tertiary education (compared with the OECD average of 1.5%). Canada ranks 21st of 32 OECD countries in its spending as a percentage of GDP at primary level, and is fourth only after Luxembourg, the United States and Korea in its spending on tertiary education (2008 figures; OECD, 2011a).

Since each province has its own education system, curricula, assessments, accountability practices and teachers' salaries, among many other things, vary from province to province. The age until which schooling is compulsory also differs: schooling is compulsory to the age of 16 in every province except Ontario and New Brunswick, where compulsory education ends at age 18. Public education is free to all Canadians at primary and secondary levels, provided they meet various age and residence requirements. Private schools exist, but are rare and their prevalence varies by province. About 93% of Canadian students attend publicly-funded institutions at primary and secondary levels (OECD, 2011a).

Figure 2.5 provides a schematic overview, by province, of the structure of Canada's education systems. The system of Québec is distinct from that of other provinces, particularly with respect to pathways to post-secondary education.

All provinces, with the exception of Nova Scotia, provide pre-school education (i.e. ages 5 to 6). Ontario is the only province that offers junior kindergarten (i.e., for children aged 4 to 5). New Brunswick, Prince Edward Island and Saskatchewan offer schooling that is intermediate between elementary and secondary, while the other seven provinces do not. In most provinces, primary and secondary school combined encompass 12 years.

The primary school curriculum focuses on language, mathematics, social studies, science, health and physical education and arts; some provinces also offer courses in second languages. In lower secondary school, students take mostly compulsory courses. The proportion of course options increases in upper secondary so that students may take specific courses to prepare for the labour market or to meet the entrance requirements of post-secondary programmes.

Secondary school diplomas are awarded to students who complete the requisite number of compulsory and optional courses (in some instances other factors maybe considered). The secondary school diploma or its equivalent is a requirement for entry into post-secondary and tertiary education.

At post-secondary level, a distinction is made between colleges, universities and graduate schools. In colleges, the most common academic qualification granted is a diploma, following two to three years' study. In universities, a bachelor's degree is awarded after three to four years. In graduate schools, students may take a one- to two-year course to be awarded a post-graduate certificate or diploma, such as a master's degree. Doctoral degrees can take three years or more.

Québec is different than the other provinces in the manner in which students proceed from secondary school to colleges/universities. The CÉGEP system (*Collège d'enseignement général et professionnel*) aims to make post-secondary education more accessible. Completion of a CÉGEP programme is compulsory before entering university programmes. To compensate for this, there are 11 rather than 12 years of schooling at the combined primary and secondary levels. Students can choose whether they want to follow a college stream (three years of CÉGEP) or a university stream (where they enter university after two years of CÉGEP).

2. PISA-15, YITS, PISA-24, AND THE CANADIAN CONTEXT

■ Figure 2.5 ■
Overview of Canada's education systems

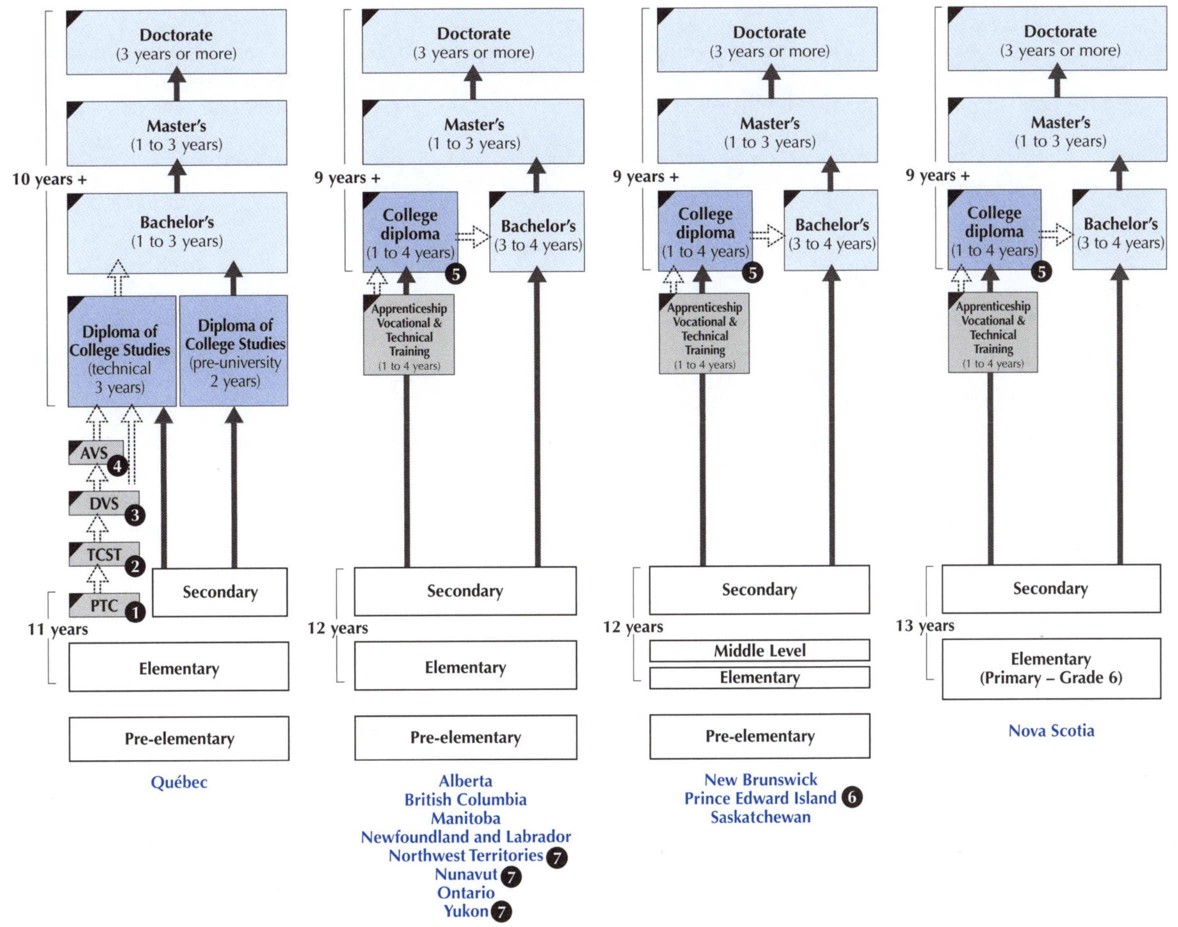

[Figure: Flowchart comparing education systems across Canadian provinces and territories]

Québec (11 years): Pre-elementary → Elementary → Secondary → PTC❶/TCST❷/DVS❸/AVS❹ → Diploma of College Studies (technical 3 years) / Diploma of College Studies (pre-university 2 years) → Bachelor's (1 to 3 years) → Master's (1 to 3 years) → Doctorate (3 years or more). 10 years +

Alberta, British Columbia, Manitoba, Newfoundland and Labrador, Northwest Territories❼, Nunavut❼, Ontario, Yukon❼ (12 years): Pre-elementary → Elementary → Secondary → Apprenticeship Vocational & Technical Training (1 to 4 years) / College diploma (1 to 4 years)❺ / Bachelor's (3 to 4 years) → Master's (1 to 3 years) → Doctorate (3 years or more). 9 years +

New Brunswick, Prince Edward Island❻, Saskatchewan (12 years): Pre-elementary → Elementary → Middle Level → Secondary → Apprenticeship Vocational & Technical Training (1 to 4 years) / College diploma (1 to 4 years)❺ / Bachelor's (3 to 4 years) → Master's (1 to 3 years) → Doctorate (3 years or more). 9 years +

Nova Scotia (13 years): Elementary (Primary – Grade 6) → Secondary → Apprenticeship Vocational & Technical Training (1 to 4 years) / College diploma (1 to 4 years)❺ / Bachelor's (3 to 4 years) → Master's (1 to 3 years) → Doctorate (3 years or more). 9 years +

Legend:
- University Education
- College Education
- Apprenticeship - Vocational & Technical Training
- To the job market
- Typical pathway
- Alternate pathway

❶ **PTC – Pre-work Training Certificate** *(3 years after Secondary II)*

❷ **TCST – Training Certificate for a Semi-skilled Trade** *(1 year after Secondary II)*

❸ **DVS – Diploma of Vocational Studies** *(600 to 1800 hrs), depending on the programme*

❹ **AVS – Attestation of Vocational Specialization** *(300 to 1185 hrs), depending on the programme*

❺ Selected institutions in Alberta, British Columbia, Ontario and Prince Edward Island offer applied degrees.

❻ In Prince Edward Island, secondary education is divided into junior high (3 years) and senior high (3 years).

❼ The territories have no degree-granting institutions. Some degrees are available through partnerships. Students may also access degrees directly from institutions outside the territories.

Notes: All colleges and universities offer certificate programmes of variable length. Continuing and adult education programmes, while not shown on this chart, may be offered at all levels of instruction.
Source: Canadian Information Centre for International Credentials, Council of Ministers of Education, 2008.

LEARNING BEYOND FIFTEEN – TEN YEARS AFTER PISA © OECD 2012

PISA-15, YITS, PISA-24, AND THE CANADIAN CONTEXT

Box 2.2 provides a snapshot of Canada's education systems from an international perspective.

> ### Box 2.2 **Highlights of Canada's education systems**
>
> Provinces have complete autonomy in determining curricula, assessments, accountability and teachers' salaries.
>
> Québec's education system differs from the other nine provinces in its entry paths to colleges and universities.
>
> There is significant diversity across provinces in terms of languages spoken, percentage of immigrants, graduation rates, GDP per capita and unemployment rates.
>
> In comparison with other OECD member countries, Canada has:
> - diverse education systems, due to the federation;
> - a multicultural population and education in two official languages;
> - medium spending as a percentage of GDP on primary, secondary and non-tertiary education;
> - high spending as a percentage of GDP on tertiary education;
> - high tertiary tuition fees, offset by well-developed student financial-assistance programmes;
> - comparatively high tertiary graduation rates (55% of 25-34 year-olds);
> - a moderate 38% earnings premium for a tertiary qualification as compared with an upper secondary qualification;
> - a modest 14% earnings premium for an upper secondary qualification as compared with a lower secondary qualification; and
> - a high proportion of tertiary-educated individuals in the working-age population.

CHAPTER SUMMARY AND CONCLUSIONS

PISA-15, YITS and PISA-24 offer a unique opportunity to measure learning gains between PISA-15 and the re-assessment in 2009 – that is, between the time the participating students were 15 years old and when they were 24. However, several technical issues must be taken into consideration when drawing conclusions from the analysis of these data. The overview of the data sources in this chapter serves as a guide for interpreting the evidence and analysis discussed in the following chapters. The description of Canada's education systems will inform the interpretation of results.

Notes

1. Marks, G.N. (2007); Bertschy, K., et al. (2009); OECD (2010a).

2. It should be noted that YITS also included a survey of older Canadian youth who were between 18 and 20 years of age in 2000. These individuals were also surveyed every two years, up to 2008, in order to have earlier information on post-secondary education participation and to compare the younger and older cohorts. However, the lack of a measure of competencies was a shortcoming in potential analyses.

3. Due to its federated structure, some statistical indicators for education published in the OECD's annual *Education at a Glance: OECD Indicators* (e.g. OECD, 2011a) are not available for Canada. Therefore, this section is unable to draw extensively on that data source.

Reading Proficiency of Canadian Youth at Ages 15 and 24

PISA-24 revealed important growth in reading skills between the ages of 15 and 24 among all individuals assessed. For example, the number of young people with scores below PISA proficiency Level 3 – a key measure of success in PISA – dropped from 21% in 2000 to 7% in 2009. However, the rate at which young people acquire skills varies considerably. Differences in performance are related to certain student characteristics that do not change over time. Though performance gaps persist, they narrowed over the nine years.

AN ASSESSMENT OF READING SKILLS AMONG 24-YEAR-OLDS AND HOW THEY RELATE TO SKILLS ACQUIRED BY THE AGE OF 15

PISA-15 provided a snapshot of what students know and can do at age 15. Canada's 2009 PISA re-assessment (PISA-24) took a second picture of the same population nearly a decade later. Both assessments not only capture the reading competencies of the youth cohort as a whole, they also collect data on individual characteristics, such as gender, family background and language spoken at home, that may be associated with performance. Analysis of this data can help in formulating policies to support struggling students.

This chapter discusses average reading scores among 15- and 24-year-old Canadians; how the distribution of reading scores has changed over time; the demographic profile of poor performers; the education and labour-market choices that predict greater reading proficiency at 24; and the risk factors associated with low reading scores for 15- and 24-year-olds.

Throughout this report, several indicators are used to describe student reading performance, including average performance, the disparity in skills, and the proportion of students with skills below PISA proficiency Level 3. Though proficiency levels may not have the same meaning for 24-year-olds and 15-year-olds, proficiency Level 3 is a well-known benchmark for PISA scores. Reading proficiency at that level has been characterised as the ability to "compare, contrast and categorise competing information according to a range of criteria" (Bussière, et al., 2001). Previous research has shown that reading performance at Level 3 or above indicates a much greater likelihood that the student will participate in post-secondary education (Bussière and Knighton, 2006).

READING PROFICIENCY AT AGES 15 AND 24

There was a marked improvement in reading proficiency among all who were re-assessed for this study. These young people had an average reading score of 541 points in PISA-15.[1] By 2009, their average reading score, measured by PISA-24, had increased by 57 points to 598 on the PISA scale (Table 3.2). In comparison, an increase of 50 score points corresponds to half a standard deviation of the original PISA scale; and the difference between two proficiency levels is more than 70 score points. Thus, the magnitude of the improvement seen among Canadian youth is similar to the difference in average proficiency scores between Canada and countries like Croatia, Israel, Luxembourg, Austria and Turkey in the recent PISA 2009 assessment (OECD, 2010b).

Canada was one of the top-performing countries in PISA-15 and one of the countries with greater equity, as measured by various indicators. For example, student outcomes in PISA 2009 were more homogeneous in Canada than in most other countries that participated in PISA-15. In PISA-15, the standard deviation – a measure of the dispersion of outcomes – was 94.6 points for Canada, as compared to the standardised measure of 100 score points across all OECD countries. Among PISA-24 participants, the standard deviation in 2000 was 92 score points. By 2009, the standard deviation had decreased by more than 14 score points to 78 points.

Reading skills generally improved between the ages of 15 and 24. Figure 3.1 shows how reading performance evolved between 2000 and 2009. In this figure, the height of the line represents the proportion of students with a particular score, shown along the X-axis. The proportions and cumulative proportions for the ranges of proficiency used in this figure are presented in Annex B, Table 3.1.

Figure 3.1 shows that at age 24 average performance has improved (the middle of the distribution has shifted to the right) and the dispersion in scores has narrowed (fewer young people now occupy the tails of the distribution, especially the left tail, which indicates the proportion of young people with very poor reading proficiency). The area under the curve, to the right of 626 score points, shows that the proportion of young people at or above proficiency Level 5 was substantially larger in 2009 than it was in 2000.

The chart at the top of Figure 3.1 shows the proportion of young people at given levels of performance, according to PISA. In 2000, 21.4% of Canadian 15-year-olds scored below 475 points, or proficiency Level 3, on the PISA scale. By 2009, this proportion had dropped to 6.7% among 24-year-olds. Similarly, in 2000, 24.8% of students scored 625 points or above, which corresponds to Level 5 on the PISA scale, while in 2009, 44.6% of those re-assessed did so. While this indicates a major positive shift in reading proficiency among Canadian youth, the nearly 7% of 24-year-olds who still failed to achieve Level 3 would benefit from general literacy training. Skills associated with proficiency Level 3 include "locating multiple pieces of information, making links between different parts of a text, and relating it to familiar everyday knowledge" (OECD 2010b).

READING PROFICIENCY OF CANADIAN YOUTH AT AGES 15 AND 24

■ Figure 3.1 ■
Comparison of distribution of reading skills, PISA-15 and PISA-24
Percentage of participants age 15 in 2000 and 24 in 2009

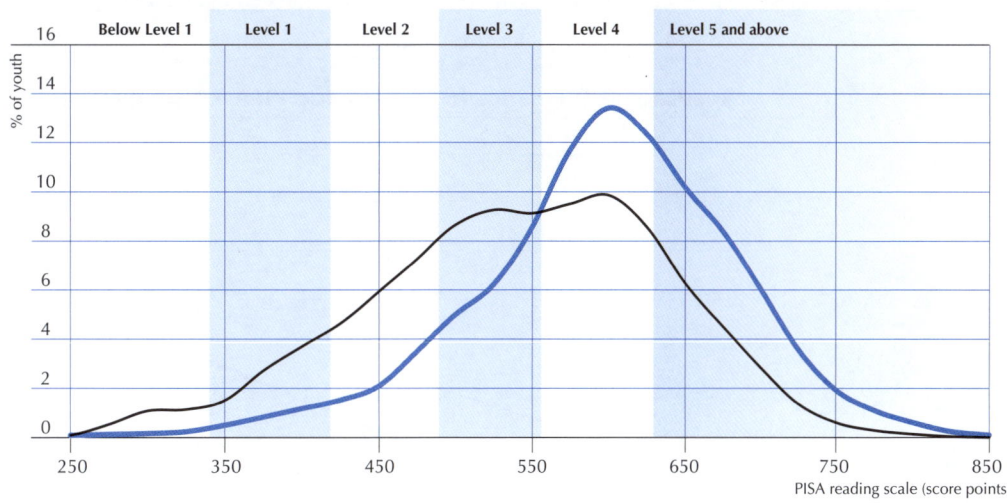

	Below Level 1	Level 1	Level 2	Level 3	Level 4	Level 5 and above
PISA-15 (2000)	2%	5%	14%	25%	29%	25%
PISA-24 (2009)	0%	2%	5%	15%	34%	45%
Difference in percentage points	-1	-4	-10	-11	5	20

Source: Table 3.1; YITS cycle 5.5: Reading Skills Reassessment.
StatLink http://dx.doi.org/10.1787/888932576795

Many improvements seen between the ages of 15 and 24 are the result of an overall shift in the distribution of reading proficiency. However, as explored in the following sections and shown in Figure 3.1, improvements were not uniform across the distribution. For instance, the distribution of proficiency in PISA-15 was relatively dispersed, with two distinct modes, or "bumps", in the distribution. In contrast, the 2009 reading proficiency distribution has only one mode and it is much narrower with a strong peak, indicating that at age 24 reading proficiency is more evenly distributed than at age 15. The rest of this chapter examines in detail how individual characteristics are associated with performance at ages 15 and 24.

DEMOGRAPHIC CHARACTERISTICS AND READING PROFICIENCY GAINS BETWEEN THE AGES OF 15 AND 24

Demographic factors, such as gender and socio-economic background, are closely related to performance differences at ages 15 and 24. The rates of skills acquisition, as measured by PISA-24, are also associated with demographic characteristics.

Gender

PISA-24 shows that by age 24, women outperform men in reading, but by a smaller margin than they did when they were 15-year-old girls and boys. Girls outperform boys in reading by a large margin in practically every country and economy that participates in PISA. Among PISA-24 participants, girls outscored boys in PISA-15 by an average of 32 points; by 2009, that gap had narrowed to 18 points. On average, these young women attained 558 points in the 2000 assessment and 608 points in the 2009 assessment – an increase of 50 points. Young men attained an average score of 526 points in the 2000 assessment and 590 points in the 2009 re-assessment – an improvement of 63 points (Table 3.2). As will be seen in many of the following cases, the poorer-performing groups acquired reading skills at a somewhat faster pace than the better-performing groups.

LEARNING BEYOND FIFTEEN – TEN YEARS AFTER PISA © OECD 2012

READING PROFICIENCY OF CANADIAN YOUTH AT AGES 15 AND 24

Figure 3.2 depicts the average performance of both girls/women (triangles) and boys/men (circles) in each assessment. The line between each measure of average performance (triangle or circle) shows the progression across assessments, or the rate of skills growth for each group (assuming that growth between the two time periods is perfectly linear). In this case, the line for young women is slightly flatter, reflecting a slower pace of improvement in reading proficiency. However, average performance is higher among young women than young men at both points in time. The difference in average performance in PISA-15 between boys and girls was large and significant; in PISA-24, however, the performance gap is narrower and the differences can be established with less confidence than in PISA-15.

■ Figure 3.2 ■
Reading performance in PISA-15 and PISA-24, by gender

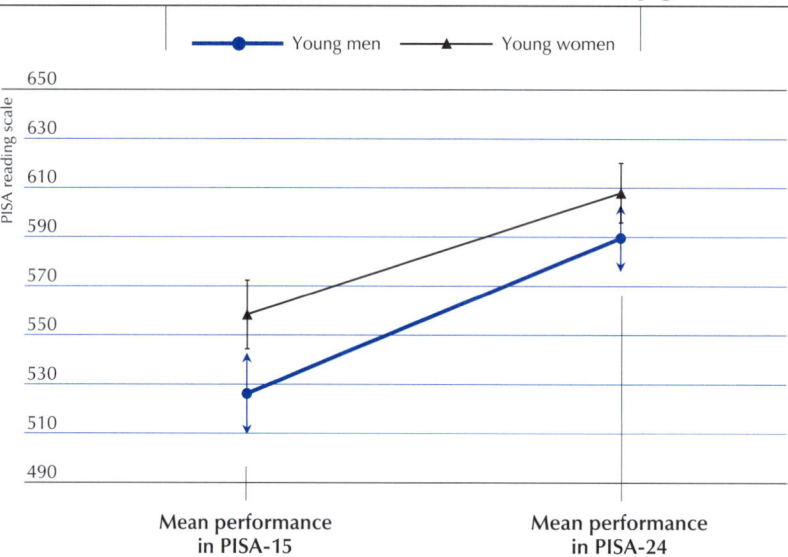

Note: The vertical lines on each measure of mean performance indicate the degree of precision with which these average scores are calculated. In statistical terms, the range of performance covered by these lines is referred to as the confidence interval. In general, overlapping vertical lines (joined confidence intervals) suggest that the differences are not statistically significant with a high degree of confidence.
Source: Table 3.2; YITS cycle 5.5: Reading Skills Reassessment.
StatLink ⟶ http://dx.doi.org/10.1787/888932576795

The distribution of scores by gender highlights important differences between young men and women at ages 15 and 24 (Figure 3.3). In particular, the difference in average performance between boys and girls at age 15 is largely the result of two large clusters, or subpopulations, of boys with low proficiency, visible as two bumps in the distribution, one centred at approximately 300 points and the other at approximately 500 points. These subpopulations are no longer present in the distribution of 24-year-old men, hence the distribution among men is similar to that among women. However, there remains a large number of poorly performing men, as seen by the "heavy tail" at the lower end of the distribution. This accounts for the lingering difference in average performance between 24-year-old men and women, despite near-identical shapes at the high end of the scale. The large proportion of men with low reading proficiency reflects initial poor performance among 15-year-old boys; however, changes to the distribution between the ages of 15 and 24 suggest that this disadvantage may decrease with time. Table 3.3 in Annex B shows the performance distribution in both assessments for both young men and women.

Immigrant background

Canadian students who were born outside of Canada performed relatively well, by international standards, in PISA-15.[2] In fact, the performance gap between students born in Canada and those born outside of Canada was particularly narrow.

Figure 3.4 shows mean student performance in both assessments by location of birth. Students born outside of Canada scored an average of 524 points in PISA-15, while those born in Canada averaged 545 points. In the 2009 re-assessment, all participants scored around 600 points, whether they were born in Canada or not. The growth in skills among foreign-born youth in Canada is remarkable and highlights the learning gains possible beyond compulsory education. Measured in score points, the skills growth among foreign-born students amounted to 77 points – more than one proficiency level on the PISA reading scale – and 54 points among those students born in Canada (Table 3.2).

READING PROFICIENCY OF CANADIAN YOUTH AT AGES 15 AND 24

■ Figure 3.3 ■
Comparison of the distribution of young men's and women's reading skills, PISA-15 and PISA-24

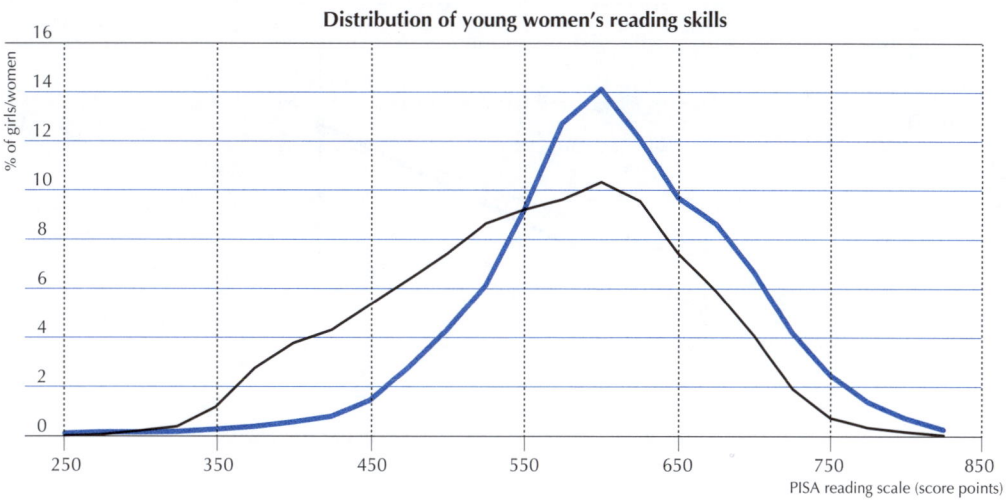

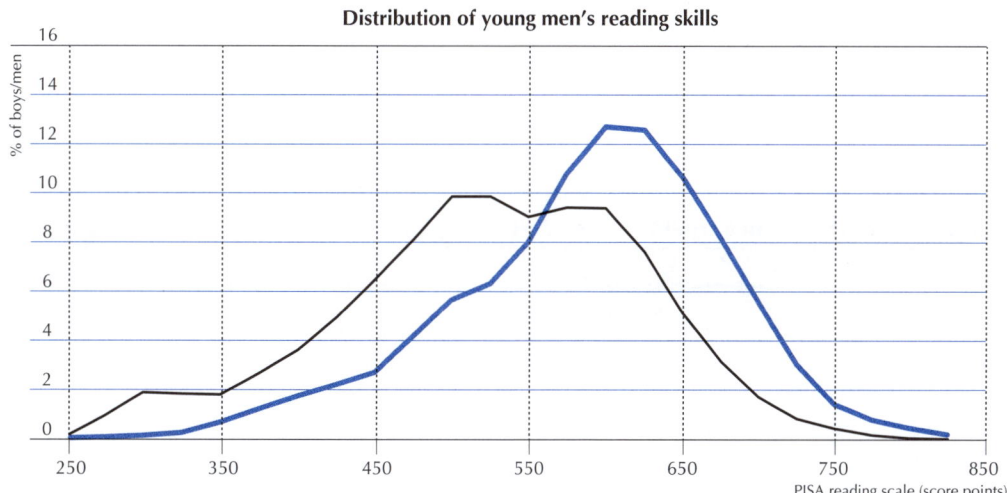

Source: Table 3.3; YITS cycle 5.5: Reading Skills Reassessment.
StatLink http://dx.doi.org/10.1787/888932576795

Family socio-economic background

Results from every PISA cycle and other international and national data show that students' socio-economic background is strongly related to their performance in school. This was also true for Canadian youth in 2000. PISA-24 provides the opportunity to analyse the evolution of skills according to socio-economic background and to determine if a disadvantaged background at age 15 continues to influence performance and the acquisition of skills beyond compulsory education.

The evidence from PISA-24 suggests that a disadvantaged background at age 15 does not impede the acquisition of skills after compulsory education. However, students who came from a disadvantaged background still have poorer skills at age 24 than their more advantaged peers. In other words, while equity in reading skills improved after compulsory education, in the sense that the more disadvantaged youth were catching up somewhat, the differences were not completely eliminated.

READING PROFICIENCY OF CANADIAN YOUTH AT AGES 15 AND 24

■ Figure 3.4 ■
Reading performance in PISA-15 and PISA-24, by country of birth

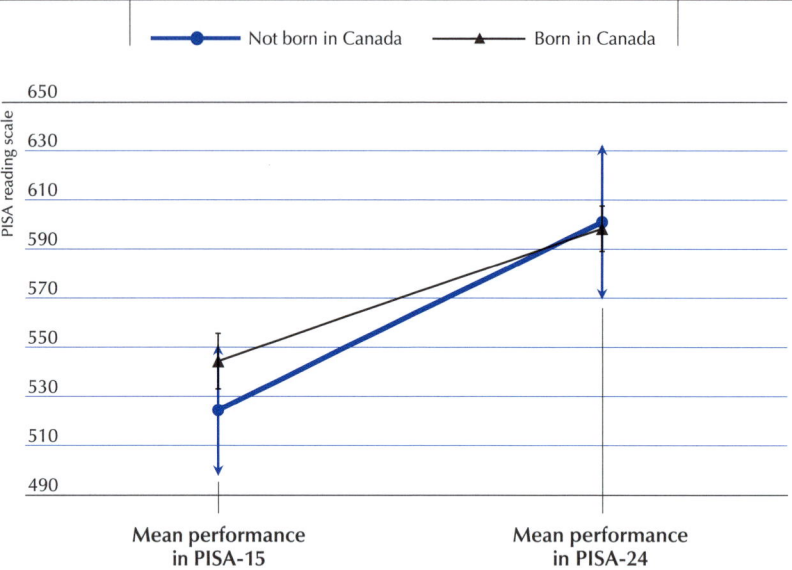

Note: The vertical lines on each measure of mean performance indicate the degree of precision with which these average scores are calculated. In statistical terms, the range of performance covered by these lines is referred to as the confidence interval. In general, overlapping vertical lines (joined confidence intervals) suggest that the differences are not statistically significant with a high degree of confidence.
Source: Table 3.2; YITS cycle 5.5: Reading Skills Reassessment.
StatLink http://dx.doi.org/10.1787/888932576795

■ Figure 3.5 ■
Reading performance in PISA-15 and PISA-24, by socio-economic background

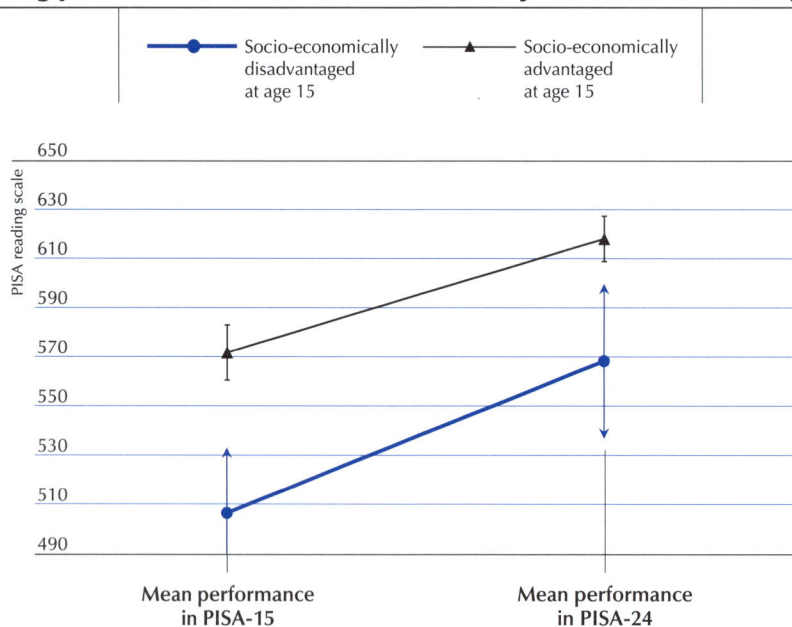

Note: The vertical lines on each measure of mean performance indicate the degree of precision with which these average scores are calculated. In statistical terms, the range of performance covered by these lines is referred to as the confidence interval. In general, overlapping vertical lines (joined confidence intervals) suggest that the differences are not statistically significant with a high degree of confidence.
Source: Table 3.2; YITS cycle 5.5: Reading Skills Reassessment.
StatLink http://dx.doi.org/10.1787/888932576795

Figure 3.5 plots the average performance among students from advantaged backgrounds and among those from disadvantaged backgrounds. For this analysis, students were grouped in thirds according to the *PISA index of economic, social and cultural status*. The bottom third of students – referred to here as socio-economically disadvantaged students – were compared to the top third of students – socio-economically advantaged students. This classification is country specific and therefore these students are advantaged or disadvantaged relative to their peers in Canada, but they might or might not be so with respect to students or individuals in other countries. Because the socio-economic status of PISA-24 participants was measured in PISA-15, this variable refers to their family background when they were 15 years old and not to how their individual socio-economic status might have evolved between 2000 and 2009.

As Figure 3.5 shows, in 2000, socio-economically disadvantaged PISA-15 participants attained an average of 506 score points in the PISA reading assessment, just above the OECD average. The average performance of those from an advantaged background was almost one full proficiency level higher, at 572 score points. By 2009, the average performance among those from a disadvantaged background improved by more than 62 score points, reaching 568 points; however, this is still below the average performance of the more advantaged youth at age 15. Meanwhile, the average performance of socio-economically advantaged participants increased by a smaller margin, 46 score points, up to 618 score points (Table 3.2).

Figure 3.5 also shows just how convincing the evidence of this persistent gap is. The confidence intervals for each of the four measures highlighted in the figures are relatively large, given the large variations in performance within each group and relatively fewer individuals assessed in each of these groups (a third of the whole sample in each case). Despite this lack of precision in the measures of average performance, the confidence intervals observed in 2000 and 2009 are not overlapping for the two groups (the upper ends of the confidence intervals in 2000 are below the lower ends of the intervals in 2009).

As the results of Chapters 4 and 5 of this report suggest, the persistent performance gap between these two groups is partly related to differences in educational pathways. Previous research (OECD, 2010a) shows that socio-economically disadvantaged students take longer to finish high school, have lower educational attainment, and are more likely to enter the labour market earlier. These factors are related to lower rates of skills acquisition and may partly explain persistently poorer reading proficiency among socio-economically disadvantaged students.

Language

Canada has two official languages, and compulsory education is provided in both English and French. The distribution of Francophones and Anglophones varies across the ten provinces. While Francophones are the majority in Québec, they are a minority in the other provinces. The following analysis considers both these aspects of language in the context of improvements in reading proficiency. The four categories are not mutually exclusive: for instance, the category of minority-language speakers consists of both Anglophones and Francophones, as does majority-language speakers. In the following analysis, language is determined by the language of the PISA test.

Anglophones outscored Francophone students by 16 score points in PISA-15, with average performances of 546 and 530 score points, respectively. The gap between minority and majority speakers in 2000 was similar (17 score points), with average performances of 545 score points for majority-language speakers and 528 score points for minority-language speakers (Table 3.2).

While the performance gap between minority and majority speakers narrowed to nearly no difference in 2009, the differences between Anglophones and Francophones remained fairly stable. The average score of minority speakers increased by 69 points compared to 54 points for majority-language speakers. As a result, average reading scores among both groups were nearly identical in 2009: 597 points for minority-language speakers and 600 points for majority-language speakers. In contrast, improvements in scores were similar among Anglophone and Francophone youth (about 56 and 58 score points, respectively). This resulted in a relatively consistent gap in reading proficiency between the average performance of Anglophone and Francophone youth in 2009. At age 24, young Anglophones had an average score of 602 points compared to 588 points for young Francophones (Table 3.2).

Figure 3.6 highlights the main differences in the distribution and the evolution of reading proficiency between Anglophone and Francophone youth in Canada. At age 15, the distribution of reading proficiency among the two groups differed in two ways. First, there were relatively fewer Francophone students (top panel of Figure 3.6) with high PISA scores – above 550, or approximately Level 4 in the PISA reading scale – than Anglophone students. Second, while there was a cluster of poorly-performing students, with scores of around 400 points, among Francophone participants, there was no such cluster of poor performers among Anglophone students.

READING PROFICIENCY OF CANADIAN YOUTH AT AGES 15 AND 24

At age 24, the difference at the high end of the distribution persists (bottom panel of Figure 3.6), while it has disappeared at the lower end. In other words, French speakers remain less likely to be highly proficient in reading at age 24, but the cluster of poor performers no longer exists. The differences between the top ends of the French and English distributions look almost identical in 2000 and 2009, despite the systematic improvement in proficiency across the entire distribution. Table 3.4 in Annex B describes the performance distribution for young Anglophone and Francophone men and women in both assessments.

■ Figure 3.6 ■
Comparison of the distribution of reading skills in PISA-15 and PISA-24, by test language

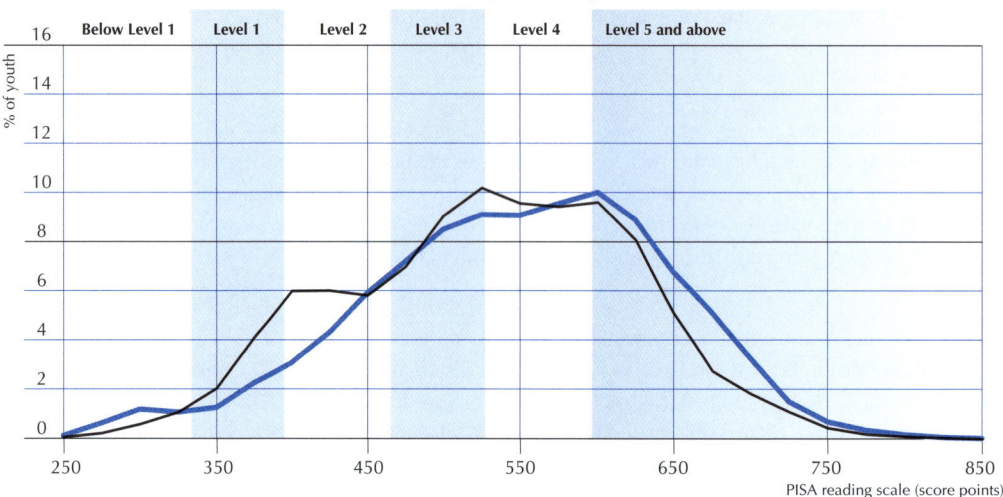

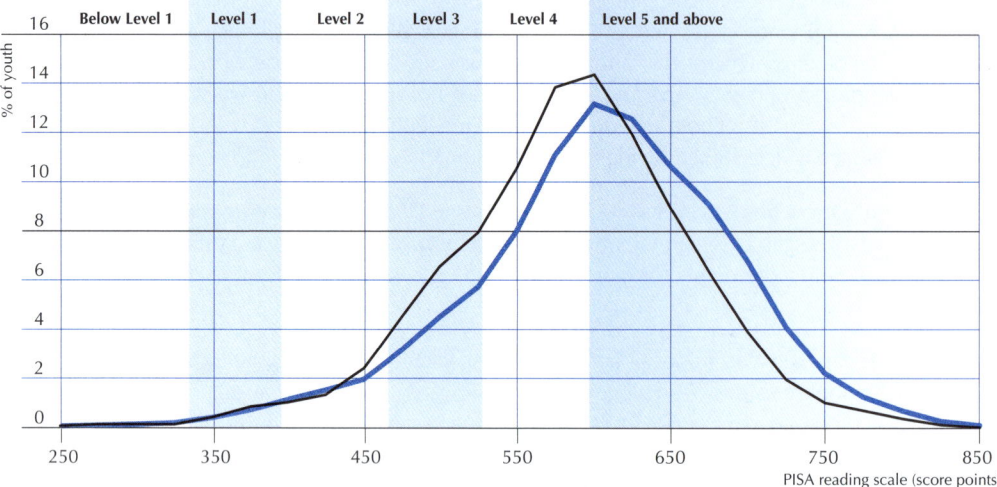

Source: Table 3.4; YITS cycle 5.5: Reading Skills Reassessment.
StatLink http://dx.doi.org/10.1787/888932576795

Urban and rural schools

Students in rural schools tend to come from socio-economically disadvantaged families (Bussière, et al., 2001). In addition, students in rural areas tend to have less access to educational resources outside of their homes and schools. For example, there may be fewer public libraries in these areas or they are less accessible. Museums and other cultural institutions are also relatively rare in rural areas compared to urban areas. These disadvantages were evident in the relationship between school location and student performance in PISA-15.

PISA-24 participants who had attended a rural school when they were 15 – a school in a community described as "a village, hamlet or rural area; with fewer than 3 000 people" – scored, on average, 23 points lower in the 2000 PISA reading assessment than those who had attended an urban school. The average PISA-15 performance among those who had attended rural schools at age 15 stood at 523 score points, while those who had attended urban schools at age 15 reached 546 score points (Table 3.2).

By age 24, individuals who had attended rural schools in 2000 had been able to overcome much of the performance disadvantage. By 2009, the average performance of PISA-24 participants who had attended rural schools when they were 15 was 590 points, a skills growth of 67 points. The average 2009 performance of PISA-24 participants who had attended urban schools when they were 15 was 600 score points, a smaller skills gain of 54 points (Table 3.2). Thus, while still evident, the gap between these two groups had narrowed to about 10 score points, a relatively small difference.

DIFFERENCES IN READING PROFICIENCY BY EDUCATION AND LABOUR-MARKET PATHWAYS, AGES 15 AND 24

The previous section has shown that a high proportion of young people can overcome disadvantages associated with demographic characteristics or school location. Where students do not converge in reading proficiency, the persistent gaps appear to be the consequence of explicit student behaviours between the ages of 15 and 24, rather than demographic characteristics. This section focuses on actual behaviour and individual choices of educational and labour-market pathways. It describes performance gaps in both PISA-15 and PISA-24 by groups of students identified by their educational attainment at age 24 and whether or not they have acquired labour-market experience.

The descriptive analysis in this section supports one of the main messages emerging from the analysis of PISA-24: sustained engagement in education is associated with strong growth in reading skills by the age of 24.

Educational attainment at age 24

Differences in reading skills among Canadian youth are associated with differences in educational attainment. In 2009, 24-year-old university graduates had higher average scores than young people with non-university level post-secondary education, who, in turn, had higher scores than those whose highest level of educational attainment was high school. Performance in PISA-24 mirrored that in PISA-15, when these groups of young people were 15 years old (Figure 3.7).

■ Figure 3.7 ■
Comparison of reading performance in PISA-15 and PISA-24, by educational attainment at age 24

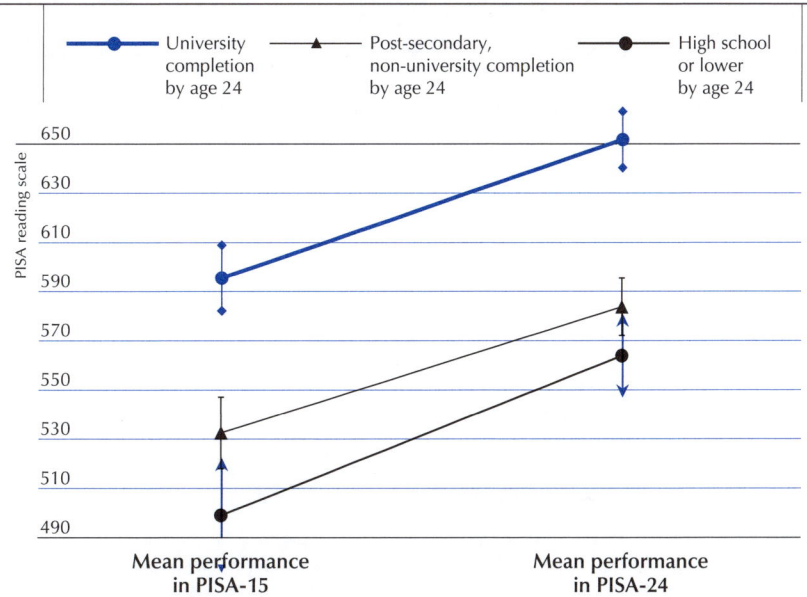

Note: The vertical lines on each measure of mean performance indicate the degree of precision with which these average scores are calculated. In statistical terms, the range of performance covered by these lines is referred to as the confidence interval. In general, overlapping vertical lines (joined confidence intervals) suggest that the differences are not statistically significant with a high degree of confidence.
Source: Table 3.5; YITS cycle 5.5: Reading Skills Reassessment.
StatLink http://dx.doi.org/10.1787/888932576795

For example, on average, young people who graduated from university by 2009 achieved 596 score points in PISA-15 and 652 in PISA-24. In contrast, non-university, post-secondary graduates had an average score of 533 points in PISA-15 and 584 points in PISA-24; and those individuals whose highest level of educational attainment was high school had scores of only 499 points in PISA-15 and 564 points in PISA-24 (Table 3.5).

Despite a faster rate of skills acquisition among young adults who have only a high-school education – indicated by the steeper line in Figure 3.7 – these youth continue to show the weakest performance at age 24. In fact, they have lower scores at age 24 than individuals with a university education had when they were 15.

The strong associations between performance and higher levels of educational attainment suggest that education is related both to initial skills at age 15 and to skills growth between the ages of 15 and 24. Nevertheless, evidence of skills growth among those with the lowest levels of educational attainment shows that skills acquisition, as measured by PISA-15 and PISA-24, occurs through various pathways.

Many factors are related to these differences in average performance. For example, the socio-economic background of those who follow an educational pathway leading to a university degree is likely to be very different than the socio-economic background of those whose highest level of attainment was a high school degree. In general, young women have higher levels of educational attainment than young men, and this is likely to have an impact on these observed differences. Individual characteristics explain some of the performance differences depicted in Figure 3.7. Chapters 4, 5 and 6 present more details and comprehensive analyses that show that even after taking these factors into account, educational attainment and years spent in education are strongly related to skills acquisition between the ages of 15 and 24.

Education pathways

Pathways through education can vary. For example, some individuals go from one stage of their education career to the next without taking any time out. This is known as a linear education pathway. For others, the path to post-secondary education is not so straightforward. They may have delayed beginning their post-secondary education to work or travel, or interrupted their studies part-way through.

Those who chose a non-linear pathway had an average score of 559 points in PISA-15, when they were 15 – some 20 points higher than those 15-year-olds who later continued along a linear pathway. However, as Figure 3.8 shows, by the age of 24, the gap in proficiency was narrowed to only 8 score points, as those who followed a linear pathway showed greater improvements in their scores.

■ Figure 3.8 ■
Comparison of reading performance in PISA-15 and PISA-24, by educational pathways

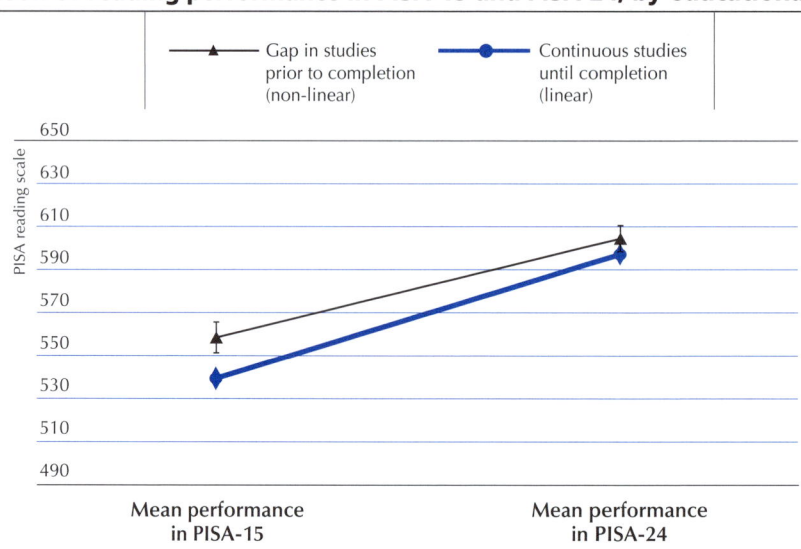

Note: The vertical lines on each measure of mean performance indicate the degree of precision with which these average scores are calculated. In statistical terms, the range of performance covered by these lines is referred to as the confidence interval. In general, overlapping vertical lines (joined confidence intervals) suggest that the differences are not statistically significant with a high degree of confidence.
Source: Table 3.5; YITS cycle 5.5: Reading Skills Reassessment.
StatLink http://dx.doi.org/10.1787/888932576795

Professional experience at age 24

While many young people chose to focus on education between 15 and 24, others moved into the labour market more quickly and, as a result, gained significant work experience by the age of 24. Individuals who had spent three or more years in full-time employment by the age of 24 are identified here as having focused on work after age 15. In PISA-15, these individuals scored an average of 529 points (Table 3.5). In contrast, those who focused on education, thus limiting their work experience to less than three years by the age of 24, scored, on average, 549 points in PISA-15. The performance gap between these two groups did not narrow in PISA-24: those with more than three years of work experience had an average score of 585 points in 2009, while those with less than three years of work experience had an average score of 606 points (Figure 3.9). This finding is particularly interesting since, in this case, the group with the lower average score did not narrow the gap between 2000 and 2009.

■ Figure 3.9 ■
Comparison of reading performance in PISA-15 and PISA-24, by professional experience at age 24

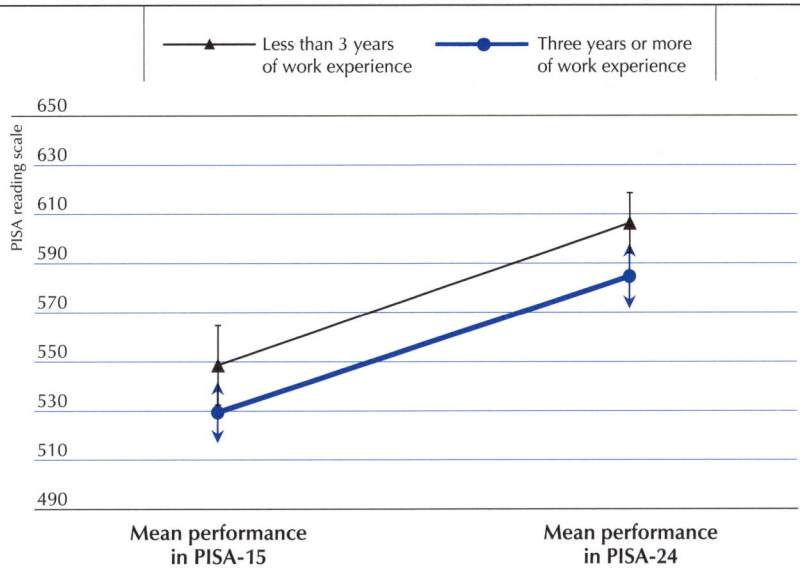

Note: The vertical lines on each measure of mean performance indicate the degree of precision with which these average scores are calculated. In statistical terms, the range of performance covered by these lines is referred to as the confidence interval. In general, overlapping vertical lines (joined confidence intervals) suggest that the differences are not statistically significant with a high degree of confidence.
Source: Table 3.5; YITS cycle 5.5: Reading Skills Reassessment.
StatLink ⌛ http://dx.doi.org/10.1787/888932576795

CHAPTER SUMMARY AND CONCLUSIONS

Ideally, compulsory education should equip students with a level of reading proficiency that will serve them well beyond school. By re-testing the students who participated in PISA-15, PISA-24 shows that reading skills continue to be acquired between the ages of 15 and 24, after compulsory education ends. The results show that Canadian youth made significant improvements in reading proficiency between the ages of 15 and 24. On average, young people in Canada had a gain of 57 score points in the PISA reading scale between 2000 and 2009, improving from 541 to 598 score points–or almost three-quarters of a PISA proficiency level.

PISA-24 shows that the strongest predictor of reading proficiency at age 24 is, in fact, reading proficiency at age 15. While not surprising, this is a significant result. It confirms that the investments in compulsory education made by governments, and the efforts parents and teachers make in helping their children and students learn, have a lasting impact. Further, it corroborates findings that young people can build on their reading proficiency at age 15. It also validates PISA's approach to measuring skills at age 15.

Comparing the degree of skills growth observed between the ages of 15 and 24 with skills acquisition by age 15, it is clear that the largest gains in reading proficiency occur during the years spent in compulsory education. Given the true costs of dropping out of school, efforts to prevent dropping out are more economical than applying corrective policies later. Results show that formal education continues to be the most effective means of acquiring skills.

One of the major goals of compulsory education is to ensure that all students graduate from compulsory education with the essential foundation skills. An indication of this would be a narrow distribution of proficiency, with the average located above Level 3. The distribution of reading proficiency scores was narrower in 2009 than in 2000, with a standard deviation of 78 points in 2009, compared to 92 points in 2000.

The proportion of young people with a score above the baseline proficiency Level 3 increased from 79% at age 15 to 93% at age 24. Level 3 is a key measure of success in PISA. Individuals proficient at this level are adept at "locating multiple pieces of information, making links between different parts of a text, and relating it to familiar everyday knowledge". This represents an important increase in the number of students who have attained a level of proficiency that will enable them to participate fully in society. Since the odds of participating in higher education are greatest among individuals at these levels, learning gains between the ages of 15 and 24 increased the pool of students who could succeed at post-secondary education to over 90%.

PISA-24 also identifies and quantifies a small but significant group of individuals with poor reading skills at age 24. The proportion of young people who scored below PISA reading proficiency Level 3 fell substantially between 2000 and 2009, but in 2009, 7% of 24-year-old Canadians still performed below this important threshold. These young people would likely benefit from general literacy training. Since the proportion of young people below proficiency Level 3 on the PISA scale dropped from 21% at age 15 to 7% at age 24, policy makers could more easily target and design programmes to improve the reading skills of these young Canadians. These findings highlight the need for continued attention to reading skills beyond compulsory education and into adulthood.

Improvements in reading proficiency do not necessarily occur at a faster pace among those students who are highly proficient. In fact, most disadvantages tend to decrease over time as the distribution of reading proficiency tends towards convergence. While some observers might have expected a "fanning-out" of skills levels and proficiencies between the ages of 15 and 24, PISA-24 shows no evidence to support this assumption.

Where skills acquisition has not tended towards convergence, the descriptive analyses suggest that education pathways may influence the differences. Young people who completed university-level studies maintained a large performance advantage over their peers. These issues are examined in subsequent chapters.

Young men, Francophones, rural students, and those from more socio-economically disadvantaged backgrounds were able to narrow the gap in performance that was evident at age 15, and a large proportion scored above Level 3 at age 24. But the gaps between these groups and others are still a concern. Characteristics associated with poorer proficiency at age 15 were still associated with lower proficiency at age 24. Socio-economically advantaged students outscored their disadvantaged peers by more than 66 score points in PISA-15; by 2009 that gap had narrowed to 50 score points. However, by age 24, the average performance of young people who were considered socio-economically disadvantaged at age 15 (568 score points in PISA-24) remained below the average performance of socio-economically advantaged students nine years earlier (572 score points in PISA-15). From a policy point of view, the persistent gap between these two groups indicates that students from low-income families and whose parents have low levels of education continue to be disadvantaged. Even if fewer individuals from these groups scored at Levels 1 and 2 at age 24, they still deserve the attention of policy makers.

The first key insight emerging from PISA-24 is that the disadvantages observed at age 15 are, for the most part, still evident at age 24. Those who underperformed in PISA-24 were more likely to be from a socio-economically disadvantaged background, to be Francophone, and to be male. These are the same individual characteristics that were associated with underperformance in PISA-15. While skills acquisition takes place at slightly different rates among the various groups of students, for the most part, these differences are not large enough to compensate for initial gaps in reading skills. In other words, performance gaps are not easily narrowed over time.

The exception to this pattern is seen in immigrant status. Most countries are hosting growing numbers of children from immigrant backgrounds. These students tend to come from disadvantaged backgrounds and speak a language at home that is not the same as the language of the PISA test. Reading proficiency among students with immigrant backgrounds was lower than that of native-born students in most countries in PISA-15. However, in Canada, students with an immigrant background, though initially disadvantaged, show that it is possible to catch up with their native peers. By age 24, young people with an immigrant background fully bridged the gap that separated them from 15-year-olds born in Canada. Students born outside of Canada scored an average of 524 points in PISA-15, while those born in Canada averaged 545 points.

In the 2009 re-assessment, all participants scored around 600 points on average, whether they were born in Canada or not. In addition to highlighting the value of integration, this shows that appropriate policies can help to reduce, if not eliminate, differences in student performance.

This finding also shows that it is possible for groups of students who perform poorly at age 15 to acquire skills and catch up with the rest of the population in the years following compulsory education. Further analysis of this group may help to determine the behaviours, attitudes and education and professional pathways that are related to faster skills acquisition.

Notes

1. The mean score of 541 points among those in the PISA-24 sample who were assessed in 2000 is somewhat higher than the mean score of 534 points for the full sample of Canadian students who participated in PISA-15. The higher average of the PISA-24 subsample is the result of differences in the two samples that were not accounted for by the survey weights. Changes to the sample composition in longitudinal surveys are often referred to as sample attrition. Sample attrition bias can occur when certain characteristics make some individuals more likely to respond to the survey than others. Survey weights are used to keep the composition of the sample representative of the population in question, in this case 15-year-old students in Canada in 2000. However, sample attrition can affect the degree to which the results can be generalised to the population level.

2. Note that the distinction here is made based on the country where the student was born. Some students who were born in Canada might have parents born outside of Canada. In other PISA reports, these students would be typically considered as students with an immigrant background, and they are commonly referred to as second-generation students.

Growth in Reading Proficiency over Time

This chapter examines improvements in reading proficiency observed between the ages of 15 and 24 and determines whether they meet, exceed or fall short of expectations. For example, PISA-15 and PISA-24 show that approximately 59 score points were gained annually while students remained in formal education, but that the level of reading proficiency at age 24 was lower than that estimated for students at the end of compulsory education. This suggests that skills gains do not continue at the same annual rate as measured in 2000 when students were 15. Skills acquisition in PISA-24 is then analysed within the PISA reading framework.

GROWTH IN READING PROFICIENCY OVER TIME

HOW DO YOUNG PEOPLE'S READING SKILLS EVOLVE AFTER COMPULSORY EDUCATION?

Although reading proficiency improved among nearly all Canadian youth, as represented by participants in PISA-24, the rate of growth was not necessarily constant between the ages of 15 and 24. Rather, the rate of skills growth was influenced by the life transitions that occurred during this time. This chapter analyses these learning gains in greater depth, providing a conceptual framework for the analysis of skills growth. The chapter also explores skills growth within the PISA reading framework, and analyses the various patterns of skills acquisition across contexts, text structures, and reading processes.

PISA-15 data provides a frame of reference for the evidence on skills growth in PISA-24. The PISA population is defined as 15-year-olds in education, regardless of the grade in which they are placed and regardless of why they might be in different grades. Comparing student performance across adjacent grades, with some technical adjustments, provides a measure of expected skills growth as students progress from one grade to the next.

Combining data from PISA-15 and PISA-24, the rate of growth expected from regular grade progression (measured using PISA-15) is compared to actual reading proficiency measured at age 24 (measured using PISA-24 and PISA-15). This comparison can provide some insights into the dynamic nature of skills gain and loss. For example, does the skills growth observed in PISA-24 measure up to the skills growth predicted using grade projections from PISA-15?

As young people move from grade to grade, and from education to work, the types and complexity of materials that they are required to read and understand also change. PISA assesses overall reading skills within an array of contexts and texts types. By comparing differences in performance among the kinds of questions used in PISA, it is possible to analyse how improvements in reading proficiency vary depending on these contexts and types of texts.

GRADE PROGRESSION AND GROWTH IN READING SKILLS

At the time of the PISA-15 test, participating students were enrolled in different grades. Most of the students were enrolled in grade 10, but some were enrolled in grades 9, 8 and 7 and a few of them were enrolled in grades 11 and 12.

There are various explanations for these differences. For example, the month of birth determining the age of entry into school, and the rules determining the normal progression through grades, vary from province to province; so even though all students were 15 at the time of the first PISA test, they were enrolled in different grades. The analysis presented here adjusts for differences between regions and for students of various ages.

Figure 4.1 illustrates the relationship between years in school and reading proficiency. The horizontal axis represents the relative grade of each student. This is calculated by subtracting the actual grade of each student from the most common grade of students in the same province who were born in the same month (the modal grade in that province has the value zero on the horizontal axis). For example, if the student is in grade 9 and the modal grade among respondents from his or her province is grade 10, then the relative grade of this student will be minus one. The horizontal axis begins three grades below the modal grade, as this is the lowest relative grade observed in PISA-15. Secondary education in Canada provides at least 11 years of formal education and in most cases 12 years.[1] Therefore, the horizontal axis in Figure 4.1 ends two units above the modal grade because most students who were in the modal grade when they took the PISA exam at age 15 could expect to receive an additional two years of formal education, not counting any post-secondary education.

The vertical axis in Figure 4.1 shows the relative PISA score in reading. This score is relative to the average proficiency of students of the same age in the same province, in order to control for differences in average proficiency by province and month of birth.[2] Each of the dots along the resulting data co-ordinates of grade and proficiency represents the estimated relationship between years of schooling and reading proficiency. The solid line describes the linear relationship between grade level and average performance. This "line of best fit" minimises the distance between each of the points and the line; in other words, it is the closest line to all points. As such, the line, or more precisely, its slope, represents the best possible approximation of a measure of expected skills growth associated with grade progression. The slope of the line of best fit is approximately 59, indicating that each year of education is associated with a learning gain of 59 score points on the PISA scale.[3]

Assuming there is no development, either gain or loss, in skills after the end of compulsory education, one implication of the results presented in Figure 4.1 is that young people who progressed through secondary education should have an average reading proficiency of about 640 score points. This score represents the predicted average performance of students two grades above the modal grade in their region.

GROWTH IN READING PROFICIENCY OVER TIME

■ Figure 4.1 ■
Relative grade level and average reading proficiency at age 15

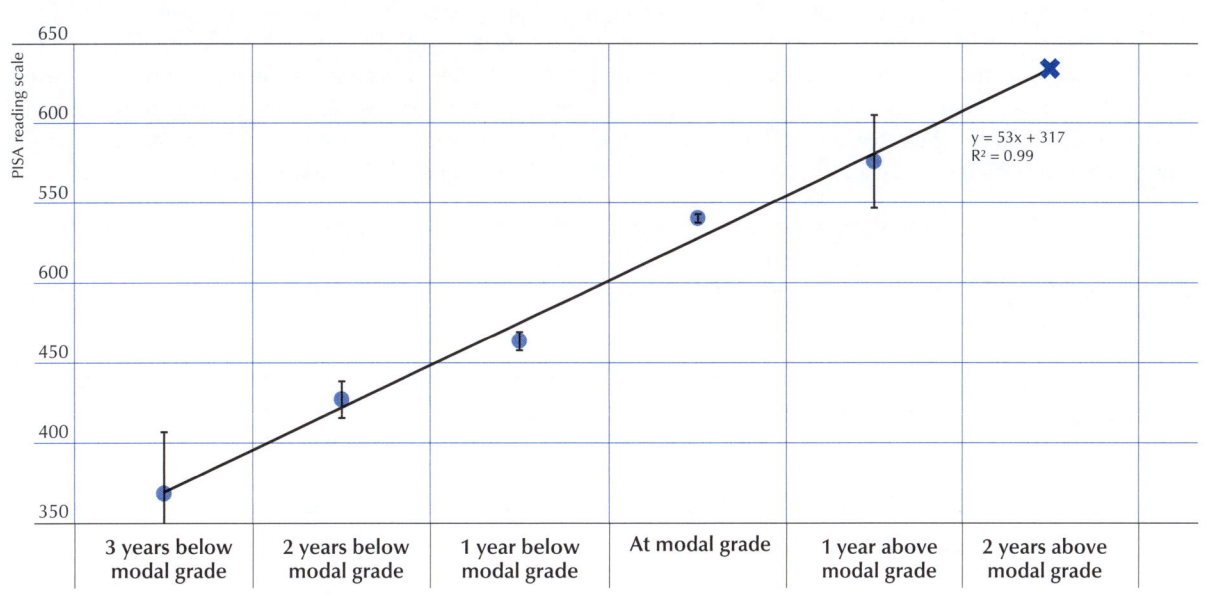

✖ Expected reading proficiency for students 2 years above modal grade

$y = 53x + 317$
$R^2 = 0.99$

(x-axis: 3 years below modal grade, 2 years below modal grade, 1 year below modal grade, At modal grade, 1 year above modal grade, 2 years above modal grade)

Source: Table 4.1; YITS cycle 5.5: Reading Skills Reassessment.
StatLink http://dx.doi.org/10.1787/888932576814

However, PISA-24 paints a very different picture. Figure 4.2 depicts the actual evolution of skills between 2000 and 2009, by relative grade, for three groups of students: students above the most common grade in 2000; students at the most common grade; and students below the most common grade.

■ Figure 4.2 ■
Comparison of reading performance in PISA-15 and PISA-24, by relative grade at age 15

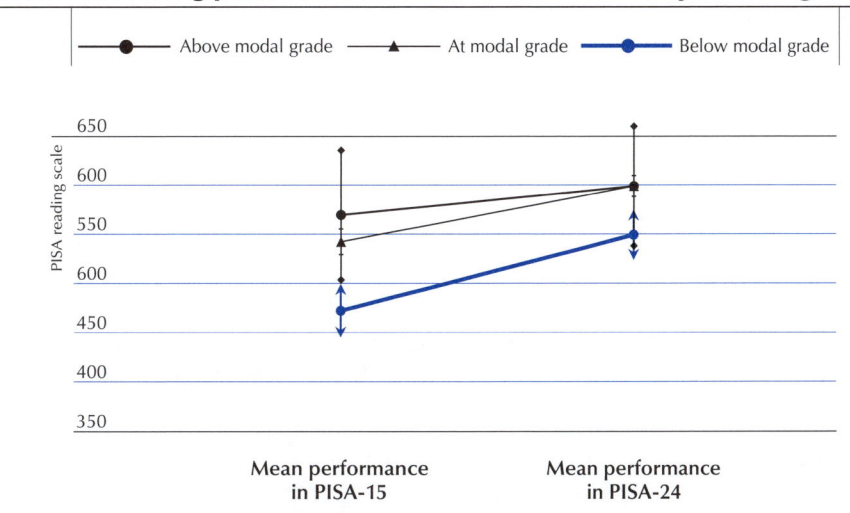

— ● — Above modal grade   — ▲ — At modal grade   — ● — Below modal grade

(x-axis: Mean performance in PISA-15, Mean performance in PISA-24)

Note: The vertical lines on each measure of mean performance indicate the degree of precision with which these average scores are calculated. In statistical terms, the range of performance covered by these lines is referred to as the confidence interval. In general, overlapping vertical lines (joined confidence intervals) suggest that the differences are not statistically significant with a high degree of confidence.
Source: Table 4.1; YITS cycle 5.5: Reading Skills Reassessment.
StatLink http://dx.doi.org/10.1787/888932576814

LEARNING BEYOND FIFTEEN – TEN YEARS AFTER PISA © OECD 2012

The group of students below the most common grade was the group with the lowest average score in PISA-15 and the fastest rate of skills acquisition between 2000 and 2009. On average, those 15-year-old students below the most common grade averaged 472 points in PISA-15 compared to 543 points for the group in the most common grade, and 570 points for the group above the most common grade. By the time these students were 24, those who had been below the most common grade at 15 still had the lowest average score (549 points), while there was virtually no difference between those who had been at or above the modal grade when they were 15 (599 points for both groups). Yet those below the modal grade showed the fastest rate of growth in reading skills. The average score among this group improved by almost 77 score points – more than an entire proficiency level. In contrast, the average score among those who were above the modal grade when they were 15 improved by less than 30 points. This is shown in Figure 4.2 by the two converging lines, which indicate a loss of advantage for students who were initially in higher grades.

By the age of 24, the level of reading proficiency among all three groups is below that predicted by the relationship between skills and grade progression (Figure 4.1). After two or more years in compulsory education and a number of years either in the labour market on in post-secondary education, the average score among these groups is below the predicted 634 points.

This evidence suggests that reading proficiency develops more slowly after formal schooling, and that loss of skills could begin before the age of 24. However, by the age of 24, most young people will have specialised in a particular field, and general reading proficiency will have ceased to be the goal of their education and training.

DYNAMIC LEARNING IN THE CONTEXT OF THE PISA READING FRAMEWORK

Since PISA-24 shows evidence of widespread skills gains, it is difficult to identify the specific reading skills that are subject to deterioration over time. One possibility is that reading proficiency may be improving or deteriorating depending on the type of texts read.

During late adolescence, as young people focus on more specialised learning, the brain becomes more efficient in performing tasks that are done more frequently, while it also becomes less efficient in functions that are infrequently used.[4] For proficiency in reading, the context of reading and the type of texts read become important factors influencing growth and decline.

As discussed in Chapter 2, the PISA reading framework groups assessment questions into three main categories: context, text structure and reading process (Adams and Wu, 2002). Since many of the questions in the PISA-15 were also used in PISA-24, it is possible to compare the relative performance on each test question across individuals. The analyses presented here describe patterns of performance taking into account the difficulty of the questions. Annex A provides details on the methodology underpinning this analysis.

A number of examples of PISA reading units and questions are presented at the end of this chapter. The units, and the questions within each unit, are not those selected for inclusion in PISA-24, as these are used to anchor other questions and construct trends within PISA, and therefore represent confidential material; but they do provide examples of the differences across contexts, text structures and reading processes assessed in PISA. They also exemplify how, for example, context and text structure interact with one another, or the differences between reading process and text structure.

The PISA reading framework distinguishes four levels within the "context" dimension of reading proficiency: educational, occupational, personal and public. In the "text structure" dimension, there are two levels: continuous and non-continuous. In the "reading process" dimension, there are three levels: retrieving, interpreting, and reflecting on information. Sample PISA test questions are included at the end of this chapter. The question entitled "brushing your teeth" is an example of a continuous, educational, interpreting question. "Mobile phone safety" is an example of a non-continuous, public, interpreting question. These examples cover all these dimensions and illustrate how they are used in the actual PISA test.

The proportion of students who answered a question correctly provides a simple way to analyse performance on a particular question, or group of questions. This is referred to as the item-correct score expressed on a scale of zero to one for each item.[5] Table 4.2 in Annex B provides details on item-correct scores for each of the 28 questions that appeared in PISA-15 and PISA-24.

The difference between the item-correct score in PISA-24 and the item-correct score in PISA-15 shows whether respondents improved or not on a particular question in the nine years between tests. The average difference for a group of questions shows whether there was improvement on a particular type of question, for instance, if questions of a similar context showed more or less improvement than other types of questions.

The more difficult the question, the smaller the proportion of students who answered it correctly in PISA-15, thus the more room for improvement by the time of the PISA re-assessment in 2009. For this reason, the more difficult questions may provide greater insight as to how skills growth varied across the PISA dimensions. The analysis presented here first looks at patterns of improvement and then relates those to the difficulty of the questions.

Improvements in performance across question types in the PISA reading framework

Figure 4.3 shows the average difference in item-correct scores for each level of the questions. In other words, it is the average improvement between PISA-15 and PISA-24 on questions categorised by their context, text structure and reading process. These are displayed in the box on the right vertical axis. The bars in Figure 4.3 show the proportion of questions in which there was an improvement and the proportion in which there was no change. This provides complementary evidence to the average difference.

All dimensions assessed by PISA showed significant improvement between 2000 and 2009. The average change in item-correct score was 0.10. However, as Figure 4.3 indicates, the change in proficiency is not uniform across the cognitive dimensions that comprise the reading domain. Average change varied from a low of 0.08 to a high of 0.14.

Of the four types of contexts represented in the PISA questions, the average difference is largest for those related to personal contexts. This is also the context that had the largest proportion of questions showing an improvement. Questions in the education and occupation contexts showed the smallest average differences. These are the contexts most often referenced by texts encountered in formal education, so it is not surprising that improvements in skills were smaller on these questions, as most young people would have left formal education well before the age of 24. Finally, the average item-correct difference for PISA items related to the public context was around the average. Although this context had the smallest proportion of questions showing improvements, the improvements on these questions tended to be greater. These average changes need to be interpreted with caution as they hide differences across groups of individuals who have followed different education and labour-market pathways.

Surprisingly, given the relative balance of text structures in various environments, there is little difference between the improvements in average performance on questions involving continuous versus non-continuous text structures. However, a slightly larger proportion of questions related to non-continuous texts showed improvement compared to continuous texts.

■ Figure 4.3 ■
Improvements between PISA-15 and PISA-24, by question type within the PISA reading framework

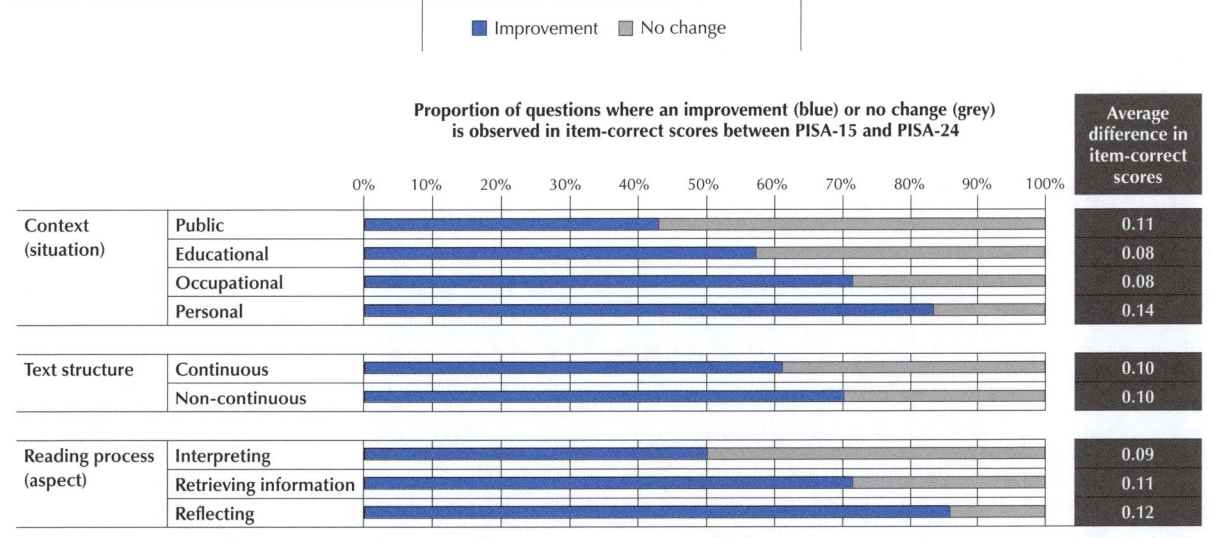

		Proportion of questions where improvement/no change	Average difference in item-correct scores
Context (situation)	Public		0.11
	Educational		0.08
	Occupational		0.08
	Personal		0.14
Text structure	Continuous		0.10
	Non-continuous		0.10
Reading process (aspect)	Interpreting		0.09
	Retrieving information		0.11
	Reflecting		0.12

Source: Table 4.2; YITS cycle 5.5: Reading Skills Reassessment.
StatLink http://dx.doi.org/10.1787/888932576814

Questions categorised by the reading process of reflecting showed the largest gain among the three levels of this dimension. It also had the largest proportion of questions that showed improvements. Questions categorised as reflecting require individuals to relate texts to their own conceptual and experiential frames of reference. Since young people have gained considerable life experience in the nine years between 15 and 24 it is not surprising to see greater improvements in this process. Questions requiring retrieval and interpretation did not show as large an improvement.

Question difficulty and improvements in performance

Contexts: Personal, occupational, public and educational

Taking the difficulty of the questions into account, skills gains appear more frequently in questions framed in a personal context and less frequently when framed in an educational context. Skills gains are more mixed for questions framed in occupational and public contexts. These findings show that individual experience plays an important role in skills gains after compulsory education. While there is no evidence of skills loss among the questions in the educational context, performance improvements tend to be smaller and less frequent in this area.

Questions framed in a personal context are found along the entire spectrum of difficulty, and improvements in item-correct statistics are relatively larger among these questions than among other types of questions (Table 4.2).

The evidence of skills growth among questions framed in occupational contexts is somewhat weakened after taking into account the difficulty of the questions. In both PISA-15 and PISA-24, these types of questions tended to be of average difficulty. While, in general, the more difficult the question, the greater the improvement observed, very little improvement is seen in one relatively difficult question (Employment, Question 2 or R219Q01T). Questions framed in a public context are distributed along the entire range of difficulty in PISA-24. Above average improvements in item-correct scores are observed among difficult questions. Slightly below-average improvements are seen on questions of average difficulty; and there are no or only slight improvements on easy questions in this context (Table 4.2).

Improvements on questions framed in an educational context are minimal. With the exception of educational questions in the middle range of difficulty, the improvements observed between 2000 and 2009 are smaller than average, given the difficulty of the questions. There are small improvements on the easier questions in this context, as would be expected, although there are questions of similar difficulty that show more marked improvement. Improvements on the difficult questions in this context are particularly small. The item-correct scores are the lowest among questions of similar difficulty among all four contexts (Table 4.2).

Text structure: Continuous and non-continuous texts

The only appreciable difference between the questions involving continuous and non-continuous text is found among the most difficult questions of each type. For non-continuous text questions, the observed improvements between 2000 and 2009 are large and greater than average, given their difficulty level. For continuous text questions, the improvements are not as large, and in some cases they are smaller than average, given their difficulty (Table 4.2).

Reading process: Reflecting on texts, interpreting texts, retrieving information

Results from PISA-24 do not show faster or slower rates of skills acquisition for any one of the three types of reading processes examined after question difficulty is taken into account. This suggests that skills growth is similar across all three reading processes.

The overall improvements observed for reflecting on texts and, to a lesser extent, for retrieving information, appear to depend partly on the difficulty of the questions. There is only one easy question related to reflecting on texts in PISA-24, which might explain why there are more of these types of questions that show improvements in item-correct scores than other types of questions: the more difficult the question, the larger the improvement over time tended to be. Yet, the observed improvements on these difficult reflecting questions are relatively weak and smaller than the improvements observed on questions related to the other reading processes.

For the reading process involving retrieving information, the results on item-correct scores are equally mixed. There are two relatively difficult questions related to retrieving information. On one, the observed improvements in item-correct scores are large – in fact, slightly larger than average. But on the other, the opposite is true: there is basically no noticeable improvement. The same mixed pattern is observed on easy or moderately difficult questions related to the same reading process (Table 4.2).

The questions related to interpreting texts span the whole range of difficulty in PISA-24, and the observed improvements in item-correct scores largely correspond to the difficulty of each question. The only deviations from this norm are the two most difficult questions related to this process, where observed improvements are particularly large–larger, for example, than those on questions of similar difficulty related to reflecting on texts (Table 4.2). It is possible that these differences are related to the context in which these questions are asked. In fact, the difficult interpreting questions are posed on personal contexts, whereas the reflecting questions are posed on an educational context.

Box 4.1 Perceived and actual reading loss

Text structure appears to have a strong association with how individuals perceive their reading proficiency. For example, Canadian youth who took part in PISA in 2000 and who were followed longitudinally in YITS were asked to rate their own reading proficiency at each data collection every two years. Using these data for the PISA-24 sample, a small number of respondents (only 61 participants report a perceived loss of skills) rated their reading skills lower in 2009 as compared with 2000. The question performance of these respondents is compared with that of other respondents who did not perceive some loss of skills (Table 4.2). In fact, neither group showed a skills loss; both groups had net improvements in their performance on questions in almost all classifications of questions.

However, there are differences in performance on questions between those who perceived a skills loss and those who did not, depending on structure of the text. For those who had not perceived a skills loss, there are variations across reading processes (retrieving, interpreting and reflecting) in continuous texts but not in non-continuous texts. For continuous texts, performance improvements are greater in retrieving information and reflecting on texts than for interpreting, perhaps because of differences in the purpose of reading in adult contexts between reading for pleasure and reading to acquire specific information.

The differences are even more pronounced for the group who perceived a skills loss. Although there is no such decline evident, there is relative stagnation in performance on questions involving continuous texts compared with those involving non-continuous texts. Similarly, across text types, questions requiring reflecting processes also have relatively smaller improvements in performance. In contrast, performance on questions requiring interpretation of non-continuous texts improved substantially. These results suggest that the nature of "reading proficiency" may be narrowly defined in popular understanding, related to the specific activities associated with the construction of meaning from continuous texts.

CHAPTER SUMMARY AND CONCLUSIONS

PISA-15 provides a framework for analysing skills gains in at least two respects. First, performance differences across grades allow researchers to estimate skills acquisition resulting from students' progress through compulsory education. Given that most students had completed secondary education by age 24, this estimate of skills growth provides a baseline from which to measure the development of skills between the ages of 15 and 24. Second, skills acquisition is analysed along the different building blocks of the PISA reading framework. By analysing performance on specific questions across assessments, it is possible to study, for example, if the overall skills acquisition evident in PISA-24 hides variations across the different aspects covered by the PISA reading assessment.

By examining the grades in which 15-year-old students were placed when they took the PISA-15 test, it is estimated that students gained around 59 score points in each year of compulsory education. This is a notable increase, equal to nearly three-quarters of a proficiency level. Reading proficiency at age 24 was, in fact, poorer than it was projected to be among students at the completion of compulsory education (grade 12 or two additional years for most PISA-15 participants).

Results from PISA-24 suggest, therefore, that skills gains do not continue at the same rate as measured at age 15. Not only was the development of reading proficiency slower after the completion of compulsory education, it appears likely that skills loss could have begun prior to age 24. These results also point to the possibility that compulsory schooling is effective in improving reading proficiency and therefore suggest that efforts should be targeted at those students who are likely to drop out of school.

Using the PISA reading framework as a reference, PISA-24 provides evidence that skills growth and maintenance occur in specific contexts and depend on individual experiences. As the contexts in which individuals use their reading skills change when they move from compulsory education into the labour market or continue with their education, it is only natural that the pace and type of learning change as well. Between the ages of 15 and 24, development of language skills was most evident in personal contexts and least evident in educational contexts. It is possible that as youth moved out of compulsory education it is in this context that reading skills have experienced the lowest amount of skill use. The findings on skills improvement related to text structure is more nuanced, as there is only weak evidence of faster skills growth in non-continuous text questions as compared with continuous text questions. The reading process of reflecting appears to have improved the most, but differences among the reading processes were quite small.

A key factor in the dynamic process of learning is the use of reading in daily life. Overall, the patterns of improvements in reading proficiency show that using reading skills regularly is a strong determinant of learning gain. While improvements in proficiency were widespread between the ages of 15 and 24, some evidence suggests that reading proficiency among young adults may already be in decline. For example, PISA-15 and PISA-24 show that approximately 59 score points were gained annually while students remained in formal education, but that the level of reading proficiency at age 24 was lower than that estimated for students at the completion of grade 12. Even after taking into consideration that PISA was not designed with to test skills at age 24, this evidence suggests that the acquisition of skills does not continue at the same annual rate as measured in 2000 when students were 15.

Substantial skills growth is apparent in each of the main dimensions considered in the PISA reading framework (context, text structure and reading process), but the rate of change in proficiency is not uniform across these key dimensions. For example, larger gains were made on reading questions related to personal, rather than educational, contexts, due to the completion of compulsory education for most people between the ages of 15 and 24.

This evidence confirms the importance of reading activities to maintain and ensure high levels of proficiency into adulthood, and supports earlier evidence from the International Adult Literacy Survey that showed that a decline in skills may begin quite early in adult life.

EXAMPLES OF PISA READING UNITS

The following questions are presented in the order in which they appeared within the unit in the main survey. Percentages of student responses are not provided in the tabulation of framework characteristics (as they were in the parallel material in the 2006 international report) because several of the units were only administered by some of the countries, and the comparison of percentages between questions in those units and other units might lead to a misinterpretation of task difficulty.

GROWTH IN READING PROFICIENCY OVER TIME

■ Figure 4.4 ■
BRUSHING YOUR TEETH

Do our teeth become cleaner and cleaner the longer and harder we brush them?

British researchers say no. They have actually tried out many different alternatives, and ended up with the perfect way to brush your teeth. A two minute brush, without brushing too hard, gives the best result. If you brush hard, you harm your tooth enamel and your gums without loosening food remnants or plaque.

Bente Hansen, an expert on tooth brushing, says that it is a good idea to hold the toothbrush the way you hold a pen. "Start in one corner and brush your way along the whole row," she says. "Don't forget your tongue either! It can actually contain loads of bacteria that may cause bad breath."

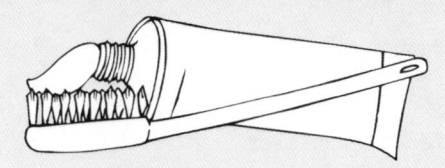

"Brushing your Teeth" is an article from a Norwegian magazine.

Use "Brushing Your Teeth" above to answer the questions that follow.

BRUSHING YOUR TEETH – QUESTION 1

Situation: *Educational*
Text format: *Continuous*
Text type: *Exposition*
Aspect: *Integrate and interpret – Form a broad understanding*
Question format: *Multiple choice*
Difficulty: *353 (1a)*

What is this article about?

A. The best way to brush your teeth.

B. The best kind of toothbrush to use.

C. The importance of good teeth.

D. The way different people brush their teeth.

Scoring
Full Credit: The best way to brush your teeth.

Comment

This task requires the reader to recognise the main idea of a short descriptive text. The text is not only short, but about the very familiar, everyday topic of brushing one's teeth. The language is quite idiomatic ("loads of bacteria", "bad breath"), and the text is composed of short paragraphs and familiar syntactic structures, with a straightforward heading and a supporting illustration. All of these features combine to make the text very approachable.

The difficulty of this question is located towards bottom of Level 1a, among the easier PISA reading questions. The question stem is rather open and broad, directing the reader to look for a broad generalisation as an answer. The words of the key ("The best way to brush your teeth") include a term that is part of the title ("brush(ing) your teeth"), and if – drawing on knowledge about the conventional structures and features of texts – there is an expectation that a title is likely to summarise a text, the reader need go no further than the title to find the key. Should confirmation be sought, the first three sentences of the body of the text also encapsulate the main idea, and it is repeated by illustration and elaboration in what little remains of this short piece. Thus the required information is both prominent and repeated in a short and simple text: all markers of relatively easy reading tasks.

BRUSHING YOUR TEETH – QUESTION 2

Situation: *Educational*
Text format: *Continuous*
Text type: *Exposition*
Aspect: *Access and retrieve – Retrieve information*
Question format: *Multiple choice*
Difficulty: *358 (1a)*

What do the British researchers recommend?

A. That you brush your teeth as often as possible.
B. That you do not try to brush your tongue.
C. That you do not brush your teeth too hard.
D. That you brush your tongue more often than your teeth.

Scoring

Full Credit: C. That you do not brush your teeth too hard.

Comment

Another question located at Level 1a, this task requires readers to retrieve a specific piece of information from the text rather than recognise a broad generalisation (as in the previous task); the question is therefore classified as **access and retrieve** *by aspect. The task explicitly directs the reader to the second paragraph with the literal match to "British researchers". It nevertheless requires some synthesis and some inference, to understand that the British researchers referred to at the beginning of paragraph 2 are those giving the advice throughout the paragraph, and that "gives the best results" is synonymous with "recommend". Performance on this task showed that the distractor providing most competition for the key is the first one, "That you brush your teeth as often as possible", presumably because it draws on a plausible misconception based on prior knowledge.*

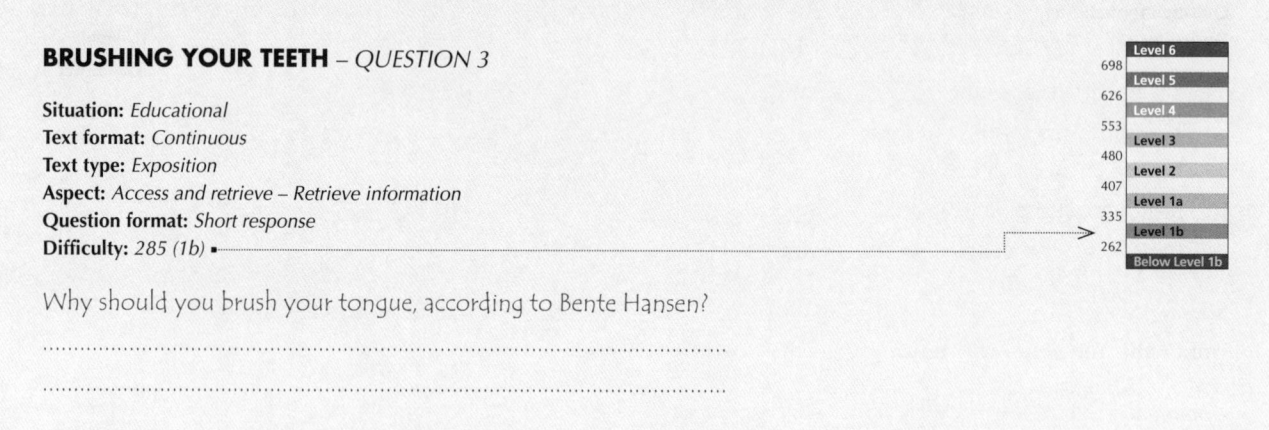

BRUSHING YOUR TEETH – QUESTION 3

Situation: *Educational*
Text format: *Continuous*
Text type: *Exposition*
Aspect: *Access and retrieve – Retrieve information*
Question format: *Short response*
Difficulty: *285 (1b)*

Why should you brush your tongue, according to Bente Hansen?

....
....

Scoring

Full Credit: Refers either to the <u>bacteria</u> OR <u>getting rid of bad breath</u>, OR <u>both</u>. Response may paraphrase or quote directly from the text.

- To get rid of bacteria.
- Your tongue can contain bacteria.
- Bacteria.
- Because you can avoid bad breath.
- Bad breath.
- To remove bacteria and therefore stop you from having bad breath. *[both]*
- It can actually contain loads of bacteria that may cause bad breath. *[both]*
- Bacteria can cause bad breath.

Comment

The wording of the question provides two terms that can be used literally to find the relevant section of the text: "Bente Hansen" and "tongue". Moreover, the term "Bente Hansen" occurs in a prominent position at the very beginning of the last paragraph. In the same paragraph the term "tongue" occurs, giving an even more precise clue for locating the exact place in which the required information is to be found. Each of these terms occurs only once in the text, so the reader does not need to deal with any competing information when matching the question to the relevant part of the text.

With a difficulty located in the lowest described level, Level 1b, this is one of the easiest questions in the PISA 2009 reading assessment. It does nevertheless require a low level of inference, since the reader has to understand that "it" in the last sentence refers to "your tongue". A further element that might be expected to contribute to difficulty is that the focus of the question is relatively abstract: the reader is asked to identify a cause ("Why?"). Mitigating this potential difficulty, however, is the fact that the word "cause" is explicitly used in the text ("that may cause bad breath"), providing a clear pointer to the required answer, so long as the reader infers the semantic relationship between "why" and "cause". It is worth noting that tasks at this lowest described level of PISA reading still demand some reading skill beyond mere decoding. It follows that students described as performing at Level 1b have demonstrated that they can read with a degree of **understanding**, in a manner consistent with the PISA definition of reading.

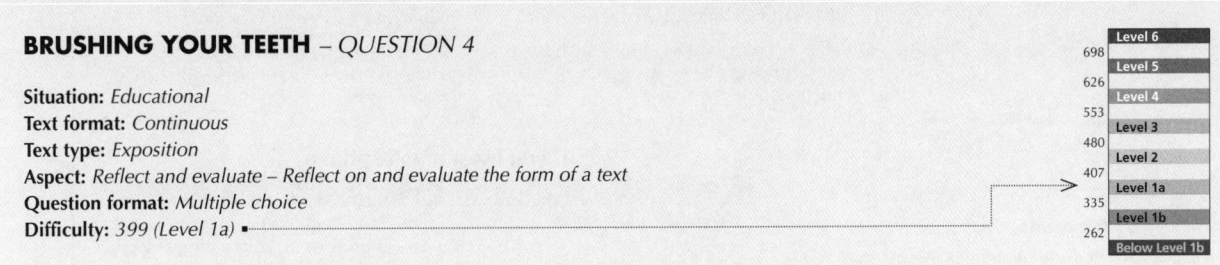

BRUSHING YOUR TEETH – *QUESTION 4*

Situation: *Educational*
Text format: *Continuous*
Text type: *Exposition*
Aspect: *Reflect and evaluate – Reflect on and evaluate the form of a text*
Question format: *Multiple choice*
Difficulty: *399 (Level 1a)*

Why is a pen mentioned in the text?

A. To help you understand how to hold a toothbrush.
B. Because you start in one corner with both a pen and a toothbrush.
C. To show that you can brush your teeth in many different ways.
D. Because you should take tooth brushing as seriously as writing.

Scoring

Full Credit: A. To help you understand how to hold a toothbrush.

Comment

The last of the tasks in this unit is located near the top of Level 1a in difficulty. Its aspect is **reflect and evaluate** because it requires standing back from the text and considering the intention of one part of it. Although this is a relatively abstract task in comparison with others in this unit, the wording of both the question stem and the key gives substantial support. The reference to "pen" in the stem directs the reader to the third paragraph. The wording of the key has a direct match with the wording in the relevant part of the text: "how to hold a toothbrush" and "hold the toothbrush the way …" respectively. The task requires the reader to recognises an analogy, but the analogical thinking is, again, explicitly there in the text: "hold the toothbrush the way you hold a pen".

The familiar content and the brevity of the text help to explain why this question is relatively easy, while its somewhat abstract focus accounts for the fact that it is the most difficult of the unit.

Figure 4.5
MOBILE PHONE SAFETY

Are mobile phones dangerous?

Yes	No
1. Radio waves given off by mobile phones can heat up body tissue, having damaging effects.	Radio waves are not powerful enough to cause heat damage to the body.
2. Magnetic fields created by mobile phones can affect the way that your body cells work.	The magnetic fields are incredibly weak, and so unlikely to affect cells in our body.
3. People who make long mobile phone calls sometimes complain of fatigue, headaches, and loss of concentration.	These effects have never been observed under laboratory conditions and may be due to other factors in modern lifestyles.
4. Mobile phone users are 2.5 times more likely to develop cancer in areas of the brain adjacent to their phone ears.	Researchers admit it's unclear this increase is linked to using mobile phones.
5. The International Agency for Research on Cancer found a link between childhood cancer and power lines. Like mobile phones, power lines also emit radiation.	The radiation produced by power lines is a different kind of radiation, with much more energy than that coming from mobile phones.
6. Radio frequency waves similar to those in mobile phones altered the gene expression in nematode worms.	Worms are not humans, so there is no guarantee that our brain cells will react in the same way.

Key points
- Conflicting reports about the health risks of mobile phones appeared in the late 1990s.
- Millions of pounds have now been invested in scientific research to investigate the effects of mobile phones.

If you use a mobile phone …

Do	Don't
Keep the calls short.	Don't use your mobile phone when the reception is weak, as the phone needs more power to communicate with the base station, and so the radio-wave emissions are higher.
Carry the mobile phone away from your body when it is on standby.	Don't buy a mobile phone with a high "SAR" value[1]. This means that it emits more radiation.
Buy a mobile phone with a long "talk time". It is more efficient, and has less powerful emissions.	Don't buy protective gadgets unless they have been independently tested.

Key points
- Given the immense numbers of mobile phone users, even small adverse effects on health could have major public health implications.
- In 2000, the Stewart Report (a British report) found no known health problems caused by mobile phones, but advised caution, especially among the young, until more research was carried out. A further report in 2004 backed this up.

1. SAR (specific absorption rate) is a measurement of how much electromagnetic radiation is absorbed by body tissue whilst using a mobile phone.

"Mobile Phone Safety" on the previous two pages is from a website.
Use "Mobile Phone Safety" to answer the questions that follow.

MOBILE PHONE SAFETY – QUESTION 2

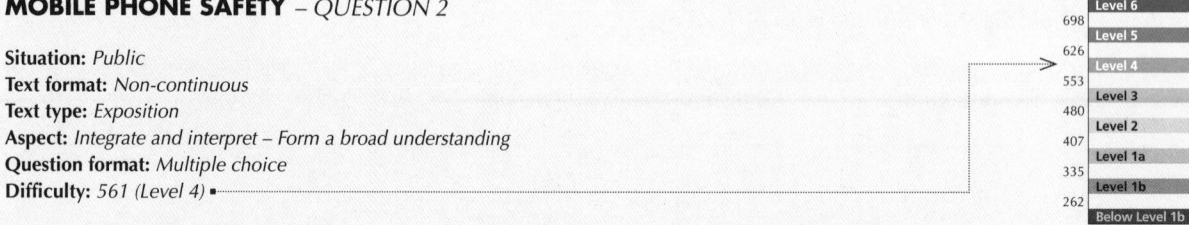

Situation: Public
Text format: Non-continuous
Text type: Exposition
Aspect: Integrate and interpret – Form a broad understanding
Question format: Multiple choice
Difficulty: 561 (Level 4)

What is the purpose of the Key points?

A. To describe the dangers of using mobile phones.
B. To suggest that debate about mobile phone safety is ongoing.
C. To describe the precautions that people who use mobile phones should take.
D. To suggest that there are no known health problems caused by mobile phones.

Scoring

Full Credit: To suggest that debate about mobile phone safety is ongoing.

Comment

Classified as a **form a broad understanding task within the integrate** *and interpret aspect, this task focuses on detecting a theme from the repetition of a particular category of information, in this case the "Key Points", a series of four boxed snippets ranged down the left hand side of the two-page text. Tasks addressing the broad understanding category are typically fairly easy, as they tend to focus on repeated and often prominent ideas in a text. However, several features of this text and task conspire to make it comparatively difficult, at Level 4. The four short Key Points tell their own story: they are related to but do not summarise the information in the body of the two main tables, so the reader needs to focus on what appears as a peripheral part of the text structure. Moreover, while all of the boxes have the caption "Key Points" the content is diverse in terms of text type, making the task of summary more difficult. The first two Key Points give a brief history of the controversy about mobile phones, the third makes a conditional proposition, and the fourth reports an equivocal finding. The fact that ambiguity, uncertainty and opposing ideas are the content of the Key Points is likely, of itself, to make the task more difficult. Here, identifying the "purpose" (which in this context is equivalent to the main theme) means establishing a hierarchy among ideas presented in the Key Points, and choosing the one that is most general and overarching. Options A and C represent different details of the Key Points, but not a single idea that could be described as overarching. Option D lifts a clause (out of context) from the fourth Key Point. Only option B, selected by 45% of students from across the OECD countries, presents a statement that synthesises the heterogeneous elements of the Key Points.*

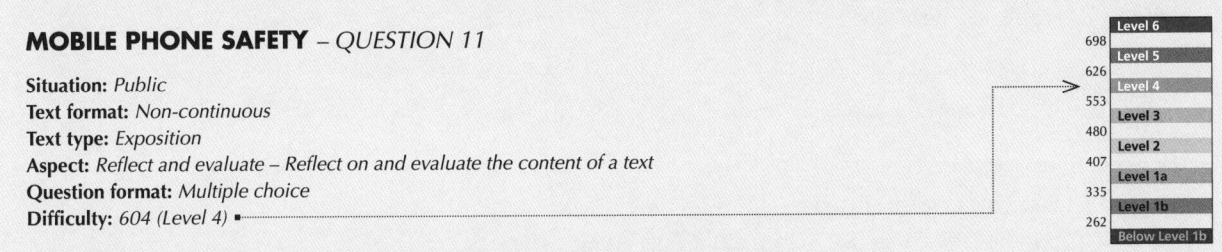

MOBILE PHONE SAFETY – QUESTION 11

Situation: *Public*
Text format: *Non-continuous*
Text type: *Exposition*
Aspect: *Reflect and evaluate – Reflect on and evaluate the content of a text*
Question format: *Multiple choice*
Difficulty: *604 (Level 4)*

"It is difficult to prove that one thing has definitely caused another."
What is the relationship of this piece of information to the Point 4 **Yes** and **No** statements in the table **Are mobile phones dangerous?**

A. It supports the Yes argument but does not prove it.
B. It proves the Yes argument.
C. It supports the No argument but does not prove it.
D. It shows that the No argument is wrong.

Scoring

Full Credit: C. It supports the No argument but does not prove it.

Comment

This task requires the reader to recognise the relationship between a generalised statement external to the text and a pair of statements in a table. It is classified as **reflect and evaluate** *in terms of aspect because of this external reference point. This is the most difficult task in the* **MOBILE PHONE SAFETY** *unit, right on the border of Level 4 and Level 5. The degree of difficulty is influenced by a number of factors. First, the stem statement uses abstract terminology ("It is difficult to prove that one thing has definitely caused another"). Secondly – a relatively straightforward part of the task – the reader needs to work out which of the two tables is relevant to this task (the first one) and which point to look at (Point 4). Thirdly, the reader needs to assimilate the structure of the relevant table: namely, that it presents opposing statements in its two columns; as we have already noted, contrary ideas are intrinsically more difficult to deal with than complementary ones. Then, the reader needs to discern precisely how the NO statement challenges the YES statement in a particular instance. Finally, logical relationship between the YES and NO statements in Point 4 must be matched, again at an abstracted level, with one of the options presented in the multiple-choice format of the task. With all these challenges intrinsic to the task, it is not surprising therefore that only a little over one-third of students across OECD countries gained credit for it.*

GROWTH IN READING PROFICIENCY OVER TIME

MOBILE PHONE SAFETY – *QUESTION 6*

Situation: *Public*
Text format: *Non-continuous*
Text type: *Exposition*
Aspect: *Reflect and evaluate – Reflect on and evaluate the content of a text*
Question format: *Open constructed response*
Difficulty: *526 (Level 3)*

```
Level 6
698
      Level 5
626
      Level 4
553
      Level 3
480
      Level 2
407
      Level 1a
335
      Level 1b
262
      Below Level 1b
```

Look at Point 3 in the **No** column of the table. In this context, what might one of these "other factors" be? Give a reason for your answer.

....

Scoring

Full Credit

Identifies a factor in modern lifestyles that could be related to fatigue, headaches, or loss of concentration. The explanation may be self-evident, or explicitly stated. For example:

- Not getting enough sleep. If you don't, you will be tired.
- Being too busy. That makes you tired.
- Too much homework, that makes you tired AND gives you headaches.
- Noise – that gives you a headache.
- Stress.
- Working late.
- Exams.
- The world is just too loud.
- People don't take time to relax anymore.
- People don't prioritise the things that matter, so they get grumpy and sick.
- Computers.
- Pollution.
- Watching too much TV.
- Drugs.
- Microwave ovens.
- Too much emailing.

Comment

Another task in which the reader needs to reflect on and evaluate the content of a text, this task calls on the ability to relate the text to knowledge external to the text. Readers must give an example from their own experience of a factor in modern life, other than mobile phones, that could explain "fatigue, headaches and loss of concentration". As in the previous task, one step in completing this task successfully is to locate the relevant information using a number reference (here, "Point 3"). The reader's subsequent steps are less complex than in the previous task, since only the YES part of Point 3 need be taken into account. In addition, the external information that needs to be drawn on is directly related to personal experience, rather than to an abstracted logical statement.

A wide range of responses earn full credit for this task. Full credit is given for producing a factor and providing an explanation as to why this might cause fatigue, headaches and loss of concentration. An example of this kind of response is "Not getting enough sleep. If you don't, you will be fatigued." Full credit is also given if it is considered that the explanation is implicit in the statement of the factor, in which case no explicit explanation is required. An example of this kind of response is "stress". On the other hand, a response such as "lifestyle" is judged too vague, without a supporting explanation or elaboration, and so is given no credit.

Towards the top of Level 3, this task was successfully completed by just over half of the students in OECD countries.

MOBILE PHONE SAFETY – QUESTION 9

Situation: *Public*
Text format: *Non-continuous*
Text type: *Exposition*
Aspect: *Integrate and interpret – Develop an interpretation*
Question format: *Multiple choice*
Difficulty: *488 (Level 3)*

Look at the table with the heading **If you use a mobile phone …**
Which of these ideas is the table based on?

A. There is no danger involved in using mobile phones.

B. There is a proven risk involved in using mobile phones.

C. There may or may not be danger involved in using mobile phones, but it is worth taking precautions.

D. There may or may not be danger involved in using mobile phones, but they should not be used until we know for sure.

E. The **Do** instructions are for those who take the threat seriously, and the **Don't** instructions are for everyone else.

Scoring
Full Credit: C. There may or may not be danger involved in using mobile phones, but it is worth taking precautions.

Comment
In this task the reader is explicitly directed to look at the second table, and to recognise its underlying assumption. In fact, the assumption isindicated in the last boxed Key Point: that in the absence of decisive evidence about the danger of mobile phones, it is advisable to take caution. The task asks readers to infer the consequences of this judgment, which can be done by checking that the table's contents are consistent with the Key Point. Alternatively, the reader can consult only the table and draw an independent conclusion from it. Option A is incorrect since it flatly contradicts the substance of the Key Point, and is inconsistent with the import of a set of injunctions that neither embargoes nor gives carte blanche to mobile phone use. Option B is rather more plausible, but the word "proven" makes it wrong in light of the information in the Key Point that no known health problems caused by mobile phones were found in the two studies that were cited. Option C presents itself as thebest answer, consistent with both the Key Point and all the detail of the DO and DON'T columns. Option D can be dismissed as nothing more than the heading of a table that reads: "If you use a mobile phone …", and option E sets up a specious opposition that has no support in the text. Just under two-thirds of students selected the correct response, making it the easiest of the four tasks related to this challenging stimulus.

4 GROWTH IN READING PROFICIENCY OVER TIME

■ Figure 4.6 ■
BALLOON

Height record for hot air balloons
The Indian pilot Vijaypat Singhania beat the height record for hot air balloons on November 26, 2005. He was the first person to fly a balloon 21 000 metres above sea level.

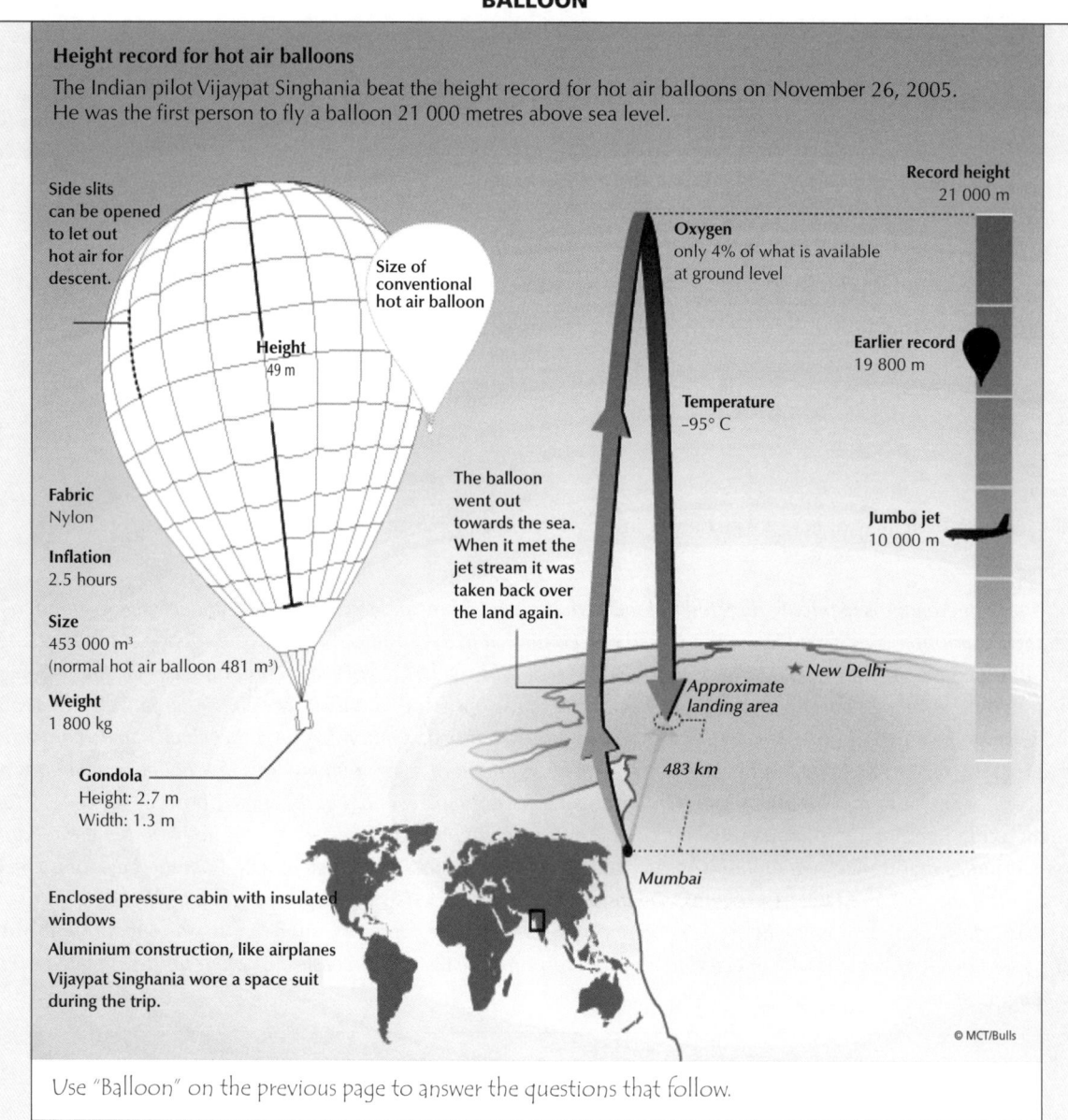

Side slits can be opened to let out hot air for descent.

Size of conventional hot air balloon

Height 49 m

Fabric
Nylon

Inflation
2.5 hours

Size
453 000 m^3
(normal hot air balloon 481 m^3)

Weight
1 800 kg

Gondola
Height: 2.7 m
Width: 1.3 m

Enclosed pressure cabin with insulated windows
Aluminium construction, like airplanes
Vijaypat Singhania wore a space suit during the trip.

Record height
21 000 m

Oxygen
only 4% of what is available at ground level

Earlier record
19 800 m

Temperature
–95° C

The balloon went out towards the sea. When it met the jet stream it was taken back over the land again.

Jumbo jet
10 000 m

New Delhi
Approximate landing area
483 km
Mumbai

© MCT/Bulls

Use "Balloon" on the previous page to answer the questions that follow.

BALLOON – QUESTION 8

Situation: Educational
Text format: Non-continuous
Text type: Description
Aspect: Integrate and interpret – Form a broad understanding
Question format: Multiple choice
Difficulty: 370 (Level 1a)

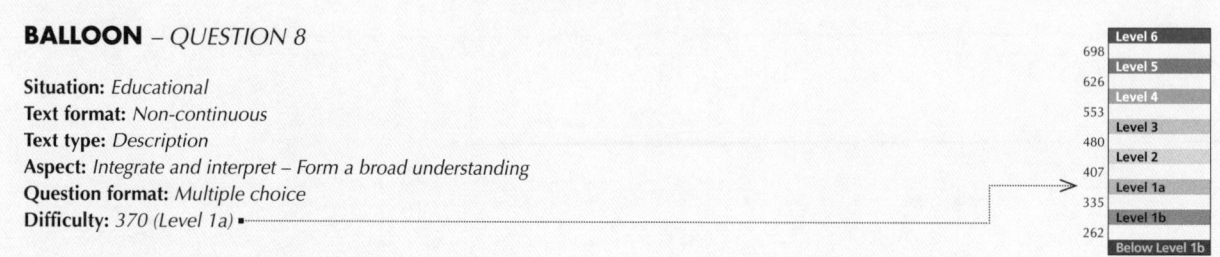

What is the main idea of this text?

A. Singhania was in danger during his balloon trip.
B. Singhania set a new world record.
C. Singhania travelled over both sea and land.
D. Singhania's balloon was enormous.

58 © OECD 2012 LEARNING BEYOND FIFTEEN – TEN YEARS AFTER PISA

Scoring

Full Credit: B. Singhania set a new world record.

Comment

The main idea of this non-continuous text is stated explicitly and prominently several times, including in the title, "Height record for hot air balloon". The prominence and repetition of the required information helps to explains its easiness: it is located in the lower half of Level 1a.

Although the main idea is explicitly stated, the question is classified as integrate and interpret, with the sub-classification forming a broad understanding, because it involves distinguishing the most significant and general from subordinate information in the text. The first option – "Singhania was in danger during his balloon trip" – is a plausible speculation, but it is not supported by anything in the text, and so cannot qualify as a main idea. The third option – "Singhania travelled over both sea and land" – accurately paraphrases information from the text, but it is a detail rather than the main idea. The fourth option – "Singhania's balloon was enormous" – refers to a conspicuous graphic feature in the text but, again, it is subordinate to the main idea.

BALLOON – QUESTION 3

Situation: *Educational*
Text format: *Non-continuous*
Text type: *Description*
Aspect: *Access and retrieve – Retrieve information*
Question format: *Short response*
Difficulty: *Full credit 595 (Level 4); Partial credit 449 (Level 2)*

Vijaypat Singhania used technologies found in two other types of transport. Which types of transport?

1. ....
2. ....

Scoring

Full Credit: Refers to BOTH airplanes AND spacecraft (in either order, can include both answers on one line). For example:

- 1. Aircraft
  2. Spacecraft
- 1. Airplanes
  2. Space ships
- 1. Air travel
  2. Space travel
- 1. Planes
  2. Space rockets
- 1. Jets
  2. Rockets

Partial Credit: Refers to EITHER airplanes OR spacecraft. For example:

- Spacecraft
- Space travel
- Space rockets
- Rockets
- Aircraft
- Airplanes
- Air travel
- Jets

Comment

In this task full credit is given for responses that lists the two required types of transport, and partial credit is given to responses that listed one type. The scoring rules reproduced above demonstrate that credit is available for several different paraphrases of the terms "airplanes" and "spacecraft".

The partial credit score is located in the upper half of Level 2 while the full credit score is located at Level 4, illustrating the fact that **access and retrieve** questions can create a significant challenge. The difficulty of the task is particularly influenced by a number of features of the text. The layout, with several different kinds of graphs and multiple captions, is quite a common type of non-continuous presentation often seen in magazines and modern textbooks, but because it does not have a conventional ordered structure (unlike, for example, a table or graph), finding specific pieces of discrete information is relatively inefficient. Captions ("Fabric", "Record height", and so on) give some support to the reader in navigating the text, but the information specific required for this task does not have a caption, so that readers have to generate their own categorisation of the relevant information as they search. Having once found the required information, inconspicuously located at the bottom left-hand corner of the diagram, the reader needs to recognise that the "aluminium construction, like airplanes" and the "space suit" are associated with categories of transport. In order to obtain credit for this question, the response needs to refer to a form or forms of transport, rather than simply transcribing an approximate section of text. Thus "space travel" is credited, but "space suit" is not. A significant piece of competing information in the text constitutes a further difficulty: many students referred to a "jumbo jet" in their answer. Although "air travel" or "airplane" or "jet" is given credit, "jumbo jet" is deemed to refer specifically to the image and caption on the right of the diagram. This answer is not given credit as the jumbo jet in the illustration is not included in the material with reference to technology used for Singhania's balloon.

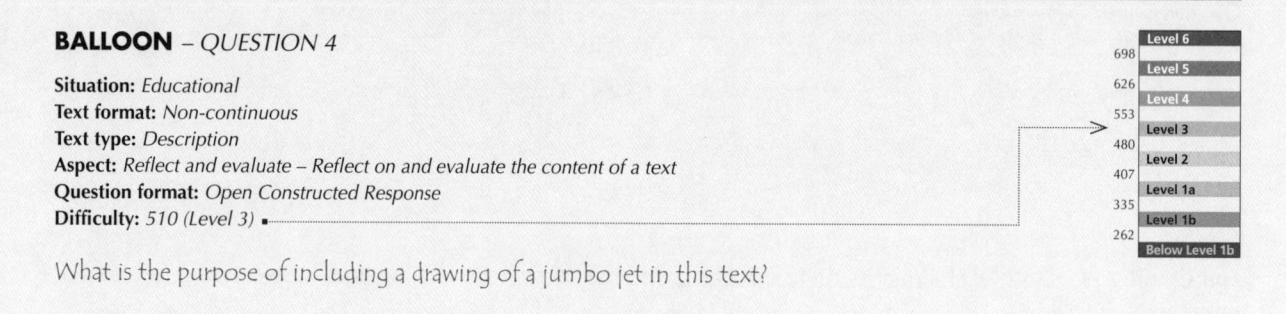

BALLOON – QUESTION 4

Situation: *Educational*
Text format: *Non-continuous*
Text type: *Description*
Aspect: *Reflect and evaluate – Reflect on and evaluate the content of a text*
Question format: *Open Constructed Response*
Difficulty: *510 (Level 3)*

What is the purpose of including a drawing of a jumbo jet in this text?
....
....

Scoring

Full Credit: Refers explicitly or implicitly to the <u>height of the balloon</u> OR to <u>the record</u>. May refer to comparison between the jumbo jet and the balloon.

- To show how high the balloon went.
- To emphasise the fact that the balloon went really, really high.
- To show how impressive his record really was – he went higher than jumbo jets!
- As a point of reference regarding height.
- To show how impressive his record really was. [minimal]

Comment

The main idea of the text is to describe the height record set by Vijaypat Singhania in his extraordinary balloon. The diagram on the right-hand side of the graphic, which includes the jumbo jet, implicitly contributes to the "wow!" factor of the text, showing just how impressive the height achieved by Singhania was by comparing it with what we usually associate with grand height: a jumbo jet's flight. In order to gain credit for this task, students must recognise the persuasive intent of including the illustration of the jumbo jet. For this reason the task is classified as **reflect and evaluate**, with the sub-category **reflect on and evaluate the content of a text**. At the upper end of Level 3, this question is moderately difficult.

GROWTH IN READING PROFICIENCY OVER TIME

BALLOON – *QUESTION 6*

Situation: *Educational*
Text format: *Non-continuous*
Text type: *Description*
Aspect: *Reflect and evaluate – Reflect on and evaluate the content of a text*
Question format: *Multiple choice*
Difficulty: *411 (Level 2)*

Why does the drawing show two balloons?

A. To compare the size of Singhania's balloon before and after it was inflated.
B. To compare the size of Singhania's balloon with that of other hot air balloons.
C. To show that Singhania's balloon looks small from the ground.
D. To show that Singhania's balloon almost collided with another balloon.

Scoring

Full Credit: B. To compare the size of Singhania's balloon with that of other hot air balloons.

Comment

It is important for readers to be aware that texts are not randomly occurring artefacts, but are constructed deliberately and with intent, and that part of the meaning of a text is found in the elements that authors choose to include. Like the previous task, this task is classified under **reflect and evaluate** *because it asks about authorial intent. It focuses on a graphic element – here the illustration of two balloons – and asks students to consider the purpose of this inclusion. In the context of the over-arching idea of the text, to describe (and celebrate) Singhania's flight, the balloon illustration sends the message, "This is a really big balloon!", just as the jumbo jet illustration sends the message, "This is a really high flight!" The caption on the smaller balloon ("Size of a conventional hot air balloon") makes it obvious that this is a different balloon to Singhania's, and therefore, for attentive readers, renders options A and C implausible. Option D has no support in the text. With a difficulty near the bottom of Level 2, this is a rather easy task.*

Figure 4.7
BLOOD DONATION

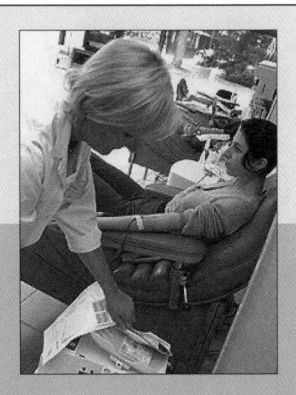

Blood donation is essential.

There is no product that can fully substitute for human blood. Blood donation is thus irreplaceable and essential to save lives.

In France, each year, 500,000 patients benefit from a blood transfusion.

The instruments for taking the blood are sterile and single-use (syringe, tubes, bags).

There is no risk in giving your blood.

Blood donation

It is the best-known kind of donation, and takes from 45 minutes to 1 hour.

A 450-ml bag is taken as well as some small samples on which tests and checks will be done.
- A man can give his blood five times a year, a woman three times.
- Donors can be from 18 to 65 years old.

An 8-week interval is compulsory between each donation.

"Blood Donation Notice" on the previous page is from a French website.
Use "Blood Donation Notice" to answer the questions that follow.

BLOOD DONATION NOTICE – QUESTION 8

Situation: Public
Text format: Continuous
Text type: Argumentation
Aspect: Integrate and interpret – Develop an interpretation
Question format: Open constructed response
Difficulty: 438 (Level 2)

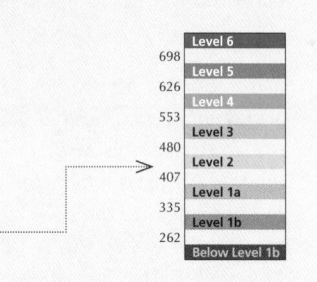

698	Level 6
626	Level 5
553	Level 4
480	Level 3
407	Level 2
335	Level 1a
262	Level 1b
	Below Level 1b

An eighteen-year-old woman who has given her blood twice in the last twelve months wants to give blood again. According to "Blood Donation Notice", on what condition will she be allowed to give blood again?

....

....

Scoring

Full Credit: Identifies that <u>enough time must have elapsed</u> since her last donation.
- Depends whether it has been 8 weeks since her last donation or not.
- She can if it has been long enough, otherwise she can't.

Comment

At a level of difficulty around the middle of Level 2, this task asks the reader to apply the information in the text to a practical case. This is the kind of reading activity that is typically associated with such a text in everyday life, and thus meets one of PISA's aims in answering questions about how well young people at the end of compulsory schooling are equipped to meet the challenges of their future lives.

The reader must match the case described in the question stem with four pieces of information provided in the second half of the text: the age and sex of the prospective donor, the number of times a person is allowed to give blood, and the interval required between donations. Reference to this last piece of information is needed in order to meet the task's requirement to stipulate the "condition" under which the young woman can give blood. As evidenced in the two examples of full credit responses, students are given credit for either a specific answer that includes reference to the interval of eight weeks between donations, or for a more generalised answer, such as "She can if it has been long enough, otherwise she can't".

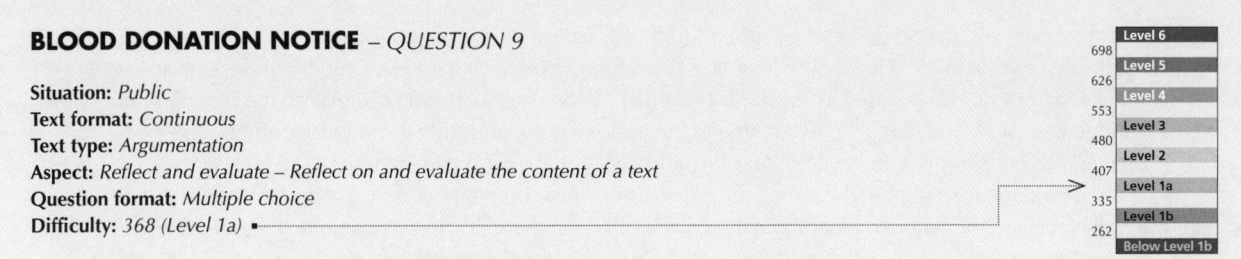

BLOOD DONATION NOTICE – QUESTION 9

Situation: Public
Text format: Continuous
Text type: Argumentation
Aspect: Reflect and evaluate – Reflect on and evaluate the content of a text
Question format: Multiple choice
Difficulty: 368 (Level 1a)

The text says: "The instruments for taking the blood are sterile and single-use … "

Why does the text include this information?

A. To reassure you that blood donation is safe.
B. To emphasise that blood donation is essential.
C. To explain the uses of your blood.
D. To give details of the tests and checks.

Scoring

QUESTION INTENT:

Reflect and evaluate: Reflect on and evaluate the content of a text.

Recognise the persuasive purpose of a phrase in an advertisement.

Full Credit: A. To reassure you that blood donation is safe.

Comment

To gain credit for this task, students must recognise the persuasive purpose of part of an advertisement. The task is classified as **reflect and evaluate** because students need to consider the wider context of what appears to be a simple statement of fact in order to recognise the underlying purpose for its inclusion.

The relative easiness of this task, which is located in the lower half of Level 1a, can be attributed to the brevity of the text and also to the fact that it deals with an everyday topic. Another characteristic of relatively easy questions exemplified here is that they typically draw on information that is consistent with common preconceptions: there is nothing contrary to expectations in the notion that people are encouraged to donate blood and reassured that donation involves no risk. Although the persuasive intent of this text is not stated explicitly in the words of the blood donation notice, the idea that it is encouraging people to donate blood and reassuring them about the safety of blood donation can be inferred from several statements. The text begins with "Blood donation is essential", a notion that is repeated and elaborated in the second paragraph ("irreplaceable and essential"). The text also refers to the absence of risk immediately after the section of text in focus in this task, though the logical connection between the two paragraphs – evidence: conclusion – must be inferred.

■ Figure 4.8 ■
MISER

THE MISER AND HIS GOLD
A fable by Aesop

A miser sold all that he had and bought a lump of gold, which he buried in a hole in the ground by the side of an old wall. He went to look at it daily. One of his workmen observed the miser's frequent visits to the spot and decided to watch his movements. The workman soon discovered the secret of the hidden treasure, and digging down, came to the lump of gold, and stole it. The miser, on his next visit, found the hole empty and began to tear his hair and to make loud lamentations. A neighbour, seeing him overcome with grief and learning the cause, said, "Pray do not grieve so; but go and take a stone, and place it in the hole, and fancy that the gold is still lying there. It will do you quite the same service; for when the gold was there, you had it not, as you did not make the slightest use of it."

Use the fable "The Miser and his Gold" on the previous page to answer the questions that follow.

MISER – QUESTION 1

Situation: *Personal*
Text format: *Continuous*
Text type: *Narration*
Aspect: *Integrate and interpret – Develop an interpretation*
Question format: *Closed constructed response*
Difficulty: *373 (Level 1a)*

Read the sentences below and number them according to the sequence of events in the text.

☐ The miser decided to turn all his money into a lump of gold.
☐ A man stole the miser's gold.
☐ The miser dug a hole and hid his treasure in it.
☐ The miser's neighbour told him to replace the gold with a stone.

Scoring
Full Credit: All four correct: 1, 3, 2, 4 in that order.

Comment

Fables are a popular and respected text type in many cultures and they are a favourite text type in reading assessments for similar reasons: they are short, self-contained, morally instructive and have stood the test of time. While perhaps not the most common reading material for young adults in OECD countries they are nevertheless likely to be familiar from childhood, and the pithy, often acerbic observations of a fable can pleasantly surprise even a blasé 15-year-old. MISER is typical of its genre: it captures and satirises a particular human weakness in a neat economical story, executed in a single paragraph.

Since **narrations** *are defined as referring to properties of objects in time, typically answering "when" questions, it is appropriate to include a task based on a narrative text that asks for a series of statements about the story to be put into the correct sequence. With such a short text, and with statements in the task that are closely matched with the terms of the story, this is an easy task, around the middle of Level 1a. On the other hand, the language of the text is rather formal and has some old-fashioned locutions. (Translators were asked to reproduce the fable-like style of the source versions.) This characteristic of the text is likely to have added to the difficulty of the question.*

GROWTH IN READING PROFICIENCY OVER TIME

MISER – QUESTION 7

Situation: Personal
Text format: Continuous
Text type: Narration
Aspect: Access and retrieve – Retrieve information
Question format: Short response
Difficulty: 310 (Level 1b)

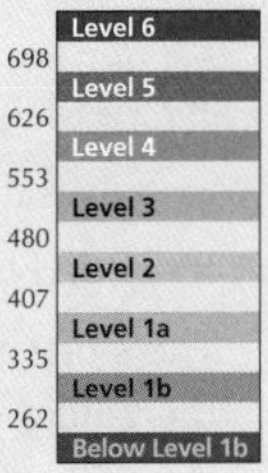

How did the miser get a lump of gold?

....

Scoring

Full Credit: States that he <u>sold everything he had</u>. May paraphrase or quote directly from the text.

- He sold all he had.
- He sold all his stuff.
- He bought it. [implicit connection to selling everything he had]

Comment

This is one of the easiest tasks in PISA reading, with a difficulty in the middle of Level 1b. The reader is required to **access and retrieve** a piece of explicitly stated information in the opening sentence of a very short text. To gain full credit, the response can either quote directly from the text – "He sold all that he had" – or provide a paraphrase such as "He sold all his stuff". The formal language of the text, which is likely to have added difficulty in other tasks in the unit, is unlikely to have much impact here because the required information is located at the very beginning of the text. Although this is an extremely easy question in PISA's frame of reference, it still requires a small degree of inference, beyond the absolutely literal: the reader must infer that there is a causal connection between the first proposition (that the miser sold all he had) and the second (that he bought gold).

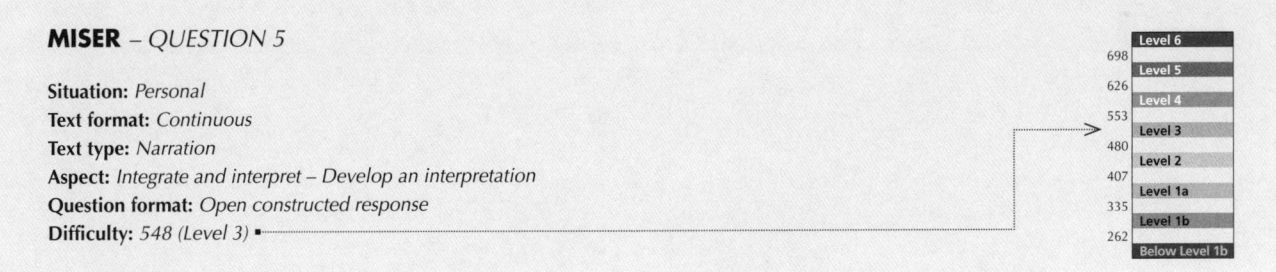

MISER – QUESTION 5

Situation: Personal
Text format: Continuous
Text type: Narration
Aspect: Integrate and interpret – Develop an interpretation
Question format: Open constructed response
Difficulty: 548 (Level 3)

Here is part of a conversation between two people who read "The Miser and his Gold".

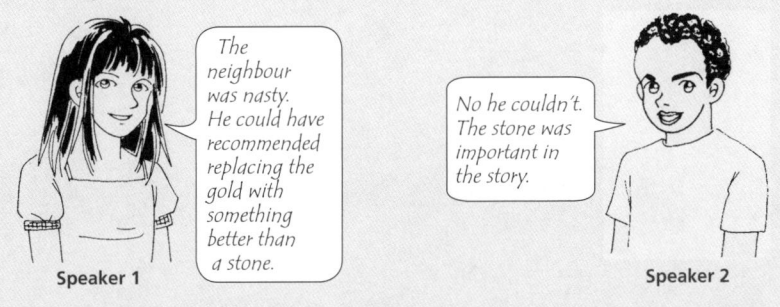

Speaker 1: The neighbour was nasty. He could have recommended replacing the gold with something better than a stone.

Speaker 2: No he couldn't. The stone was important in the story.

What could Speaker 2 say to support his point of view?

....

....

LEARNING BEYOND FIFTEEN – TEN YEARS AFTER PISA © OECD 2012

Scoring

Full Credit

Recognises that the message of the story depends on the gold being replaced by something useless or worthless.

- It needed to be replaced by something worthless to make the point.
- The stone is important in the story, because the whole point is he might as well have buried a stone for all the good the gold did him.
- If you replaced it with something better than a stone, it would miss the point because the thing buried needs to be something really useless.
- A stone is useless, but for the miser, so was the gold!
- Something better would be something he could use – he didn't use the gold, that's what the guy was pointing out.
- Because stones can be found anywhere. The gold and the stone are the same to the miser. ["can be found anywhere" implies that the stone is of no special value]

Comment

This task takes the form of setting up a dialogue between two imaginary readers, to represent two conflicting interpretations of the story. In fact only the second speaker's position is consistent with the overall implication of the text, so that in providing a supporting explanation readers demonstrate that they have understood the "punch line" – the moral import – of the fable. The relative difficulty of the task, near the top of Level 3, is likely to be influenced by the fact that readers needs to do a good deal of work to generate a full credit response. First they must make sense of the neighbour's speech in the story, which is expressed in a formal register. (As noted, translators were asked to reproduce the fable-like style.) Secondly, the relationship between the question stem and the required information is not obvious: there is little or no support in the stem ("What could Speaker 2 say to support his point of view?") to guide the reader in interpreting the task, though the reference to the stone and the neighbour by the speakers should point the reader to the end of the fable.

As shown in examples of responses, to gain full credit, students could express, in a variety of ways, the key idea that wealth has no value unless it is used. Vague gestures at meaning, such as "the stone had a symbolic value", are not given credit.

■ Figure 4.9 ■
THE PLAY'S THE THING

Takes place in a castle by the beach in Italy.

FIRST ACT
Ornate guest room in a very nice beachside castle. Doors on the right and left. Sitting
5 *room set in the middle of the stage: couch, table, and two armchairs. Large windows at the back. Starry night. It is dark on the stage. When the curtain goes up we hear men conversing loudly behind the door on the left.*
10 *The door opens and three tuxedoed gentlemen enter. One turns the light on immediately. They walk to the centre in silence and stand around the table. They sit down together, Gál in the armchair to the left, Turai in the one on*
15 *the right, Ádám on the couch in the middle. Very long, almost awkward silence. Comfortable stretches. Silence. Then:*

GÁL
Why are you so deep in thought?

20 **TURAI**
I'm thinking about how difficult it is to begin a play. To introduce all the principal characters in the beginning, when it all starts.

ÁDÁM
25 I suppose it must be hard.

TURAI
It is – devilishly hard. The play starts. The audience goes quiet. The actors enter the stage and the torment begins. It's an eternity,
30 sometimes as much as a quarter of an hour before the audience finds out who's who and what they are all up to.

GÁL
Quite a peculiar brain you've got. Can't you
35 forget your profession for a single minute?

TURAI
That cannot be done.

GÁL
Not half an hour passes without you
40 discussing theatre, actors, plays. There are other things in this world.

TURAI
There aren't. I am a dramatist. That is my curse.

45 **GÁL**
You shouldn't become such a slave to your profession.

TURAI
If you do not master it, you are its slave.
50 There is no middle ground. Trust me, it's no joke starting a play well. It is one of the toughest problems of stage mechanics. Introducing your characters promptly. Let's look at this scene here, the three of
55 us. Three gentlemen in tuxedoes. Say they enter not this room in this lordly castle, but rather a stage, just when a play begins. They would have to chat about a whole lot of uninteresting topics until it came out

60 who we are. Wouldn't it be much easier to start all this by standing up and introducing ourselves? *Stands up. Good evening. The three of us are guests in this castle. We have just arrived from the*
65 dining room where we had an excellent dinner and drank two bottles of champagne. My name is Sándor TURAI, I'm a playwright, I've been writing plays for thirty years, that's my profession. Full stop.
70 Your turn.

GÁL
Stands up. My name is GÁL, I'm also a playwright. I write plays as well, all of them in the company of this gentleman
75 here. We are a famous playwright duo. All playbills of good comedies and operettas read: written by GÁL and TURAI. Naturally, this is my profession as well.

GÁL and **TURAI**
80 *Together.* And this young man …

ÁDÁM
Stands up. This young man is, if you allow me, Albert ÁDÁM, twenty-five years old, composer. I wrote the music for these kind
85 gentlemen for their latest operetta. This is my first work for the stage. These two elderly angels have discovered me and now, with their help, I'd like to become famous. They got me invited to this castle. They got
90 my dress-coat and tuxedo made. In other words, I am poor and unknown, for now. Other than that I'm an orphan and my grandmother raised me. My grandmother has passed away. I am all alone in this world. I
95 have no name, I have no money.

TURAI
But you are young.

GÁL
And gifted.

100 **ÁDÁM**
And I am in love with the soloist.

TURAI
You shouldn't have added that. Everyone in the audience would figure that out anyway.

105 *They all sit down.*

TURAI
Now wouldn't this be the easiest way to start a play?

GÁL
110 If we were allowed to do this, it would be easy to write plays.

TURAI
Trust me, it's not that hard. Just think of this whole thing as …

115 **GÁL**
All right, all right, all right, just don't start talking about the theatre again. I'm fed up with it. We'll talk tomorrow, if you wish.

"The Play's the Thing" is the beginning of a play by the Hungarian dramatist Ferenc Molnár.

Use "The Play's the Thing" on the previous two pages to answer the questions that follow. (Note that line numbers are given in the margin of the script to help you find parts that are referred to in the questions.)

4 GROWTH IN READING PROFICIENCY OVER TIME

THE PLAY'S THE THING – *QUESTION 3*

Situation: *Personal*
Text format: *Continuous*
Text type: *Narration*
Aspect: *Integrate and interpret – Develop an interpretation*
Question format: *Short response*
Difficulty: *730 (Level 6)*

698	Level 6
626	Level 5
553	Level 4
480	Level 3
407	Level 2
335	Level 1a
262	Level 1b
	Below Level 1b

What were the characters in the play doing **just before** the curtain went up?

....

Scoring

Full Credit: Refers to <u>dinner</u> or <u>drinking champagne</u>. May paraphrase or quote the text directly.
- They have just had dinner and champagne.
- "We have just arrived from the dining room where we had an excellent dinner." *[direct quotation]*
- "An excellent dinner and drank two bottles of champagne." *[direct quotation]*
- Dinner and drinks.
- Dinner.
- Drank champagne.
- Had dinner and drank.
- They were in the dining room.

Comment

This task illustrates several features of the most difficult tasks in PISA reading. The text is long by PISA standards, and it may be supposed that the fictional world depicted is remote from the experience of most 15-year-olds. The introduction to the unit tells students that the stimulus of **THE PLAY'S THE THING** is the beginning of a play by the Hungarian dramatist Ferenc Molnár, but there is no other external orientation. The setting ("a castle by the beach in Italy") is likely to be exotic to many, and the situation is only revealed gradually through the dialogue itself. While individual pieces of vocabulary are not particularly difficult, and the tone is often chatty, the register of the language is a little mannered. Perhaps most importantly a level of unfamiliarity is introduced by the abstract theme of the discussion: a sophisticated conversation between characters about the relationship between life and art, and the challenges of writing for the theatre. The text is classified as narration because this theme is dealt with as part of the play's narrative.

While all the tasks in this unit acquire a layer of difficulty associated with the challenges of the text, the cognitive demand of this task in particular is also attributable to the high level of interpretation required to define the meaning of the question's terms, in relation to the text. The reader needs to be alert to the distinction between characters and actors. The question refers to what the characters (not the actors) were doing "just before the curtain went up". This is potentially confusing since it requires recognition of a shift between the real world of a stage in a theatre, which has a curtain, and the imaginary world of Gal, Turai and Adam, who were in the dining room having dinner just before they entered the guest room (the stage setting). A question that assesses students' capacity to distinguish between real and fictional worlds seems particularly appropriate in relation to a text whose theme is about just that, so that the complexity of the question is aligned with the content of the text.

A further level of the task's difficulty is introduced by the fact that the required information is in an unexpected location. The question refers to the action "before the curtain went up", which would typically lead one to search at the opening of the scene, the beginning of the extract. On the contrary, the information is actually found about half-way through the extract, when Turai reveals that he and his friends "have just arrived from the dining room". While the scoring for the question shows that several kinds of response are acceptable, to be given full credit readers must demonstrate that they have found this inconspicuous piece of information. The need to assimilate information that is contrary to expectations – where the reader needs to give full attention to the text in defiance of preconceptions – is highly characteristic of the most demanding reading tasks in PISA.

THE PLAY'S THE THING – QUESTION 4

Situation: *Personal*
Text format: *Continuous*
Text type: *Narration*
Aspect: *Integrate and interpret – Develop an interpretation*
Question format: *Multiple choice*
Difficulty: *474 (Level 2)*

"It's an eternity, sometimes as much as a quarter of an hour … " (lines 29-30)
According to Turai, why is a quarter of an hour "an eternity"?

A. It is a long time to expect an audience to sit still in a crowded theatre.
B. It seems to take forever for the situation to be clarified at the beginning of a play.
C. It always seems to take a long time for a dramatist to write the beginning of a play.
D. It seems that time moves slowly when a significant event is happening in a play.

Scoring

Full Credit: B. It seems to take forever for the situation to be clarified at the beginning of a play.

Comment

Near the borderline between Level 2 and Level 3, this question together with the previous one illustrates the fact that questions covering a wide range of difficulties can be based on a single text.

Unlike in the previous task, the stem of this task directs the reader to the relevant section in the play, even quoting the lines, thus relieving the reader of any challenge in figuring out where the necessary information is to be found. Nevertheless, the reader needs to understand the context in which the line is uttered in order to respond successfully. In fact, the implication of "It seems to take forever for the situation to be clarified at the beginning of a play" underpins much of the rest of this extract, which enacts the solution of characters explicitly introducing themselves at the beginning of a play instead of waiting for the action to reveal who they are. Insofar as the utterance that is quoted in the stem prompts most of the rest of this extract, repetition and emphasis support the reader in integrating and interpreting the quotation. In that respect too, this task clearly differs from Question 3, in which the required information is only provided once, and is buried in an unexpected part of the text.

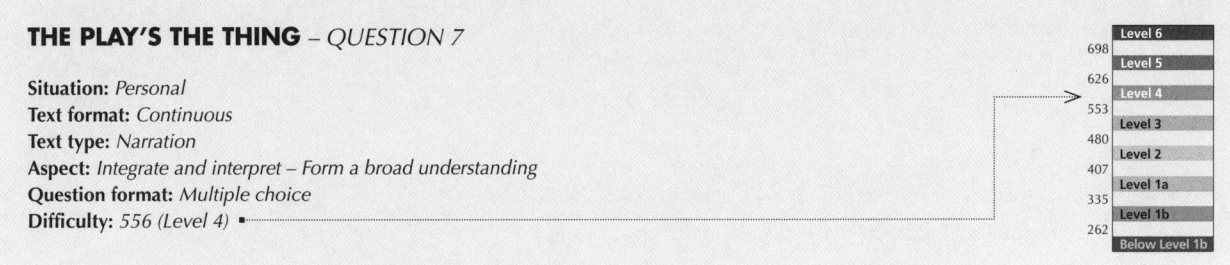

THE PLAY'S THE THING – QUESTION 7

Situation: *Personal*
Text format: *Continuous*
Text type: *Narration*
Aspect: *Integrate and interpret – Form a broad understanding*
Question format: *Multiple choice*
Difficulty: *556 (Level 4)*

Overall, what is the dramatist Molnár doing in this extract?

A. He is showing the way that each character will solve his own problems.
B. He is making his characters demonstrate what an eternity in a play is like.
C. He is giving an example of a typical and traditional opening scene for a play.
D. He is using the characters to act out one of his own creative problems.

Scoring

Full Credit: D. He is using the characters to act out one of his own creative problems.

Comment

In this task the reader is asked to take a global perspective, **form a broad understanding** by integrating and interpreting the implications of the dialogue across the text. The task involves recognising the conceptual theme of a section of a play, where the theme is literary and abstract. This relatively unfamiliar territory for most 15-year-olds is likely to constitute the difficulty of the task, which is located at Level 4. A little under half of the students in OECD countries gained full credit for this task, with the others divided fairly evenly across the three distractors.

GROWTH IN READING PROFICIENCY OVER TIME

■ Figure 4.10 ■
TELECOMMUTING

The way of the future

Just imagine how wonderful it would be to "telecommute"[1] to work on the electronic highway, with all your work done on a computer or by phone! No longer would you have to jam your body into crowded buses or trains or waste hours and hours travelling to and from work. You could work wherever you want to – just think of all the job opportunities this would open up!

Molly

Disaster in the making

Cutting down on commuting hours and reducing the energy consumption involved is obviously a good idea. But such a goal should be accomplished by improving public transportation or by ensuring that workplaces are located near where people live. The ambitious idea that telecommuting should be part of everyone's way of life will only lead people to become more and more self-absorbed. Do we really want our sense of being part of a community to deteriorate even further?

Richard

---

1. "Telecommuting" is a term coined by Jack Nilles in the early 1970s to describe a situation in which workers work on a computer away from a central office (for example, at home) and transmit data and documents to the central office via telephone lines.

Use "Telecommuting" above to answer the questions that follow.

TELECOMMUTING – QUESTION 1

Situation: *Occupational*
Text format: *Multiple*
Text type: *Argumentation*
Aspect: *Integrate and interpret – Form a broad understanding*
Question format: *Multiple choice*
Difficulty: *537 (Level 3)*

What is the relationship between "The way of the future" and "Disaster in the making"?

A. They use different arguments to reach the same general conclusion.

B. They are written in the same style but they are about completely different topics.

C. They express the same general point of view, but arrive at different conclusions.

D. They express opposing points of view on the same topic.

Scoring

Full Credit: D. They express opposing points of view on the same topic.

Comment

The stimulus for the unit **TELECOMMUTING** *is two short texts that offer contrasting opinions on telecommuting, defined in a footnote to the text as "working on a computer away from a central office". The only addition to the originally submitted text that was made by PISA test developers was this footnote. It was assumed that the term "telecommuting" would be unfamiliar to most 15-year-olds. The footnote was included in order to avoid giving an advantage to students whose language would allow them to unpack the meaning of this compound word. For example, students tested in English may have been able to infer the meaning of the word by combining the meaning of "tele" (distant) and "commute". By contrast, some countries in which English is not the testing language used the English term or a transliteration, which would not provide the same clues to the meaning.*

The purpose of each of the short texts in the stimulus is to persuade readers to a point of view, so the stimulus is classified as **argumentation**. Given that the purpose of the stimulus material is to discuss an issue related to working life, the text is classified as occupational in terms of situation. The two pieces that make up the stimulus are both continuous, but because they were generated independently and juxtaposed for the purpose of the assessment, the text format classification of this text is **multiple**.

This question requires students to recognise the relationship between the two short texts. To answer correctly, students must first form a global understanding of each of the short texts, and then identify the relationship between them: that is, that they express contrasting points of view on the same topic. A factor contributing to the difficulty of this question is the level of interpretation required to identify the position that is expressed in each text. In the first text the author's position is signalled clearly early in the text ("Just imagine how wonderful it would be to 'telecommute' to work ...") and reinforced throughout. In contrast the second piece contains no direct statement of the author's own position: instead, it is written as a series of responses to arguments that the author opposes, so understanding the position of the second author requires a greater level of interpretation than understanding the position of the first author. Once the work of interpreting the position of each author has been done, recognising that the positions are contrasting is relatively straightforward. The weakest students chose option B. These students fail to recognise that the two texts are about the same topic. Students who chose options A and C recognise that the two texts are about the same topic, but fail to identify that they express contrasting views. At Level 3, just over one-half of the students in OECD countries gained credit for this question.

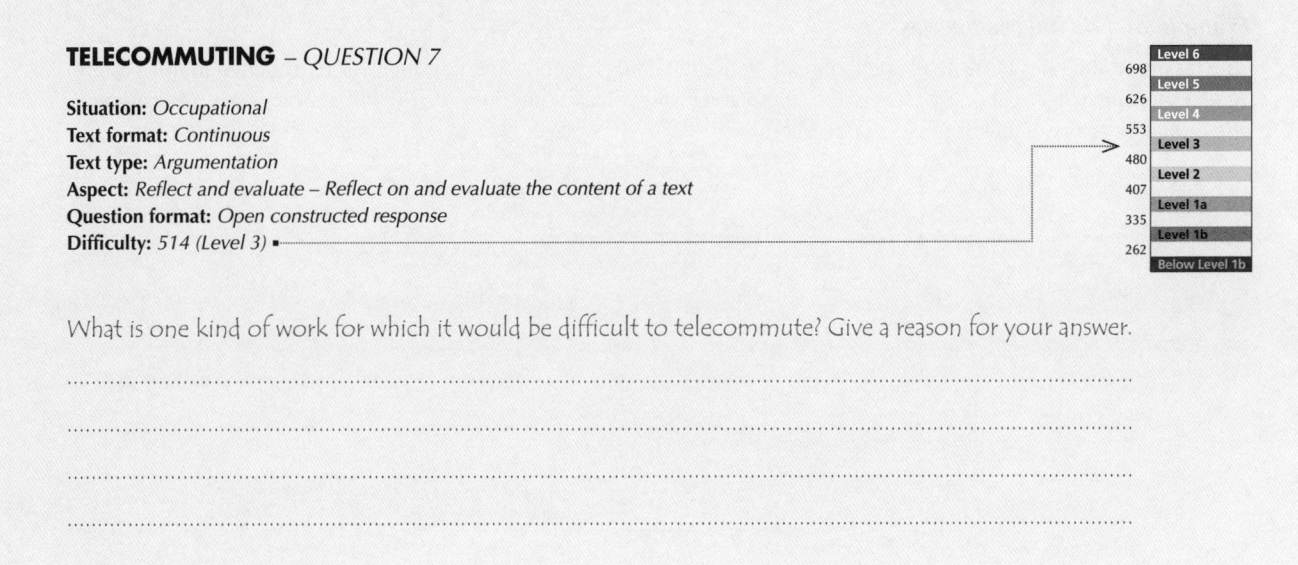

TELECOMMUTING – *QUESTION 7*

Situation: *Occupational*
Text format: *Continuous*
Text type: *Argumentation*
Aspect: *Reflect and evaluate – Reflect on and evaluate the content of a text*
Question format: *Open constructed response*
Difficulty: *514 (Level 3)*

What is one kind of work for which it would be difficult to telecommute? Give a reason for your answer.

....
....
....
....

Scoring

QUESTION INTENT:

Reflect and evaluate: Reflect on and evaluate the content of a text

Use prior knowledge to generate an example that fits a category described in a text

Full Credit: <u>Identifies a kind of work</u> and gives a <u>plausible explanation as to why a person who does that kind of work could not telecommute</u>. Responses MUST indicate (explicitly or implicitly) that it is necessary to be physically present for the specific work.

- Building. It's hard to work with the wood and bricks from just anywhere.
- Sportsperson. You need to really be there to play the sport.
- Plumber. You can't fix someone else's sink from your home!
- Digging ditches because you need to be there.
- Nursing – it's hard to check if patients are ok over the Internet.

Comment

This question requires students to generate an example (a profession) that fits a given category. The textual information required for this question is found in the footnote definition of telecommuting. Therefore, although the stimulus is comprised of multiple texts, this question is classified as **continuous** in terms of text format because it only refers to one text element.

To provide an example of a job in which telecommuting would be difficult, students must link their comprehension of the text (the definition of telecommuting) with outside knowledge, since no specific profession is mentioned in the text. This question is therefore classified as **reflect and evaluate**, with the sub-category **reflect on and evaluate the content of a text.**

In order to gain credit for this question, students needed to give an example and to justify why their example fitted the given category, and the explanation needed to refer either explicitly or implicitly to the fact that the worker would need to be physically present in order to perform their job. Although the range of responses eligible for full credit was very wide, many students failed to gain credit because they did not provide an explanation at all, or they gave an explanation that did not show that they understood that the job they listed would require the worker's physical presence. An example of the latter is, "Digging ditches because it would be hard work." Compare this with the credited response, "Digging ditches because you need to be there."

Nearly 60% of students gained full credit for this question.

Example of a digital reading task

One task from the PISA 2009 assessment of reading of digital texts, comprising four items, is reproduced in this section. Screen shots are used to illustrate parts of the stimulus relevant to each question. The digital version of this unit and other released tasks are available at *www.pisa.oecd.org*.

Notes

1. In the Province of Québec, there are only 11 years of compulsory education before students move on to post-secondary studies.

2. This analysis uses a subset of the Canadian PISA students who have never received remedial or enrichment support. Relative proficiency controls for the effects of differences in proficiency between provinces and month of birth within each grade. Although grade level is, strictly speaking, not an interval variable, the consistency of the differences in proficiency between all pairs of adjacent grade levels lends credibility to a quasi-interval interpretation. In other words, a pairwise comparison of differences between adjacent grades would produce approximately the same graph.

3. A similar analysis was undertaken by Willms (2004), who found that for the 12 countries with similar variations in the age cut-off for school registration, the average increase in PISA scores was 34 points per grade level.

4. During late adolescence, a period of increased synaptic pruning occurs in the prefrontal cortex (Paus, 2005; Giedd, et al., 1999; Abitz, et al., 2007) which is the center of language function. In normal development, synaptic pruning renders the brain more efficient by eliminating inefficient neural pathways. Since neuronal efficiency increases with repetitive firing of a pathway, the end result of synaptic pruning is decreased cognitive capacity with infrequently used functions.

5. More precisely, since it is possible to earn partial credit on some items, the item-correct score is the total credit received for a particular question by all participants, divided by the total credit available to all participants. The scores are weighted by the student weights from PISA-24, but all questions are given an equal weight towards the overall average.

Proficiency Growth before and after Age 15

A defining feature of proficiency growth after the age of 15 is that high performers did not acquire skills as fast as low performers and, as a result, some groups of students who had performed poorly at the age of 15 were able to close some of the gap in reading skills by the age of 24. This chapter provides further evidence of proficiency convergence by examining how family and school environments are related to reading proficiency at age 15 and to skills growth between the ages of 15 and 24. One important finding is that individuals who are more inclined to self-directed learning do not do as well in the highly structured environments often found in compulsory education, but they appear to thrive in environments that allow for greater autonomy.

SKILLS GROWTH IN PISA-24

One of the most striking findings of the descriptive analysis presented in Chapter 3 was the varying rate of growth in reading skills between the ages of 15 and 24 that, in many cases, led to a narrowing of the skills gap and allowed certain groups, particularly immigrant students, to eliminate entirely the gap that had previously separated them from high-performing students.

This chapter expands on the descriptive analysis presented in Chapter 3 by examining the relationship between positive early environments and continuing improvements in proficiency. The chapter begins by considering how initial reading proficiency is related to skills growth after age 15. It examines the relationship between reading proficiency at age 15 and improvements in reading proficiency growth between the ages of 15 and 24; the influence of positive early environments later on in a young person's life; and the specific student characteristics that translate into greater improvements in reading proficiency after 15.

SKILLS GROWTH AND INITIAL READING PROFICIENCY AT AGE 15

The observed relationship between skills at age 15 and skills growth

The difference in PISA scores between 15-year-olds and 24-year-olds shows that students who scored the lowest at the younger age tended to make the largest gains in proficiency by the time they were 24. In other words, PISA-24 shows evidence of convergence in skills between the ages of 15 and 24.

Figure 5.1 offers a first glimpse of the relationship between all of the assessment data in PISA-24. With skills at age 15 represented on the horizontal axis and skills growth on the vertical axis, each dot represents an individual who participated in both PISA-15 and PISA-24. Table 5.1 in Annex B presents the details of this analysis. As the table shows, this estimated difference in skills growth remains practically unchanged after individual student characteristics and other relevant factors are taken into account.

Figure 5.1 shows that the higher the initial level of skills, the smaller the improvement in skills over the nine years. Because of the nature of the reassessment, this is the expected pattern. However, it is unclear to what extent this pattern is an artefact of the assessment mechanism. As discussed in Chapter 2, however, these simple estimates of skills growth may overstate the rate of catching-up among poor performers due to the potential bias introduced by regression towards the mean (see Annex A for a technical discussion).

■ Figure 5.1 ■
Observed relationship between reading skills at age 15 and growth in reading skills between the ages of 15 and 24

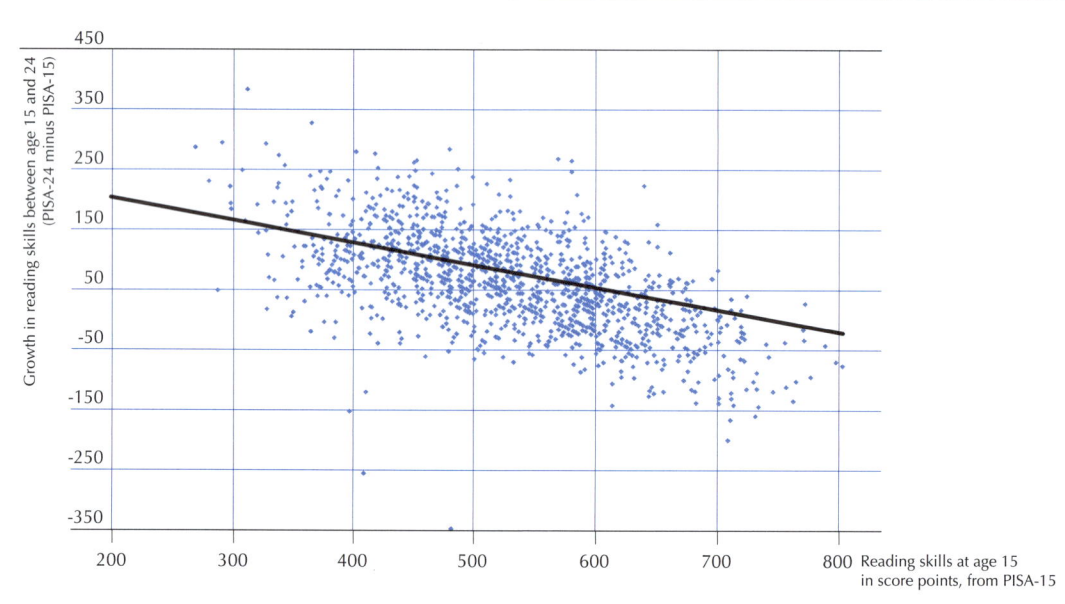

Source: Table 5.1; YITS cycle 5.5: Reading Skills Reassessment.
StatLink http://dx.doi.org/10.1787/888932576833

PROFICIENCY GROWTH BEFORE AND AFTER AGE 15

■ Figure 5.2 ■
Development of reading skills by PISA proficiency levels and school marks at age 15

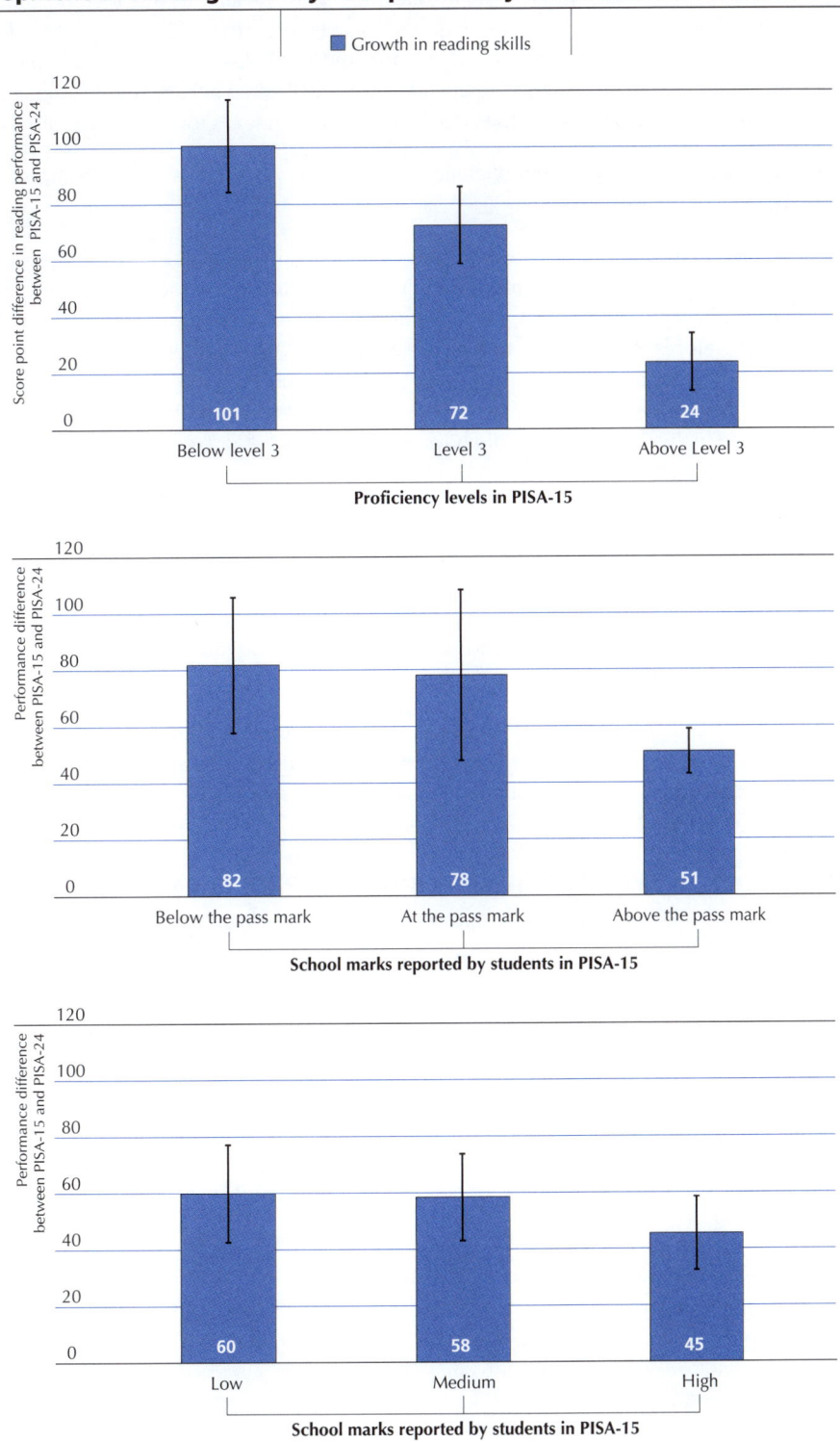

Growth in reading skills

Chart 1 — Score point difference in reading performance between PISA-15 and PISA-24, by Proficiency levels in PISA-15:
- Below level 3: 101
- Level 3: 72
- Above Level 3: 24

Chart 2 — Performance difference between PISA-15 and PISA-24, by School marks reported by students in PISA-15:
- Below the pass mark: 82
- At the pass mark: 78
- Above the pass mark: 51

Chart 3 — Performance difference between PISA-15 and PISA-24, by School marks reported by students in PISA-15:
- Low: 60
- Medium: 58
- High: 45

Note: The second figure refers to the self reported grades in language by the participants when they were 15 years old in PISA 2000. "Low" refers to obtaining below 70%, "Medium" refers to obtaining from 70% to 79% and "High" refers to obtaining at or above 80%. The vertical lines on each measure of mean skill growth indicate the degree of precision with which these average scores are calculated. In statistical terms, the range of score points in terms of skill growth covered by these lines is referred to as the confidence interval. In general, overlapping vertical lines (joined confidence intervals) suggest that the differences are not statistically significant with a high degree of confidence (95% in this case).
Source: Table 5.1; YITS cycle 5.5: Reading Skills Reassessment.
StatLink ⟶ http://dx.doi.org/10.1787/888932576833

Adjusting for initial skills with school marks

Analysing skills growth across proficiency levels in PISA offers a way of looking at this phenomenon. For instance, Figure 5.2 shows that skills growth between the ages of 15 and 24 averaged around 24 points for students above PISA proficiency Level 3 in 2000, but was more than 100 points for students below Level 3 (Table 5.1). As discussed in Chapter 2, however, these simple estimates of skills growth may overstate the rate of catching-up among poor performers due to the potential bias introduced by regression towards the mean (see Annex A for a technical discussion).

One way to verify the relationship between early proficiency and skills growth is to examine learning gains by a different measure of early ability, namely school marks.

PISA-15 asked students to report their most recent school marks in reading, mathematics and science. Only self-reported school marks in high school language classes were used in this analysis due to the focus on reading skills in PISA-24. Two measures of school marks were used to test the relationship between initial skills and skills growth. In the first instance, students reported their marks in relation to the passing grade – 9% were below the passing mark, 12% were at the passing mark, and 76% were above the passing mark. In the second instance, students reported their marks as a percentage. These have been categorised into three groups, low school marks (below 70%), medium school marks (between 70% and 79%), and high school marks (at or above 80%), with each group containing approximately one-third of students (Table 5.1).

The results, presented in Figure 5.2, provide evidence that supports the argument that skills growth was in fact greater among students with lower proficiency. For example, skills growth among those with marks below passing at the time of PISA-15 improved by more than 80 score points. In contrast, those with marks above passing in 2000 improved by 50 score points by 2009. The same pattern is observed using the other measure of school marks. Those with high marks show the smallest improvement in proficiency, around 45 score points, while those with low marks improved by an average of 60 score points (Table 5.1).

The relationship between learning gains and school marks in language, though weaker than that between skills growth and PISA-15 scores, provides further evidence that poorly performing students made some progress in closing the gap in reading skills. These results suggest that opportunities for learning after the completion of compulsory education can mitigate some of the inequalities observed at age 15.

A CONCEPTUAL MODEL OF IMPROVEMENT IN READING PROFICIENCY

To provide a framework for the in-depth analysis of skills growth that follows, this section presents a conceptual model for considering skills acquisition before and after the age of 15. This simplified representation of reality offers a stylised model to analyse the data. PISA-15 and PISA-24 represent a three-point measurement cycle during a person's early life: at birth, at age 15 and at age 24 (Figure 5.3). The three time points define two distinct phases of skills growth. Although the PISA reading proficiency scale has no relevance for young children, it is constructed to measure skills that students have accumulated from birth to age 15 (OECD, 2001).

The first phase in skills development in this model takes place from birth to age 15, and is measured by PISA-15. This phase is characterised by natural variations in cognitive skills and the quality of the individual's learning environment in and outside school. During this phase, the most important determinants of proficiency development are parents, teachers and formal schooling.

The second phase of learning on this model takes place between the ages of 15 and 24, and is measured by the difference in performance between PISA-15 and PISA-24. Phase two marks the transition from extrinsic and passive reception of learning (in compulsory education) to intrinsic and active self-determination (after the completion of compulsory education). This phase is characterised by more individual choices regarding education and training, and practicing existing skills in work and leisure.

In both phases, learning opportunities are not distributed equally among young people. Up to the age of 15, many students will enjoy environments and support networks that provide rich learning opportunities. Of course, students will differ in the extent to which they enjoy and benefit from these resources, depending on, for example, whether they live in urban or rural areas, or whether their families provide additional support and opportunities to learn.

The transition from extrinsic and passive reception of learning opportunities to intrinsic and active self-determination can be either beneficial or detrimental to the rate of development of an individual's reading proficiency. Young people who benefited from advantageous early environments may be unable to replicate the richness of their early learning experiences. The cost of developing certain skills, through post-secondary education, for example, may be too high. However, it is also possible that students who lacked adequate learning support during the first phase of their reading development may later be able to seek out positive learning environments.

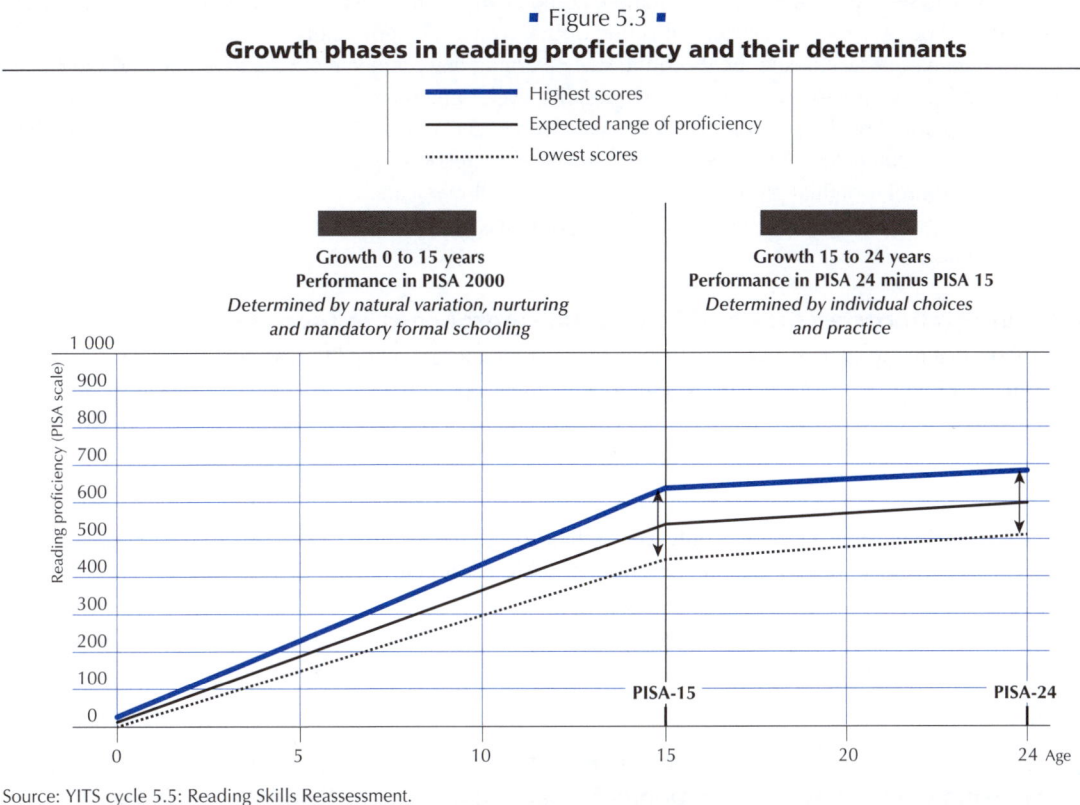

■ Figure 5.3 ■
Growth phases in reading proficiency and their determinants

- Highest scores
- Expected range of proficiency
- Lowest scores

Growth 0 to 15 years
Performance in PISA 2000
Determined by natural variation, nurturing and mandatory formal schooling

Growth 15 to 24 years
Performance in PISA 24 minus PISA 15
Determined by individual choices and practice

Source: YITS cycle 5.5: Reading Skills Reassessment.
StatLink http://dx.doi.org/10.1787/888932576833

Ideally, the freedom of choice in the years after compulsory education would allow for remediation of any inequities that arose during earlier learning. However, at least three factors limit such remediation. First, freedom of choice in learning opportunities depends on having universal access to those opportunities, which requires well-funded and well-distributed post-secondary and adult secondary learning programmes. Second, individuals must be assisted in bearing the short-term costs associated with long-term learning pathways, particularly if they come from socio-economically disadvantaged backgrounds. Third, disadvantages in the first phase of learning may limit the capacity of an individual to develop new skills, a factor that increases in importance with advancing age and slower neural development.

POSITIVE LEARNING ENVIRONMENTS BEFORE AND AFTER AGE 15

PISA-15 showed that a number of factors were associated with better individual performance at age 15 (phase one). PISA-24 offers an opportunity to examine the relationship between these factors and skills growth after 15 (phase two).

PISA-24 suggests that, as the opportunities for learning become more diverse, self-directed individuals are more successful in seizing those opportunities. In the transition out of compulsory education into post-secondary education or the labour market, skills acquisition is greater among those who thrive on their own or can successfully replicate the kinds of support mechanisms offered by their families, teachers and schools. In fact, the factors that tend to be associated with better performance at age 15 do not, in general, continue to have a positive relationship to skills growth after 15. In some cases, the opposite is true: factors that had a negative association with performance at age 15 tend to be weakly but positively related to skills growth after age 15. A negative relationship does not mean that individuals experienced skills loss, but rather that their pace of growth was slower.

PROFICIENCY GROWTH BEFORE AND AFTER AGE 15

PISA-15 collected information from students and their parents on their family background, learning environments and approaches towards learning. From school principals, PISA-15 collected information on the school environment. This section examines some of the data gathered from these two questionnaires, dividing them into two broad categories: the family environment and individual engagement, and the school environment.

This section describes the simple observed relationships between these factors and skills growth in phases one and two. The next section analyses these relationships in a more complex model that investigates how these factors interact with one another. In particular, the initial skills level is one of the strongest determinants of skills growth after age 15. Therefore, when examining the relationship between the early learning environments of young people and their skills growth in phase two, it is important to control for the initial skills level. Otherwise, the raw correlations of the variables with skills gains may be caused by the overriding effect of skills convergence, rather than the true effect of the variables themselves. As has been documented in Chapter 2 and elsewhere, regression towards the mean renders the PISA-15 score an inappropriate control for initial proficiency. As a result, the following analysis was conducted for three groups of students defined by their school grades, in order to control for differences in results among students with higher and lower initial reading skills.

Supportive family characteristics and individual approaches to learning

PISA evidence shows that many student and family characteristics are closely related to performance at age 15. While these characteristics provided an advantage in early skills growth, they appear to be either negatively related or unrelated to skills growth after age 15, with one exception. A student's belief that he or she is in control of his/her life had a positive impact on skills growth. Interestingly, this characteristic was associated with slower skills growth in the first phase of a young person's development.

Figure 5.4 depicts the relationship between family and individual characteristics with skills growth in phases one and two. The variables are classified along three dimensions: socio-economic status, family support, and individual approaches to learning. A positive sign represents a positive relationship; the more positive signs, the stronger the relationship. The inverse holds for negative signs. Statistically significant estimates are marked in bold. Table 5.2 in Annex B provides detailed results.

■ Figure 5.4 ■
Relationship between supportive family characteristics and individual approaches to learning, reading performance at age 15, and improvement in reading skills between the ages of 15 and 24

Criteria for:

+	Stands for a positive correlation	−	Stands for a negative correlation
++	Stand for a positive correlation above 0.07	− −	Stand for a negative correlation above 0.07
+++	Stand for a positive correlation above 0.15	− − −	Stand for a negative correlation above 0.15

School marks in language

Supportive family characteristics and individual approaches to learning	High Phase 1 (PISA-15)	High Phase 2 (PISA-24 - PISA-15)	Medium Phase 1 (PISA-15)	Medium Phase 2 (PISA-24 - PISA-15)	Low Phase 1 (PISA-15)	Low Phase 2 (PISA-24 - PISA-15)
Socio-economic status						
Highest parental education	+ +	−	+ +	−	**+ + +**	−
Highest parental occupation	+ +	+	**+ + +**	− −	**+ + +**	−
Family support of learning						
Cultural communication	**+ + +**	+	**+ + +**	− −	**+ + +**	−
Family educational support	+ +	−	− −	+ +	− −	+
Individual approaches to learning						
Sense of mastery[1]	−	+	− − −	+ +	−	+

1. Sense of mastery is a variable collected only in Canada through the PISA-24 survey implemented along with PISA-15.
Note: An statistically significant correlation is highlighted in bold.
Low school marks refers to obtaining below 70%, Medium school marks refers to obtaining from 70% to 79% and High school marks refers to obtaining at or above 80%.
Source: Table 5.2; YITS cycle 5.5: Reading Skills Reassessment.

Socio-economic status

Parents' education and occupation are two components of family background that are closely related to student performance at age 15 but are not related to skills growth after 15. Parents' education and occupation are measured by the highest level of achievement in the respective areas by the father and the mother. Parents' education and occupation are both closely related to student performance, particularly among those students with average and high school marks at age 15. The relationships are strong and substantial. For example, among those with high school marks the correlation between the highest parental occupational status and performance in PISA-15 is 0.24. However, the correlation between the highest parental occupational status and skills growth after 15 is negative and very weak, -0.02 (Table 5.2). The same pattern is seen for both these variables, regardless of the students' school marks. If anything, the negative relationship to skills growth was more pronounced among those individuals who, at age 15, had medium school marks.

Family support of learning

PISA-15 collected data on two aspects of family support for learning: parental cultural communication with their 15-year-olds and help with schoolwork and homework.

Cultural communication refers to the frequency with which parents discuss political or social issues, talk about books, films or television programmes, or listen to classical music with their children, as reported by the students at age 15. Cultural communication in the family has been shown to have a positive relationship with performance at age 15 (*PISA 2009 Results*, Volume II, OECD 2010c).

Cultural communication at home helps students thrive at age 15, but it has no lasting effect on skills growth beyond then. It is possible that students who had enjoyed higher levels of parental engagement do not maintain the same intrinsic motivation after they lose this support. The correlations between performance in PISA-15 and cultural communication are positive across all groups of students, regardless of their school marks. This positive relationship is particularly strong (positive correlation of 0.29, among the strongest of all analysed here) among those who, at age 15, had medium school marks. Yet it is precisely for this group that the relationship between cultural communication and skills growth after 15 is most negative (-0.11). While this negative relationship is not statistically significant, it is among the most negative observed in this analysis. For individuals with high school marks at 15, the relationship is also positive at age 15 and turns negative, although the relationship is weaker. For those with low marks, the relationship at age 15 is still positive, but weak, and the relationship with skills growth after 15 remains positive (Table 5.2).

Assistance with schoolwork and homework refers to the frequency with which parents or siblings worked with 15-year-olds. In contrast to cultural communication, help with schoolwork has a complex association with performance at age 15. PISA data suggest that when students struggle with their homework, parents are more likely to offer assistance. Therefore, the relationship between support for schoolwork and performance in PISA tends to be negative. As shown in Figure 5.4, the relationship with skills growth after 15 is weak, but positive (Table 5.2).

Individual approaches to learning

Beyond the variables measured by PISA-15 across all countries, Canada extended the student questionnaire to include questions relating to an individual's sense of mastery – the belief that one has control over one's destiny. The inspiration for this scale is the concept of external versus internal locus of control. A large body of research literature has highlighted this issue in the context of learning.[1]

PISA-24 results highlight the importance of a strong sense of self-determination for learning beyond compulsory education. During compulsory education, which is usually characterised as a supportive environment, a sense of mastery appears to be associated with less skills growth. However, beyond compulsory education, when learning takes place in a less structured manner, a sense of mastery seems to be positively related to skills growth.

A respondent's sense of mastery is defined as "the extent to which one regards one's life chances as being under one's own control in contrast to being fatalistically ruled" (Pearlin and Schooler, 1978). The concept of mastery was measured using the student questionnaire in YITS that was distributed with PISA-15.[2] Individuals were asked about the extent to which they agreed with the following statements: "I often feel helpless in dealing with the problems of life"; "I have little control over the things that happen to me"; "There is little I can do to change many of the important things in life"; "There is really no way I can solve some of the problems I have"; "Sometimes I feel I'm being pushed around in life"; "I can do just about anything I really set my mind to"; and "What happens to me in the future mostly depends on me". The sense-of-mastery scale was then developed by combining their answers.

5
PROFICIENCY GROWTH BEFORE AND AFTER AGE 15

While a sense of mastery is negatively related to performance at age 15, it is positively related to skills growth after age 15. For example, for the group of individuals with medium school marks at age 15, the correlation between a sense of mastery at age 15 and performance in PISA-15 is -0.30 and the correlation with skills growth after 15 is 0.12. In both cases, the correlations are consistent across groups, but they are not statistically significant. The pattern is similar for those with high and low school marks at age 15 (Table 5.2).

Supportive school learning environments

PISA-15 collected a wealth of information from students and school principals about school policies and practices. Focusing on those shown to have had a positive relationship to performance, this section classifies them into the following subcategories: school characteristics (size and average socio-economic intake); student perceptions of the school environment; school resources; teacher characteristics and engagement; school use of resources for instruction; school governance; and school climate.

The analysis of supportive school environments reveals similar findings to that of supportive family structures. In general, supportive school characteristics and policies that have a positive relation to skills acquisition at age 15 do not have a positive effect on skills development after age 15. In contrast, several factors that were negatively related to performance at 15 were positively related to skills growth after 15.

The relationships between the environment at school and skills at 15 and skills development after 15 are explored in Figure 5.5. A positive sign represents a positive relationship; the more positive signs, the stronger the relationship. The inverse holds for negative signs. Statistically significant estimates are marked in bold. Table 5.2 in Annex B provides detailed results.

■ Figure 5.5 ■
Relationship between supportive school learning environments, reading performance at age 15, and improvement in reading skills between the ages of 15 and 24

Criteria for:
+	Stands for a positive correlation	-	Stands for a negative correlation
++	Stand for a positive correlation above 0.07	- -	Stand for a negative correlation above 0.07
+++	Stand for a positive correlation above 0.15	- - -	Stand for a negative correlation above 0.15

	School marks in language					
	High		Medium		Low	
	Phase 1 (PISA-15)	Phase 2 (PISA-24 - PISA-15)	Phase 1 (PISA-15)	Phase 2 (PISA-24 - PISA-15)	Phase 1 (PISA-15)	Phase 2 (PISA-24 - PISA-15)
School characteristics						
Average school socio-economic profile	+++	- -	+++	- -	+++	-
School size	+++	- -	++	-	+++	- -
Student perception of school environment						
Student-teacher relations	+	-	++	- -	++	+
School achievement pressure	- - -	++	- - -	++	- -	++
School resources						
School education resources	- -	+	-	+	- -	+
School material resources	-	+	++	+	+	-
Teacher characteristics and engagement						
Student-teacher ratio	+	++	+++	- - -	++	-
Teacher shortage	- - -	++	+	-	-	-
Proportion of specialized reading teachers	+++	- - -	-	++	++	-
Teacher morale	++	++	-	+	+	-
Teacher participation in decision making	+++	- -	- -	++	+	++
Instructional time						
Total instructional hours	+	-	-	+	+	++
School governance						
School autonomy	+	+	+++	- -	+	++
School climate						
Supportive school environment	+++	- -	++	- -	++	+
Student behaviours	- -	+	+	- -	-	-
Teacher behaviours		+	+	- -	-	+

Note: An statistically significant correlation is highlighted in bold.
Low school marks refers to obtaining below 70%, Medium school marks refers to obtaining from 70% to 79% and High school marks refers to obtaining at or above 80%.
Source: Table 5.2; YITS cycle 5.5: Reading Skills Reassessment.

School characteristics: School socio-economic intake and school size

The average socio-economic background of students in a school – the school's socio-economic intake – is strongly and positively related to student performance in PISA-15, and weakly and negatively related to skills growth after 15. This pattern is evident across all groups of students, regardless of school marks at age 15. As with other variables, the result is most noticeable for students with medium school marks. The correlation between school socio-economic intake and student performance in PISA-15 is 0.32, the strongest correlation estimated in this exercise; its correlation with skills growth after age 15 is -0.09, a weak correlation (Table 5.2). The pattern is similar for those with high and low school marks at age 15. In general, a more advantaged socio-economic intake can mean a more supportive environment for learning: for example, it is associated with a better disciplinary climate. It is also possible that socio-economically advantaged students have a positive effect on the learning outcomes of their peers. However, PISA-24 results suggest that individual socio-economic background at age 15 does not continue to have a positive effect in phase two. In fact, those without this supportive environment at age 15 tend to acquire skills at a faster rate once they leave school. The results for school size are mixed and inconsistent, particularly for age 24.

Student perceptions of the school environment

PISA-15 asked students to report on a number of issues related to their school environment. The analysis here focuses on two that were shown to be particularly relevant in the Canadian context: teacher-student relations and school pressure to achieve.

The scale of teacher-student relations at age 15 was based on the answers students provided when they were asked to report the extent to which they agree with the following statements: "Students get along well with most teachers"; "Most teachers are interested in students' well-being"; "Most of my teachers really listen to what I have to say"; "If I need extra help, I will receive it from my teachers"; and "Most of my teachers treat me fairly".

School pressure to achieve at age 15 measured the extent to which students' felt that teachers emphasise academic performance and are demanding of their students.[3] The scale was built on students' reports on the frequency with which "the teacher wants students to work hard"; "the teacher tells students that they can do better"; "the teacher does not like it when students deliver careless work"; and "students have to learn a lot".

In general, a positive and supportive environment at school – as measured by teacher-student relations reported by the students – is weakly but positively related with performance at age 15 and weakly but negatively related with skills growth after 15. The change is most dramatic among those with average school marks at age 15. For this group, the correlation between teacher-student relations and skills at 15 is 0.14; the correlation with skills growth after 15 is -0.13 (Table 5.2). Neither correlation is particularly substantial, but they are not inconsequential either. For the group of students who had low school marks, the pattern is similar but the relationships are weaker. For the group that achieved high school marks, however, both relationships are positive, but they are also weak. This mixed evidence suggests that if a supportive school environment does have a positive impact on skills at age 15 that impact does not continue beyond compulsory education.

Pressure to achieve was weakly and negatively related to performance in PISA-15 across all groups of students, regardless of their school marks; in contrast, it was weakly and positively related to skills growth after 15, although the estimates of the relationships with both outcomes are statistically imprecise. For the group of students with high school marks, the relationship with performance at 15 is negative, but not very substantial (the actual correlation is -0.13, one of the lowest statistically significant correlations estimated for this exercise). The correlation with skills growth after 15, however, is 0.11 (Table 5.2). For the other groups of students, the correlations are approximately the same size and in the same direction, i.e. negative for skills at 15 and positive for skills growth after 15. These results confirm the longer-term associations (albeit weak) between pressure to achieve and performance after compulsory education, and suggest a need to better understand how achievement pressure operates in both the longer and shorter terms among students with differing achievement levels

School resources

PISA-24 evidence on school resources is inconclusive. There is no consistent relationship between either educational or material resources and performance at age 15 or skills growth after 15, regardless of the students' school marks. All relationships are weak and change from positive to negative or vice versa. For example, better educational resources are negatively related to performance at age 15, but positively related to skills growth after age 15 across all groups.

In contrast, better material resources are negatively related to performance at age 15 for those with low school marks, but positively related for those with high or average school marks.

That resources are only weakly related to skills is not surprising. The evidence from every PISA cycle shows that resources *per se* are not the main driver of school success. A large body of evidence from national assessments and other research and policy studies concludes the same. In general, the emphasis is on quality and how resources are used. For example, *Quality Time for Students: Learning in and out of School* (OECD, 2011b) argues that it is not so much the amount of time students spend learning, but rather how they use that time that counts.

Teacher characteristics and engagement

PISA-15 asked school principals about school enrolment and the size of their teacher staff to calculate student-teacher ratios. They were also asked to assess whether a shortage of teachers was hindering learning in their school. To evaluate teacher quality, the questionnaire distributed to principals asked about the proportion of teachers who were specialised in language instruction, given the focus on reading in PISA-15.

The importance of teachers and teaching for skills at age 15 is highlighted in this analysis; but PISA-24 also shows that, with some exceptions, this positive relation does not translate into positive effects on the rate of skills acquisition after the age of 15. The exceptions are found among measures of teacher engagement at school (morale and participation) that appear to be positively, albeit weakly, related to skills growth as well as skills acquisition at 15.

PISA moved beyond these relatively simple and objective measures and assessed teacher engagement at school. In particular, principals were asked to report on teacher morale and teacher participation in decision making. The scale of teacher morale was based on principals' reports on the extent to which they agree with the following statements: "The morale of teachers in this school is high"; "Teachers work with enthusiasm"; "Teachers take pride in this school"; and "Teachers value academic achievement." The teacher participation scale was based on principals' reports on the number of areas (staffing, budgeting and instruction) where teachers have the main responsibility (Adams and Wu, 2003 and OECD, 2001 provide more details on how each of these scales were built).

The availability of teachers, particularly specialised language teachers, has a weakly positive relationship to skills at 15 and a complex relationship to skills growth after 15. The proportion of specialised teachers is positively related to performance in PISA-15 and negatively related to performance in PISA-24 among those with low school marks at age 15. For the group of individuals with high school marks at 15, the relationships follow the same pattern, but they are weaker. For the group with medium school marks, the relationship changes from negative to positive. Across the other two measures of human resources at school, the results are equally mixed. For example, the student-teacher ratio is weakly and positively associated with performance at 15 and skills growth after 15 among those with low school marks. Teacher shortage is weakly and negatively associated with performance at age 15 and with skills growth after 15.

Teacher morale and teacher participation in decision making are generally only weakly related to skills growth in either PISA or PISA-24, and the relationships are inconsistent across grade levels, making it difficult to identify a pattern.

Instructional time and school governance

In PISA-15, school principals reported on the total number of school hours per year for the typical 15-year-old attending their school. The relationship between instructional time and skills at 15 is generally positive but weak. Among students with high school marks, group instructional time at age 15 is positively related to skills growth after the age of 15.

PISA-15 asked school principals to report on whether schools, rather than local or national authorities, had the primary responsibility for school administration, staffing, compensation, budgeting, admissions, and the curriculum. School autonomy is positively and weakly related to skills at age 15 and skills growth after age 15 among individuals with low and high school marks at age 15.

School climate

School principals provided information on student behaviour by reporting on the extent to which instruction in their school was hindered by: student absenteeism; disruption of classes by students; students skipping classes; students lacking respect for teachers; the use of alcohol or illegal drugs; and students intimidating or bullying other students. A scale for teacher behaviour was also developed based on school principals' reports on the extent to which instruction was being hindered by: low expectation of teachers; poor student-teacher relations; teachers not meeting individual students' needs; teacher absenteeism; staff resisting change; teachers being too strict with students; and students not being encouraged to achieve their full potential. A composite index of supportive school environments, produced in the context of Canada and shown to be related to skills at age 15 is also analysed.[4]

While a supportive school environment tends to be positively related to skills at age 15, there is a weak but generally negative relationship with skills growth after 15. This is particularly true for students with average or below average reading marks.

Student and teacher behaviours appear to be mostly unrelated to reading skills growth in either PISA-15 or PISA-24.

Box 5.1 Dichotomy between phase one and phase two growth

When examined individually, many of the relationships are small and statistically insignificant. However, taken together, the relationships between these variables to phase-one and phase-two growth forms a fairly consistent story.

The dichotomy between the role of positive influences at age 15 and age 24 is illustrated in Figure 13, which plots the correlations between the previously examined indices and proficiency growth in both periods of time. There are three data series in the panel of figures below that show the correlations for three different samples based on initial proficiency level. Each point in these figures gives the correlation between a given index and proficiency growth in the two time periods. The horizontal axis gives the correlation to phase-one growth, and the vertical axis to phase-two growth. Accordingly, data points in the top left of the space indicate a moderate positive correlation to growth after age 15 and a negative correlation to growth before age 15. Conversely, data points in the bottom right indicate negative correlations to growth after age 15 and positive correlations to growth prior to age 15. Data points in the bottom left and top right indicate negative and positive correlations, respectively, in both time periods.

■ Figure 5.6 ■
Relationship between correlations with PISA questionnaire indices and reading performance at age 15 and at age 24

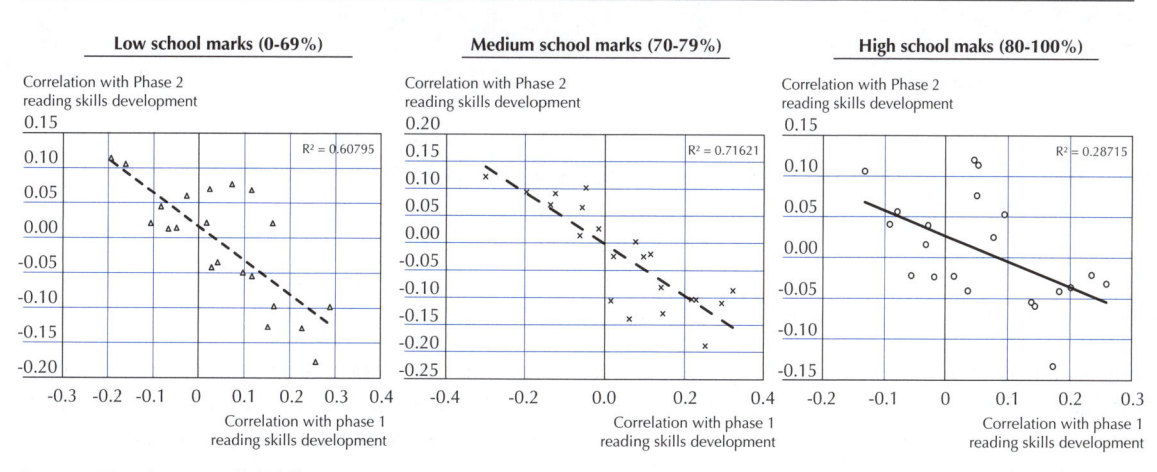

Source: YITS cycle 5.5: Reading Skills Reassessment.
StatLink http://dx.doi.org/10.1787/888932576833

The inverse relationship between proficiency growth in the two time periods indicates that students who had positive early learning conditions likely developed correspondingly strong skills, but any improvements outside of this environment were smaller. The negative correlations for later proficiency improvements do not indicate that higher values on the indices represent a reduction in skills. Rather, they indicate that skills growth did not occur as quickly as for other individuals. In short, individuals who enjoyed positive school experiences early in their lives may be unlikely to replicate those experiences later on.

PROFICIENCY GROWTH OUTSIDE THE CLASSROOM

The analysis above highlights several indices that were expected to have positive associations with reading performance at age 15 yet in fact had negative associations. These three factors are: sense of mastery, family educational support, and school pressure to achieve. To build on the results presented so far, this section analyses the relevance of these three variables jointly in a multiple regression. Two key contextual factors at age 15, socio-economic status and supportive school environment, were also included in the analysis. The same model was estimated separately for the three groups of students based on high school grades. The estimated effects on skills growth of an increase of one unit in the indices measuring these factors are shown in Table 5.3.[5]

A supportive school environment and family socio-economic status are both associated with better performance in PISA-15, after accounting for all the other factors included in this joint model. In contrast, both of these factors are negatively related to skills growth between the ages of 15 and 24. The negative relationships estimated for these two variables are indicative of skills convergence observed for youth after 15 (Table 5.3). Likewise, the effects of the sense of mastery, family educational support and school pressure to achieve change between PISA-15 and PISA-24: the impact on skills growth is negative at age 15 and positive at age 24.

While supportive school environments and socio-economic advantage benefit students generally, family educational support and pressure to achieve are specific to learning. The negative coefficients for these two factors during skills growth before the age of 15 indicate that students with poor initial reading skills tend to receive (or perceive) greater family educational support and school pressure. However, the positive coefficients for growth between the ages of 15 and 24 indicate that these personal interactions may produce residual effects that last even after students have left their school and family environments.

The relationship to sense of mastery suggests how these effects may relate to development in phase two. As discussed above, a sense of mastery describes the extent to which an individual feels he/she has control over his/her life. At age 15, students with a strong sense of mastery were not among the most proficient readers in general. For children and adolescents, successful learning and growth can be characterised as more dependent on trusting the decisions and direction of authority figures, such as teachers and parents. Therefore, it is understandable that students who may resent or resist this authority may have poorer learning outcomes. The positive estimates for skills growth in phase two suggests that once these young adults are beyond the environment where most of their learning decisions are made by external authorities, that is after the age of 15, those with a strong sense of mastery will be more likely to make decisions that result in a faster rate of skills acquisition. Youth who were pushed to succeed by their parents and teachers may similarly be more likely to choose avenues that lead to greater skills gains once they are making decisions on their own.

WHAT IS THE NET EFFECT OF POSITIVE EARLY LEARNING ENVIRONMENTS?

Although many factors related to early reading development may have a weak or negative association with skills growth after the age of 15, they are associated with other developmental outcomes and life choices that may provide even greater long-term advantages in terms of skills maintenance. Positive early learning environments tend to foster decision making associated with positive learning later on in life.

Like many other factors, even though skills growth between the ages of 15 and 24 may be slower for those in the most advantaged early environments, the initial advantage lasts. Table 5.4 presents data on skills at age 15 and 24 along four measures of learning environments at age 15: sense of mastery, family educational support, cultural communication and socio-economic background.

The results are presented for each level of parental education (Table 5.4), and for the top third and bottom third of youth on each of the indices (Figures 5.7 and 5.8).

Figure 5.7 shows, for example, that while skills growth was faster among individuals who did not enjoy frequent parental cultural communication (63 score points versus 49 score points), the average score at age 24 for those with less parental communication at age 15 (575 score points) barely catch up with the skills at age 15 of those who enjoyed more parental communication (572 score points). In general, though skills growth was greater among youth from less-advantaged environments, the faster growth was not sufficient to erase the early lead among those youth who enjoyed a more advantaged learning environment in their early years.

Figure 5.7
Improvements in reading skills between the ages of 15 and 24, by individual and family-related factors associated with skills at age 15

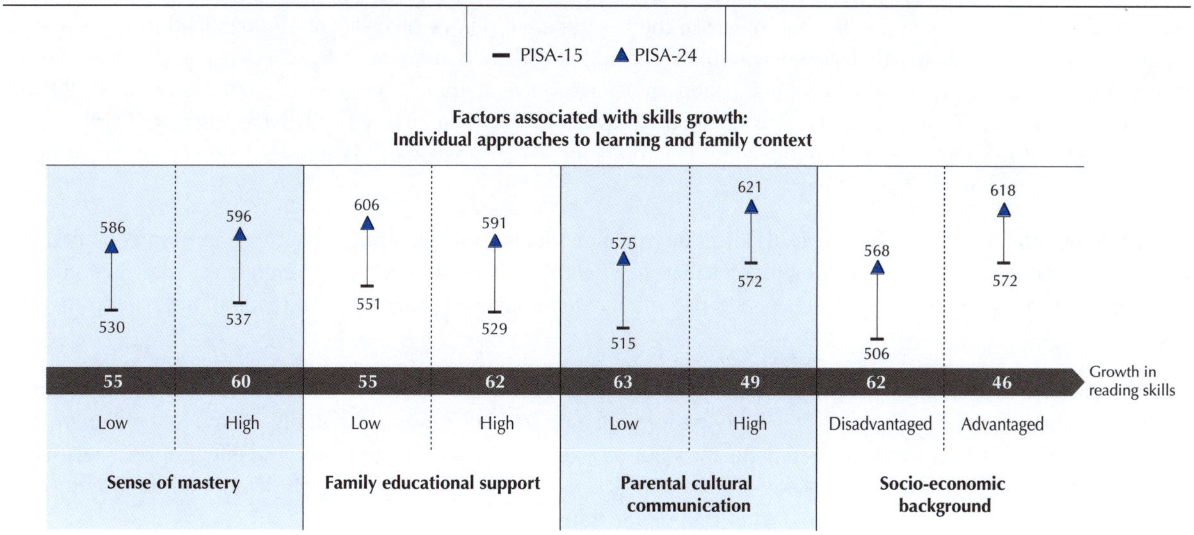

— PISA-15   ▲ PISA-24

Factors associated with skills growth:
Individual approaches to learning and family context

	Sense of mastery		Family educational support		Parental cultural communication		Socio-economic background	
PISA-24	586	596	606	591	575	621	568	618
PISA-15	530	537	551	529	515	572	506	572
Growth	55	60	55	62	63	49	62	46
	Low	High	Low	High	Low	High	Disadvantaged	Advantaged

Growth in reading skills →

Source: Table 5.4; YITS cycle 5.5: Reading Skills Reassessment.
StatLink http://dx.doi.org/10.1787/888932576833

The same pattern is observed for school factors, as evident in Figure 5.8. For example, those students whose school environment was less supportive showed faster skills growth than those whose school environment was more supportive (63 versus 54 score points). However, performance in PISA-24 was better among those whose school environment was more supportive (612 score points versus 580 score points), as had been the case in PISA-15 (559 versus 517 score points).

Figure 5.8
Improvements in reading skills between the ages of 15 and 24, by school-related factors associated with skills at age 15

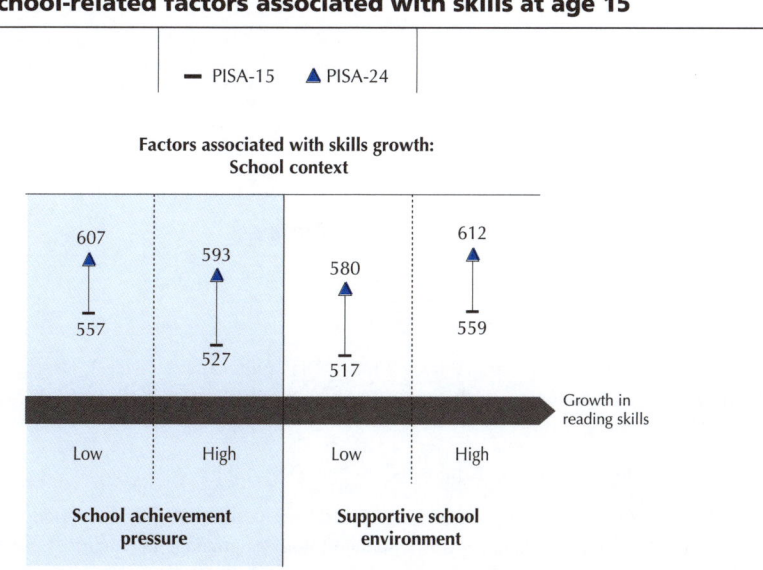

— PISA-15   ▲ PISA-24

Factors associated with skills growth:
School context

	School achievement pressure		Supportive school environment	
PISA-24	607	593	580	612
PISA-15	557	527	517	559
	Low	High	Low	High

Growth in reading skills →

Source: Table 5.4; YITS cycle 5.5: Reading Skills Reassessment.
StatLink http://dx.doi.org/10.1787/888932576833

CHAPTER SUMMARY AND CONCLUSIONS

Improvements in reading proficiency between the ages of 15 and 24 occur in environments that are much different from those up until the age of 15. Analysis of PISA-15 and PISA-24 results finds that certain attitudes and learning environments are more beneficial to young people than others in the two different phases of skills growth identified in this exercise. Students who felt they had a high degree of control over their lives did not perform as well at 15 as those who did not share this feeling. Conversely, students who felt they had a more supportive learning environment up to the age of 15 thrived. Yet after the age of 15, things changed: the more supportive early learning environments were associated with slower improvements in reading skills once out of these environments, while a sense of mastery became one of the strongest indicators of improvements in proficiency.

These findings confirm that, over time, skills levels among individuals converge. That is, young people who do not thrive early in their education have opportunities later that may better suit their abilities and preferences. Likewise, students who received extra attention from teachers and parents showed greater improvements in reading proficiency after the age of 15.

Despite the fact that students who performed poorly on PISA at age 15 showed greater improvements in reading proficiency by the time they were 24, the early performance disadvantage was not entirely overcome by age 24. This may partly be because less-proficient students miss out on later education opportunities. The effect of post-secondary education and other life transitions is taken up in the next chapter. The importance of self-determination in improving reading proficiency is also an important factor in these life transitions.

Self determination is key for improvements in proficiency among low-achievers. The degree of control one feels one has over one's life, an individual's sense of mastery, is one of the strongest factors related to improvements in reading skills after the age of 15. In contrast, the sense of self-mastery was negatively related to skills at age 15. From childhood to age 15, the strongest influences on reading proficiency are from parents and the home learning environment, and from teachers and the school learning environment. As individuals transition into adulthood, however, the emphasis shifts to the choices young people make about post-secondary education and the extent to which they practice their reading skills in employment and leisure. Greater autonomy and capacity to make individual life choices is generally related to faster skills growth, particularly when combined with participation in post-secondary education.

Notes

1. Greer, J.V. (1991), and Pearlin, L. and S. Schooler (1978).

2. Statistics Canada (2005), "Youth in Transition Survey 2000, YITS reading cohort, Cycle 1, Users guide", revised September 2005, and provides all the necessary documentation on this variable and is available for download here: http://www.statcan.gc.ca/imdb-bmdi/document/4435_D25_T1_V1-eng.pdf

3. This is referred to as the index of "achievement press" in other PISA publications.

4. The index of school supportive environment is constructed as a composite index of student-teacher relations, average sense of belonging, and proportion of language teachers with a specialisation in language instruction. Cartwright and Rhode (2010) provide all details on how this index was constructed.

5. In this context, the analysis focuses on consistency of results across groups. The uncertainty of the estimates is increased by the small sample sizes within each group.

The Effect of Education and Work Pathways on Reading Proficiency

This chapter discusses the paths young people choose towards entering further education or the labour force and their relation to skills and skills gains. Those who completed university education tended to have high PISA scores when they were 15 and they continued to have a considerable advantage at age 24 over those who did not follow this pathway. However, young people whose highest educational attainment was high school still acquired reading skills after the age of 15 – and these skills were acquired at similar or faster rates than those acquired by university-educated young adults. Meanwhile, work experience appears to play only a minor role in learning gains after the age of 15. Other life transitions, like moving out of the parental home and marriage, are also examined. The role of active self-determination appears to be a critical factor for explaining differences in skills gains across these life transitions.

THE EFFECT OF EDUCATION AND WORK PATHWAYS ON READING PROFICIENCY

LIFE CHOICES AND THE ACQUISITION OF SKILLS

The development of reading skills between the ages of 15 and 24 takes place in the context of individual life choices. After Canadian youth completed compulsory education, they were faced with the choice of attending a university or college, or attempting to enter the labour market. They also made decisions about where to live and with whom. These decisions affected their acquisition of skills during the period.

Analysis in Chapter 3 shows that there were large differences in skills at age 15 and persistent differences at age 24 for youth who followed different educational pathways. Chapter 3 also alludes to variations in the rates of skills acquisition across various education and labour-market pathways. The analysis in this chapter builds on the findings described in previous chapters and focuses on the relationship between educational and labour-market pathways and skills growth. It also provides a context for analysing skills growth more generally, by providing information on other important life decisions young people make during the transition into adulthood.

Most of the young people surveyed chose to pursue further education rather than enter the labour force immediately after compulsory education. By 2009, many of these young people had attended some kind of post-secondary education. In fact, 41% of PISA-24 respondents had completed a non-university level programme, and 29% had earned a university degree. The skills acquired by the age of 15 help shape these decisions. Previous research using the Youth in Transition Survey (YITS) has shown that PISA scores are strong predictors of participation in post-secondary education (OECD, 2010a), a finding that is strongly reflected in the PISA-24 data as well.

During this crucial transition period, there is a lot more happening in the lives of young people than acquiring skills and participating in education or work. Young men and women are also deciding where and with whom they will live. Often, these choices become the context, whether positive or negative, in which skills acquisition and further education takes place. In other cases, these choices are the consequences of other decisions made about skills acquisition and education.

This chapter examines how some key educational and demographic choices affect skills acquisition. It discusses how learning gains vary by educational attainment and by years spent in formal education; differences in skills growth based on the specific pathways chosen, for instance, by those who took a "gap year"; and how the acquisition of skills varies depending on work experience, geographic mobility, relationships or level of independence.

IMPROVEMENTS IN READING PROFICIENCY, EDUCATIONAL ATTAINMENT AND PATHWAYS

Educational attainment and growth in reading skills

Previous analysis of the YITS and PISA-15 data has shown that educational attainment and education pathway choices are influenced by individuals' reading proficiencies at age 15. In other words, reading proficiency at age 15, as measured by PISA-15, is a strong predictor of eventual educational attainment (OECD, 2010a). The PISA scores in reading for 15- and 24-year-olds, according to various educational attainment levels by age 24, are illustrated in Figure 6.1.[1]

On average, growth in reading skills between the ages of 15 and 24 for university graduates was not as large as the improvement in scores was for youth whose highest educational attainment was high school (56 compared to 65 points). However, growth in reading skills among university graduates was larger than that observed among graduates from non-university post-secondary programmes (51 points). Furthermore, the large initial advantage in reading proficiency among university graduates persisted. In fact, university graduates averaged higher reading scores at age 15 than did other youth at age 24. At 24 years old, young people with only high school attainment had an average score of 564 points, non-university post-secondary graduates had an average score of 584 points, and university graduates had an average score of 652 points (Table 6.1).

Educational pathways and growth in reading skills

Beyond educational attainment, PISA-24 provides evidence of how specific educational pathways can affect growth in reading skills. Not all individuals follow a linear pathway through education, progressing from one level to the next without any interruption until the completion of a particular degree. Many individuals decide to take a break from their studies and pursue other interests or enterprises. These individuals follow a non-linear educational pathway, defined by a break in studies of at least one "gap" year.

Figure 6.1
Growth in reading skills between the ages of 15 and 24, by educational attainment at age 24

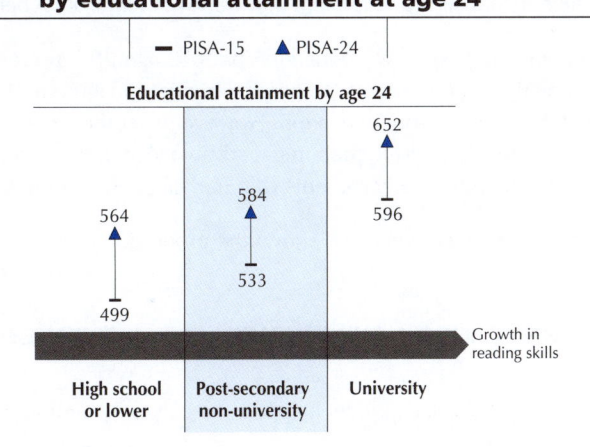

— PISA-15   ▲ PISA-24

Educational attainment by age 24

- High school or lower: 499 → 564
- Post-secondary non-university: 533 → 584
- University: 596 → 652

Growth in reading skills

Source: Table 6.1; YITS cycle 5.5: Reading Skills Reassessment.
StatLink http://dx.doi.org/10.1787/888932576852

Figure 6.2 illustrates the skills growth for young people at each level of educational attainment. Individuals are divided into those who went directly through their post-secondary education without interruption, and those who took a gap year during which they did not pursue formal education. In this study, a gap is defined as at least one year during which young people were not enrolled as full-time students, and after which they returned to full-time studies before completing their education.

For university and non-university post-secondary graduates, students who followed a more linear pathway showed greater improvements in skills between the ages of 15 and 24. Those university graduates who did not take a gap year improved by 64 score points, while those who took a gap year improved by 60 points. Non-university post-secondary graduates who did not take a gap year improved by 53 score points, while those who did take a gap year improved by 40 score points. But a gap year appears to have been beneficial for those individuals whose highest level of educational attainment was high school. Those who did not take a break from education saw a 65 score point improvement in their reading skills, while those who did take a gap year improved by 73 points.

Figure 6.2
Growth in reading skills between the ages of 15 and 24, by educational pathway

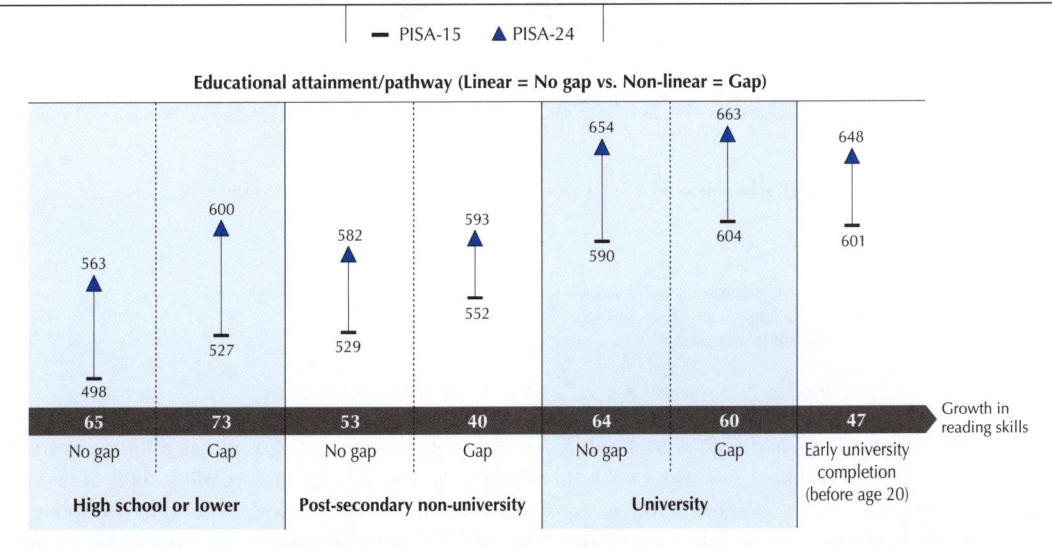

— PISA-15   ▲ PISA-24

Educational attainment/pathway (Linear = No gap vs. Non-linear = Gap)

Pathway	PISA-15	PISA-24	Growth
High school or lower — No gap	498	563	65
High school or lower — Gap	527	600	73
Post-secondary non-university — No gap	529	582	53
Post-secondary non-university — Gap	552	593	40
University — No gap	590	654	64
University — Gap	604	663	60
Early university completion (before age 20)	601	648	47

Note: A gap refers to a break of at least a year, when these individual did not pursue formal education.
Source: Table 6.1; YITS cycle 5.5: Reading Skills Reassessment.
StatLink http://dx.doi.org/10.1787/888932576852

For low-achievers, taking a break from education may be a deliberate choice to try to improve their learning environment or to postpone further education until they are better prepared to take advantage of it. In contrast, a break in education might not be beneficial for high-achieving students, as it may remove them from a beneficial environment.

The group of students who completed university education prior to age 20 represents an extreme example. Reading scores at age 15 were also very high (at 601 points, among the highest in Figure 6.2). These students entered university immediately after completing their compulsory education. However, after the age of 15, they did not acquire skills any faster than other university graduates. As a result, their initial advantage shrunk or, in some cases, disappeared and their reading skills were surpassed by other university students who had taken more time to complete their education.

Table 6.1 in Annex B includes all these statistics and shows the proportion of individuals by attainment and pathways in the PISA-24 sample.

EDUCATIONAL ATTAINMENT, WORK EXPERIENCE, AND IMPROVEMENTS IN READING PROFICIENCY

In contrast to educational attainment, work experience appears to play only a minor role in the growth of reading skills after age 15.

Figure 6.3 shows findings related to skills acquisition among youth with substantial work experience, defined as more than two years of experience, and those without substantial work experience, defined as two years or less. To account for any differences related to educational pathways, the analysis was conducted taking into account educational attainment at age 24.

■ Figure 6.3 ■
Growth in reading skills between the ages of 15 and 24, by educational attainment and professional pathways at age 24

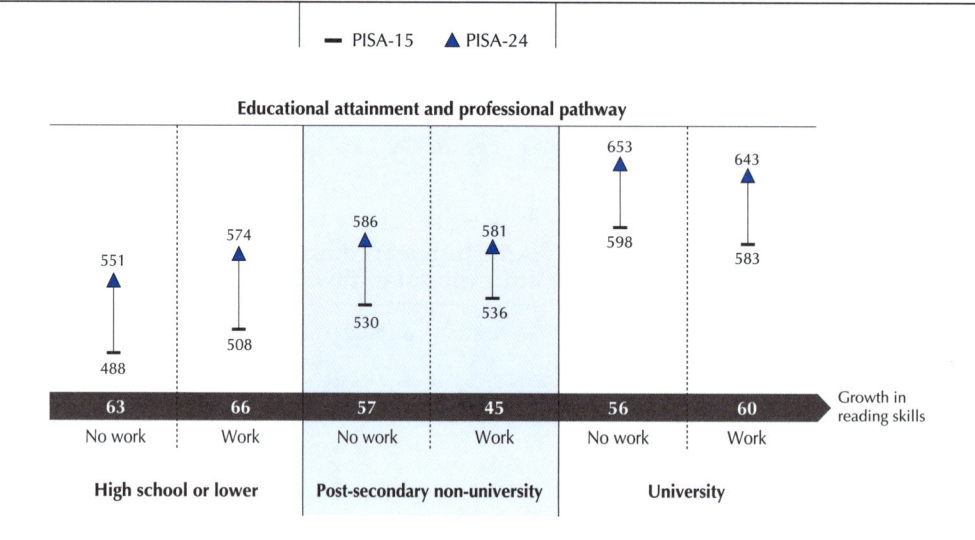

— PISA-15   ▲ PISA-24

Educational attainment and professional pathway					
488 → 551	508 → 574	530 → 586	536 → 581	598 → 653	583 → 643
63	66	57	45	56	60
No work	Work	No work	Work	No work	Work
High school or lower		Post-secondary non-university		University	

Note: Work refers to 3 years or more of professional work experience.
Source: Table 6.1; YITS cycle 5.5: Reading Skills Reassessment.
StatLink http://dx.doi.org/10.1787/888932576852

Among university graduates and high school-only graduates there is little to no advantage in terms of growth in reading skills for those with substantial work experience. In contrast, the rate of acquiring reading skills among non-university post-secondary graduates was somewhat higher for those without substantial work experience (57-point increase) than for those with substantial work experience (45-point increase). The faster rate of acquiring reading skills meant that while those without work experience started with slightly lower scores at age 15 (530 versus 536 score points), they ended up with slightly higher scores at age 24 (586 versus 581 score points) than those with work experience.

THE EFFECT OF EDUCATION AND WORK PATHWAYS ON READING PROFICIENCY

The types of reading-related tasks performed on the job vary across occupations, industries and fields of work. These differences are likely to be an important factor in explaining varying levels of skills acquisition. However, this and other workplace factors could not be rigorously analysed using this data because the number of observations would be too small to draw any meaningful conclusions.

EDUCATIONAL ATTAINMENT, TIME SPENT IN EDUCATION AND THE ACQUISITION OF SKILLS

The rate of improvement in reading proficiency is strongly related to the time spent in formal education. In fact, the length of time spent in formal education appears to be equally important for skills growth across all levels of educational attainment. Figure 6.4 shows the improvement in reading proficiency (displayed as bars) by the amount of time spent in formal education across different levels of educational attainment. The vertical lines at the end of each bar represent an estimate of the precision (the confidence intervals) with which each of these growth rates is measured. Table 6.2 in Annex B provides the detailed results.

For all levels of attainment, the more time spent in formal education, the greater the improvements in reading proficiency. Despite the imprecision with which each of these statistics is measured, a consistent pattern emerges. In Figure 6.4, the solid lines at the bars show the linear relationship between years spent in formal education and skills growth for each level of attainment. The effect size is similar across groups, ranging from 7.5 score points per year in education among university graduates to 9.8 score points per year in education among non-university post-secondary graduates. In other words, the size of the improvement associated with each additional year is approximately the same, regardless of the eventual level of attainment.

■ Figure 6.4 ■
Improvements in reading proficiency, by educational attainment and years spent in formal education

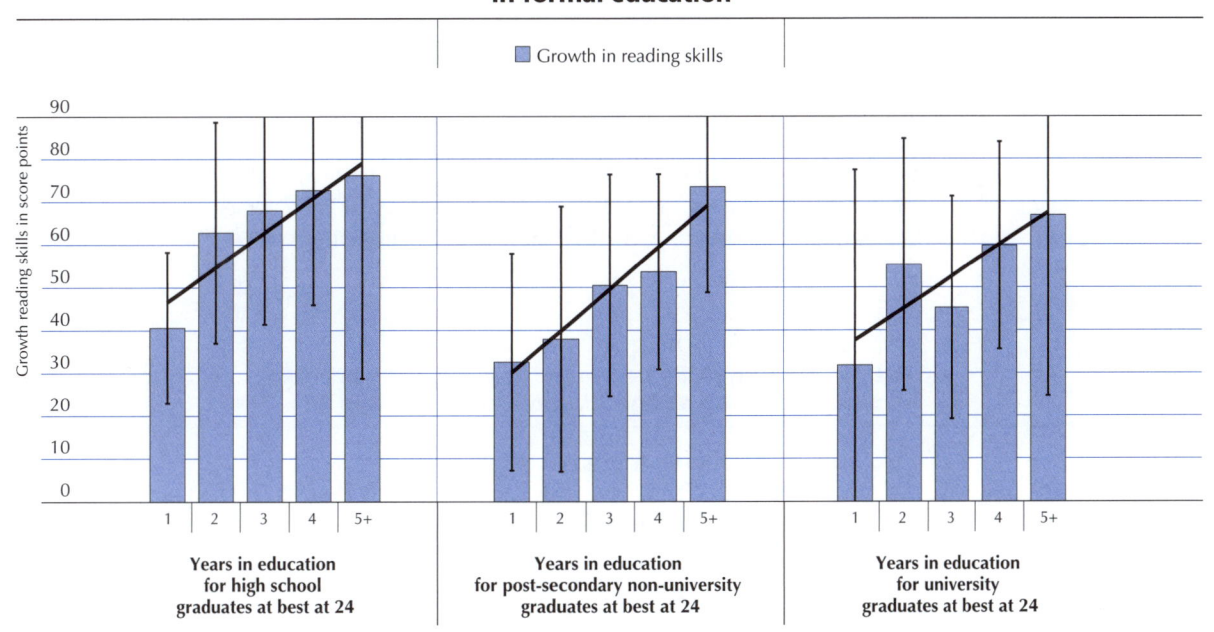

Source: Table 6.2; YITS cycle 5.5: Reading Skills Reassessment.
StatLink http://dx.doi.org/10.1787/888932576852

This general pattern is similar to the consistent effect of grade progression on skills growth discussed earlier. While there is no reason to expect that learning gains in each year of formal education would be the same, a plausible explanation for the linearity is that the amount of textual material to which students are exposed does not vary relative to their capacity. Regardless of the programme of study, curricula are designed to match the learning material given to students to their capacity to consume and absorb it. Given that initial status varies across these educational pathways, these findings present an optimistic counterpoint to the prevailing hypothesis of inexorable skills decline. They suggest that continuous lifelong learning may be more advantageous to the development of skills than programme-based study.

Beyond these estimates, obtaining a post-secondary degree or spending more time in education is strongly related to faster skills acquisition. The estimated effects of an extra year of education or obtaining a post-secondary degree are both robust and large. Even when compared with other variables, and even after accounting for other factors, such as gender, socio-economic background at age 15 or skills at age 15, staying in post-secondary education longer and obtaining a degree have impacts on skills gains similar to the estimated effects of a whole standard deviation in socio-economic background and close to half a standard deviation in skills levels at age 15. In fact, these are the only two variables related to education- and work-related pathways that seem to have an effect beyond age 15. In contrast, other factors, such as reading enjoyment at age 15, are not related to skills gains after comparing individuals who are similar in all other respects included in these combined models. Table 6.3 provides more detailed results.

LEARNING GAINS AND DEMOGRAPHIC TRANSITIONS

During this crucial transition period between the ages of 15 and 24, there is a lot more happening in the lives of young people than acquiring skills and participating in education or work. Young men and women are also making choices about where they live and their relationships.

Geographic mobility and growth in reading skills

One of the significant results of the PISA study in Canada is the persistent gap in reading proficiency between rural and urban students. An analysis of the PISA results found that reading skills are not used as much in rural communities as in urban communities, which, in turn, discourages formation of literacy skills in young students living in rural areas (Cartwright and Allen, 2002).

While this may be true for proficiency improvements up to age 15, there appears to be little or no additional impact of the setting of a school – rural or urban – on reading proficiency after the age of 15 (Table 6.4). On the contrary, as Figure 6.5 shows, students in rural areas catch up to their urban counterparts to some extent. Rural youth who migrated to an urban setting and rural youth who stayed in a rural setting improved their reading scores by 63 points and 68 points, respectively, between the ages of 15 and 24. In contrast, young people who were in an urban setting at both ages improved in reading by an average of 53 points. Moreover, urban students who migrated to rural areas improved by 64 points, which contradicts the notion that rural settings are less likely to foster skills development than urban settings.

However, two important points must be considered when interpreting this data. First, urban youth who migrated to rural areas had substantially lower scores than their peers. Second, despite the higher rate of improvement among rural youth after the age of 15, the final scores of 24-year-olds from rural settings still lag behind those of 24-year-olds from urban areas.

■ Figure 6.5 ■
Growth in reading skills between the ages of 15 and 24, by school location at age 15 and location at age 24

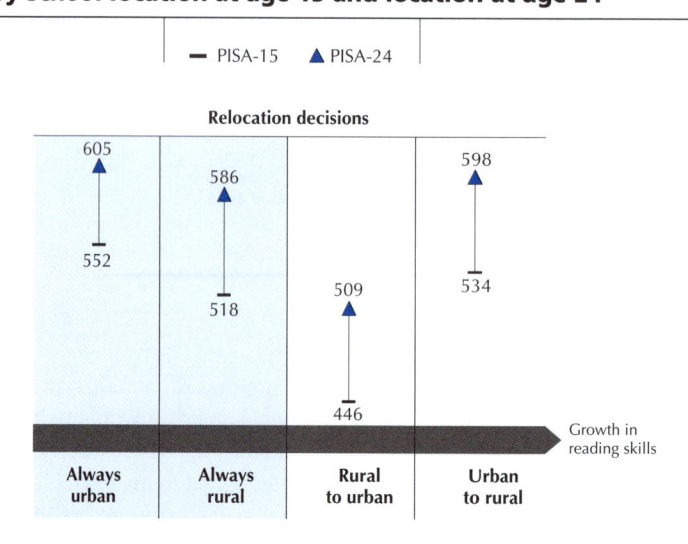

Relocation decisions

	Always urban	Always rural	Rural to urban	Urban to rural
PISA-15	552	518	446	534
PISA-24	605	586	509	598

Source: Table 6.4; YITS cycle 5.5: Reading Skills Reassessment.
StatLink http://dx.doi.org/10.1787/888932576852

Relationship choices and growth in reading skills

A common transition associated with young adulthood is the transition from dependence on parents to independence and relationships with a life partner. In order to meet the challenges associated with this transition, many young adults make short-term economic decisions, such as accepting a low-paying job to pay for monthly expenses rather than apply their income to an activity that might pay off later on, such as post-secondary education or training. The consequences of these trade-offs may not be universal; what is beneficial to some young adults may be detrimental (or at least less advantageous) to others.

The transition from single status to married or common-law (labeled "other relationship" in Table 6.5) is associated with different patterns of development of reading proficiency. For students who were highly proficient at 15, remaining single is associated with greater proficiency gains after age 15; the reverse is true among low-achievers. A tempting explanation for this pattern is that higher-achieving students may delay lifestyle decisions until they have completed their higher education. However, this does not explain the pattern among low-achievers, which shows greater improvements in reading proficiency among those who have changed their marital status.

There may be several mechanisms producing these relationships. Students with high reading proficiency at age 15 will likely have more opportunities to develop their skills by continuing their formal education. Students with low reading proficiency will likely have had limited post-secondary education options, but may have found more supportive learning environments different than those in which their initial reading scores were attained. Regardless, the principle remains the same: if early reading proficiency is a product of context, then remaining in a nurturing context is likely to sustain improvement, while shifting out of a nurturing context into greater self-determination is likely to impede it. Conversely, greater self-determination appears to be beneficial to those who had initially low scores as a result of their early learning environment.

The association between relationship choices and educational pathways is shown in Table 6.6. There is no systematic difference in the reading proficiency of 15-year-olds entering different educational pathways when compared across each of the transition groups. The average PISA score differences between young people whose highest educational attainment is high school, those who graduated from non-university post-secondary programmes, and university graduates, are about the same, regardless of the relationship choice. Furthermore, the absolute levels of reading proficiency at age 15 are also comparable across demographic groups, indicting there is little to no selection bias in the different transition groups.

The effects of these transitions become evident when looking at improvements in reading skills between the ages of 15 and 24 (see Table 6.6). There is a clear pattern showing that improvement in reading proficiency among young people with post-secondary educational attainment is higher for individuals who are single or live with their parents than for individuals who have changed their relationship or independence status. Conversely, individuals whose highest level of educational attainment is high school and who have changed their relationship status or are living independently from their parents tend to show greater improvements in proficiency.

This evidence confirms the notion that independence and self-determination primarily benefit those individuals who may be disadvantaged during their earlier development. In contrast, assuming that students who pursue higher education had more supportive learning environments when they were young, the smaller improvements in proficiency after the age of 15 imply that removing these individuals from those environments may slow the rate with which they acquire skills.

CHAPTER SUMMARY AND CONCLUSIONS

Research from YITS has already established a link between skills levels at age 15 and participation in post-secondary education, most notably at the university level (OECD, 2010a). Data on proficiency at age 24 show that the initial skills advantage for youth who go on to university persists, even though there is a general move towards skills convergence among all young people by the age of 24.

Despite the persistent performance advantage among university graduates, PISA-24 suggests that what is most important for maintaining and improving reading proficiency is participation in formal education of any type.

Furthermore, work experience is not a substitute for formal education. Spending more time in education is associated with faster rates of acquiring skills; focusing on work for longer periods of time is not. In fact, young people who went directly from compulsory education into the labour market and stayed there for much of the period between PISA-15 and PISA-24 started with lower levels of skills at age 15 and ended up with lower levels of skills at age 24. Their reading performance showed smaller improvements during this period.

This chapter has also shown that the context in which education takes place is also related to skills growth. A change can be beneficial to those who were low-achievers until the age of 15. For those who had greater proficiency, a move away from parents and into other relationships was not beneficial for skills growth. Though early skills disadvantages are persistent, these findings show that changes to the learning environment can have a strong and positive effect on skills acquisition among disadvantaged students.

Second-chance programmes and system flexibility can help young people who did not have the advantages of supportive learning environments in their school years. Educators must find a way to improve the reading proficiencies of those who do not complete compulsory education or graduate with low reading proficiency. While it is unlikely that low-achievers will be able to completely make up for initial disadvantage, this study has identified several mechanisms that could mitigate such disadvantage.

The ideal policy would be to prevent dropping out. Because of the true costs of dropping out of school, efforts to prevent it are more cost-effective than applying corrective policy later. Results show that formal education continues to be the most effective way to improve skills. Another alternative would be to provide second-chance and flexible programmes tailored to students' needs.

Across all levels of educational attainment, improvement in proficiency is strongly related to time spent in the education system. For instance, young people who never completed a programme above high school, but who spent four or more years in school (e.g. on incomplete degrees or diplomas at the post-secondary level) between the ages of 15 and 24, showed improvements in skills (70 score points or more) that were similar to or greater than those observed among young people who spent four or more years in education after high school and completed a university degree (60 score points or more).

Life choices affect reading proficiency and the rate of learning gains. Continued improvement in reading proficiency after age 15 is not necessarily associated with the same factors that were associated with reading proficiency by age 15. Once young people leave compulsory education, personal factors and choices affect the rate at which they acquire skills, underlining the importance of inculcating learning strategies, mastery and self-regulated learning during school.

Not all life transitions were associated with positive skills growth. Young people who had the advantage of supportive learning environments up to age 15 showed relatively slower improvements in reading proficiency as they made the transition to independence. In contrast, those young people who did not thrive in their early learning contexts made greater improvements if they experienced a change in their environments, for example, if they moved out of their parents' home.

Independence and self-determination allow individuals who may be disadvantaged during their younger years to find environments that foster greater proficiency later on. For example, young people who performed poorly at age 15, as measured by reading marks in school, showed greater improvements between the ages of 15 and 24 if they made a change in their life circumstances, such as changing the status of a relationship (e.g. from single to married) or moving out of their parents' home.

Formal education and higher education are key factors affecting reading performance. Participation in some form of post-secondary education is consistently, robustly and substantially related to skills growth between the ages of 15 and 24. For example, differences in reading skills at 15 and 24 are most dramatic between those young people who spent significant time in formal education and those who did not. University graduates at age 24 had an average score of 652 points in PISA-24. In contrast, those with only high school attainment scored, on average, nearly 100 points lower, at 564 points. When those with university-level attainment were 15, they averaged 596 points on PISA, substantially above the scores attained nine years later by those whose highest educational attainment was high school. This underscores the importance of ensuring good reading proficiency by the end of compulsory education.

Completing a post-secondary degree by age 24 is also strongly related with skills growth, even after accounting for skills at age 15, socio-economic background and other individual characteristics. Those with only a high school diploma at age 24 or those with substantial work experience (more than three years) by age 24 tended to attain lower scores at age 24 than those with higher educational attainment or less substantial work experience.

The choice of pathway to higher education and work had impacts on improvements in reading proficiency. However, greater proficiency at early ages prepares young people for further education and creates opportunities for additional studies that may not be as readily available to low-achievers. The lowest PISA scores at age 24 were associated with young people who had spent the least amount of time in the education system, and who had spent the most amount of time working. Therefore, compulsory education should equip all students with the reading skills necessary for further learning.

While the most common and direct path through secondary and university-level education appears to maximise reading proficiency gains, not everyone can take that route. System flexibility and second-chance programmes are important mechanisms for increasing learning gains among many youth. The evidence in this report shows that given the opportunity, many low-achievers found ways to improve their proficiency in the years following compulsory education. While not all of them catch up with the top performers, the skills they acquire later help them to fully participate in society.

Note

1. This classification is based on highest attainment at age 24. Therefore, some of the individuals classified as those whose highest level of educational attainment is high school will undoubtedly end up with a higher degree; they might even be enrolled in a university or any other post-secondary education programme, but have not completed their degree by the age of 24.

Conclusion

The Programme for International Student Assessment (PISA) measures the extent to which 15-year-olds near the end of compulsory education have acquired some of the knowledge and skills that are essential for full participation in modern societies. This triennial survey focuses on student performance in reading, mathematics and science.

Canada added a dynamic element to the snapshot provided by PISA. Over ten years, its Youth in Transition Survey followed those students who were assessed by PISA in 2000. Every two years, YITS collected data on the educational and labour market pathways of these individuals. In 2009, Canada further enriched this database with a skills re-assessment of these young people, focusing on reading skills.

The result provides a rich source of data to support evidence-based policy making in Canada and in other countries involved in PISA. Understanding how skills develop over time is increasingly important as higher levels of skills foster economic and social prosperity.

The data Canada has generated shows the dynamic nature of learning during the critical period between the ages of 15 and 24. The development of reading skills during this period builds critically on the acquisition of skills earlier in life; such that reading proficiency among 24-year-olds tends to mirror that of their 15-year-olds selves. Many of the performance gaps observed at age 15 were still present at age 24. The one exception to this rule were those born outside of Canada, who at age 24 performed as well as those born in Canada, even if they had lower levels of performance at age 15. In fact, students with poor reading proficiency at age 15 were not necessarily saddled with this deficiency for life. That is, after compulsory education, transitions through education and the labour market, and particularly the opportunity to continue education, offered plenty of opportunities to develop and improve reading skills.

Educational attainment was strongly related to improvements in reading skills between the ages of 15 and 24, even when taking into account initial levels of skills and a host of other factors. The importance of education for improving reading skills was no surprise; indeed, this evidence supports the call for flexibility in education systems. Second-chance opportunities are vital for helping those with low levels of skills at the end of compulsory education to succeed later on in life.

How individuals use their skills and the extent to which a person regards his or her life chances as being under his or her own control were also strongly related to skills growth. The transition into adulthood generally involves a move from the controlled and relatively passive learning environments of school and compulsory education into the more diverse, complex, and autonomous learning contexts of post-secondary education and the labour market. Those 15-year-olds who reported feeling more in control of their own success showed greater improvements in their reading proficiency by the time they were 24 than did those individuals who were more passive and fatalistic learners at age 15.

References

Adams, R. and **M. Wu** (eds.) (2003), Programme for International Student Assessment (PISA): PISA 2000 Technical Report, PISA, OECD Publishing.

Abitz, M., et al. (2007), "Excess of Neurons in the Human Newborn Mediodorsal Thalamus Compared with that of the Adult", *Cerebral Cortex,* 17 (11), pp. 2573-2578.

Alexander, K., D. Entwisle, and **L. Olson** (2007), *Lasting Consequences of the Summer Learning Gap,* American Sociological Review, Washington, D.C.

Beswick, J.F., E.A. Sloat, and **J.D. Willms** (2008), "Four Educational Myths That Stymie Social Justice", *The Educational Forum,* No. 72, pp. 115-28.

Bussière, P. and **T. Knighton** (2006), *Educational Outcomes at Age 19 Associated with Reading Ability at Age 15,* Statistics Canada, Ottawa.

Bussière, P., et al. (2001), *Measuring Up: The Performance of Canada's Youth in Reading, Mathematics and Science,* Statistics Canada, Ottawa.

Bynner, J. and **S. Parsons** (2009), "Insights into basic skills from a UK longitudinal study," In Reder, S., and J. Bynner (eds.), *Tracking Adult Literacy and Numeracy Skills – Findings from Longitudinal Research* (pp. 27-58), Routledge, New York.

Cartwright F. and **M.K. Allen** (2002), *Understanding the Rural-urban Reading Gap,* Statistics Canada, Ottawa.

Cartwright F. (2012), "Technical feasibility of reporting YITS 2009 skill assessment results on the PISA 2000 reading scale", *OECD Education Working Paper* No. 69, OECD Publishing.

Cattell, R.B. (1971), *Abilities: Their Structure, Growth, and Action,* Houghton Mifflin, Boston.

Cattell, R.B. (1987), *Intelligence: Its Growth, Structure and Action,* Elsevier Science New York.

Cooper, H., et al. (1996), "The effects of summer vacation on achievement test scores: A narrative and meta-analytic review", *Review of Educational Research,* No. 66, pp. 227-268.

Council of Ministers of Education Canada (2008), *Pan-Canadian Assessment Program: Report on the assessment of 13-year-olds in reading, math and science,* Council of Ministers of Education Canada, Ontario.

Desjardins, R., Y. Clermont, T.S. Murray and **P. Werquin** (2005), "Learning a Living: First Results of the Adult Literacy and Life Skills Survey", retrieved 5 January 2011 from *http://www.nald.ca/library/research/learnliv/cover.htm*

Desjardins, R and **A. J. Warnke** (2012), "Ageing and skills: a review and analysis of skill gain and skill loss over the lifespan and over time", *OECD Education Working Paper* No. 66, OECD, Paris.

Dreyfus, S. E., and **H.L. Dreyfus** (1980), *A Five-Stage Model of the Mental Activities Involved in Directed Skill Acquisition,* Storming Media, Washington, DC.

Giedd, J.N., et al. (1999), "Brain Development During Childhood and Adolescence: A Longitudinal MRI Study", *Nature Neuroscience 2(10),* pp. 861-863.

Greer, J.V. (1991), "At-risk students in the fast lanes: Let them through", *Exceptional Children* (March, April), pp. 390-391.

Heyns, B. (1978), *Summer Learning and the Effects of Schooling,* Academic Press, New York

Motte, A., Q. Hanqing , Y. Zhang and **Patrick Bussière** (2008), "The Youth in Transition Survey: Following Canadian Youth through Time", in *Who Goes? Who Stays? What Matters? Accessing and Persisting in post-Second are Education in Canada;* School of Policy Studies, Queen's University, Mc-Gill, Queen's University Press, Montréal and Kingston, pp 63-75.

OECD (2001), *Knowledge and Skills for Life: First Results from PISA 2000,* PISA, OECD Publishing.

OECD (2009), "PIAAC Literacy: A conceptual framework", *OECD Education Working Paper* No. 34, OECD Publishing.

REFERENCES

OECD (2010a), *Pathways to Success: How Knowledge and Skills at Age 15 Shape Future Lives in Canada*, PISA, OECD Publishing.

OECD (2010b), *PISA 2009 Results: What Students Know and Can Do: Student Performance in Reading, Mathematics and Science* (Volume I), PISA, OECD Publishing.

OECD (2010c), *PISA 2009 Results: Overcoming Social Background: Equity in Learning Opportunities and Outcomes* (Volume II), PISA, OECD Publishing.

OECD (2011a), *Education at a Glance 2011: OECD Indicators,* OECD Publishing.

OECD (2011b), *Quality Time for Students: Learning In and Out of School*, OECD Publishing.

Paus, T. (2005), "Mapping Brain Maturation and Cognitive Development during Adolescence", *Trends in Cognitive Science,* 9(2), pp. 60-68.

Pearlin, L. and S. Schooler (1978), "The structure of coping", *Journal of Health and Social Behaviour*, No.19, pp. 2-21.

Statistics Canada (2005), "Youth in Transition Survey 2000, YITS reading cohort, Cycle 1, Users' guide", revised September 2005, Statistics Canada, Ottawa.

Willms, D.J. (2004), *Variation in Literacy Skills Among Canadian Provinces: Findings from the OECD PISA*, Statistics Canada, Ottawa.

Wylie, C. and E. Hodgen (2011), *Forming Adulthood – Past, present and future in the experiences and views of the Competent Learners @ 20*, New Zealand Council for Educational Research (web copy: *http://www.educationcounts.govt.nz/__data/assets/pdf_file/0017/101816/981_Forming-Adulthood.pdf*).

Wylie, C., and E. Hodgen (2007), *Competent Learners @ 16: competency levels and development over time*, New Zealand Council for Educational Research (web copy: *http://www.educationcounts.govt.nz/__data/assets/pdf_file/0009/9945/cc-overtime-16.pdf*).

Yamamoto, K. (2002), *Estimating PISA Students on the IALS Prose Literacy Scale*, Educational Testing Service, Princeton, New Jersey.

Annex A
TECHNICAL ANNEX

ANNEX A: TECHNICAL ANNEX

SAMPLE DESIGN AND WEIGHTING PROCEDURES FOR THE PISA RE-ASSESSMENT

The PISA-24 sample is a representative sample of Canadian youth who were 15 years old in 2000. To ensure that the sample remains representative, the original PISA-15 sample weights applied to the data have to be modified to take into account attrition within YITS and the fact that only a sub-sample of YITS participants took part in the PISA-24 test.

The starting point for the creation of weights for PISA-24 is the final weight from YITS Cycle 5. To derive a final weight for the PISA-24, the following adjustments are applied to initial weights of the individual records on the PISA-24:

- Adjustment for sub-sampling of the Cycle 5 YITS sample

To select the PISA-24 sample, the YITS cycle 5 responding sample was stratified into 12 strata and a random sample was selected within each stratum. To adjust the initial weights to account for this sampling, the initial weight of each sampled unit in stratum h is multiplied by a factor equal to the number of Cycle 5 units in stratum h (N_h) divided by the number of units selected for the Reading Skills Re-assessment sample in stratum h (n_h).

- Adjustment for non-response

To adjust the weights for non-response to the PISA-24, a logistic regression is used to estimate the expected probability of response for each sample unit. Modelling is done within region as data allows (Atlantic, Québec, Ontario, Prairies, and British Columbia). To form response groups within which weight adjustments are to be made, the sample file is sorted by the estimated probability of response within each region. It is then divided into deciles, giving ten response adjustment groups for each region. Within each response adjustment group, the non-response adjustment factor is computed as the ratio of the sum of the weights for all units selected in the PISA-24 sample to the sum of the weights for all responding sample units.

- Adjustment for calibration to Cycle 5 gender totals

To bring estimates for the PISA-24 in line with YITS Cycle 5 estimates, a final calibration adjustment is made. Non-response weights are adjusted such that the survey weights sum to the same totals, by gender, as the Cycle 5 weights for all units in the Cycle 5 sample.

The final PISA-24 weight is the product of the initial weight multiplied by (1) the adjustment for sub-sampling of the YITS Cycle 5 sample, (2) the non-response adjustment, and (3) the calibration adjustment.

Although the participants in the PISA-24 tended to come from more advantageous socio-economic contexts than the original PISA-15 sample, population weights were calculated by Statistics Canada to adjust the representation of the current sample to the population represented by the PISA/YITS 2000 sample. The current study uses data from all cycles of YITS, including the original PISA-15 data.

DESCRIPTION OF INDICES EXAMINED IN THIS REPORT

Sense of mastery

The concept of mastery – the belief that one has control over one's destiny – was measured using the student questionnaire in YITS that was distributed with PISA-15 (Statistics Canada, 2005). The inspiration for this scale is the concept of external versus internal locus of control. A respondent's sense of mastery is defined as "the extent to which one regards one's life chances as being under one's own control in contrast to being fatalistically ruled" (Pearlin and Schooler, 1978). Individuals were asked about the extent to which they agreed with the following statements: "I often feel helpless in dealing with the problems of life"; "I have little control over the things that happen to me"; "There is little I can do to change many of the important things in life"; "There is really no way I can solve some of the problems I have"; "Sometimes I feel I'm being pushed around in life"; "I can do just about anything I really set my mind to"; and "What happens to me in the future mostly depends on me". The sense-of-mastery scale was then developed by combining their answers.

Teacher-student relations

Students' reports on their level of agreement with the following statements: Students get along well with most teachers; Most teachers are interested in students' well-being; Most of their teachers really listen to what they have to say; If they need extra help, they will receive it from their teachers; and Most of their teachers treat them fairly. Based on PISA-15 question ST30Q1-5 in the student questionnaire.

School achievement pressure

Students' reports on the frequency with which: the teacher wants students to work hard; the teacher tells students that they can do better; the teacher does not like it when students deliver careless work; and the teachers says that students have to learn a lot. Based on PISA-15 questions ST26Q2-4 and ST26Q15 in the student questionnaire.

Family educational support
Students' reports on the frequency that their parents and siblings work with them on their schoolwork. Based on PISA-15 question ST20Q01-3 in the student questionnaire.

Parental cultural communication
Students' reports on the frequency with which their parents/guardians discussed political or social issues with them; discussed books, films or television programmes; and listened to classical music. Based on PISA-15 question ST19Qo1-03 in the student questionnaire.

Total number of schooling hours per year
Instructional time for 15-year-old students in the school and derived hours of school per year. Based on PISA-15 question SC06Q01-3 in the school questionnaire.

Teacher morale
The extent to which school principals agreed with the following statements: The morale of the teachers in this school is high; Teachers work with enthusiasm; Teachers take pride in this school; and Teachers value academic achievement. Based on PISA-15 question SC20Q01-4 in the school questionnaire.

Shortage of teachers
The principals' views on how much learning by 15-year-old students was hindered by a shortage or inadequacy of teachers, in general, and in the specific courses of language, mathematics, and science. Based on PISA-15 question SC21Q01-4 in the school questionnaire.

School autonomy
School principals' reports on who had the main responsibility for school administration, staffing, compensation, financing, admission, teaching material and curriculum. A PISA index of school autonomy is derived from the number of categories that principals classified as not being a school responsibility. Based on PISA-15 question Based on PISA-15 questions SC22Q01-12 in the school questionnaire.

Teacher participation in decision making
An index of teacher autonomy was derived from the number of categories that principals classified as being mainly the responsibility of teachers. Based on PISA-15 questions SC22Q01-12 in the school questionnaire.

Student behaviour
Principals' reports on the extent to which learning by 15-year-olds in their school was hindered by: student absenteeism; disruption of classes by students; students skipping classes; students lacking respect for teachers; the use of alcohol or illegal drugs; and students intimidating or bullying other students. Based on PISA-15 questions SC19Q02,06,09,10,13,15 in the school questionnaire.

Teacher behaviour
Principals' reports on the extent to which learning by 15-year-olds was hindered by: low expectation of teachers; poor student-teacher relations; teachers not meeting individual students' needs; teacher absenteeism; staff resisting change; teachers being too strict with students; and students not being encouraged to achieve their full potential. Based on PISA-15 questions SC19Q01,03,07,08,11,14,16 in the school questionnaire.

Material resources
School principals' reports on the extent to which learning by 15-year-olds in their school was hindered by: lack of instructional material; not enough computers for instruction; lack of instructional materials in the library; lack of multi-media resources for instruction; inadequate science laboratory equipment; and inadequate facilities for the fine arts. Based on PISA-15 questions SCQ04-09 in the school questionnaire.

School size
School principals' report of the number of girls/boys enrolled in the school, the total enrolment, and the percentage of girls. Based on PISA-15 questions SC02Q01-02 in the school questionnaire.

Number of teachers
School principals' report of the number of full- and part-time teachers. Based on PISA-15 questions SC14Q01 in the school questionnaire.

Proportion of language teachers
Proportion of full- and part-time language teachers. Based on PISA-15 questions SC14Q07-08 in the school questionnaire.

MEASUREMENT ERROR AND REGRESSION TO THE MEAN

The results of PISA-24 suggest that larger gains in development of reading proficiency are made by individuals with the lower initial proficiency. The importance of this finding should not be overlooked, as it suggests that the disadvantages faced by many youth can be overcome with time. However, the problem of regression towards the mean clouds the analyst's ability to properly observe this relationship. This section looks more closely at the topic of skills convergence and the methodological issues with estimating skills growth using PISA-24. It then provides an option for dealing with regression towards the mean, which is used throughout the report.

The primary limitation to drawing inferences about changes in individuals is the imprecision with which proficiency is measured at the individual level. Although substantial documentation is available to describe in a precise manner what is meant by the construct of "reading proficiency" in the PISA assessment (OECD, 2001), because the construct must be measured by sampling behaviour that is merely indicative of its presence, there will always be imprecision in how it is assessed. Accordingly, an individual's score on the PISA-15 assessment and the PISA-24 assessment in 2009 should be though of as an imprecise signal of actual reading proficiency at ages 15 and 24 and of skills growth during this time.

In general, comparability of measurements over time or across individuals can be achieved by increasing the number of observations (i.e. test items) and the similarity in how the observations are collected between the individuals being compared. Several factors with the different test administrations in this study determine the imprecision of the resulting scores: the rotated booklet design in PISA-15 increases the differences between individuals, and the relatively small number of test items in PISA-24 increases the relative impact of random mistakes to influence proficiency estimates. Both of these factors increase the measurement error.

Since the measurements at both time periods are imprecise, the difference between those estimates (i.e. skills growth) is even more imprecise. For example, random measurement error may have resulted in an overestimate for a student at age 15 and an underestimate at age 24, artificially deflating the perceived change in proficiency or skills growth. The reverse, an underestimation at age 15 and an overestimation at age 24, is also possible. This results in a range of possible score differences that is greater than the range of either of the individual scores.

The average measurement variance gives some indication of the relative accuracy of each of the three outcomes used in this study: reading proficiency at age 15, proficiency at age 24, and the change in proficiency between the two periods. One way to consider the measurement error is to show it as a proportion of the total variation in proficiency between individuals, a statistic known as the reliability. Estimates for the amount of change that has occurred, since it has the largest measurement error and the smallest total variation, has the smallest reliability among the three proficiency estimates. The numerical reliabilities for each outcome are displayed in each bar in Figure A.1. The value of 0.67 for change indicates that one third of the individual variations in estimated change in proficiency are due to chance.

■ Figure A.1 ■
Measurement variance, total variance, and scale reliability for reading outcomes based on PISA-15

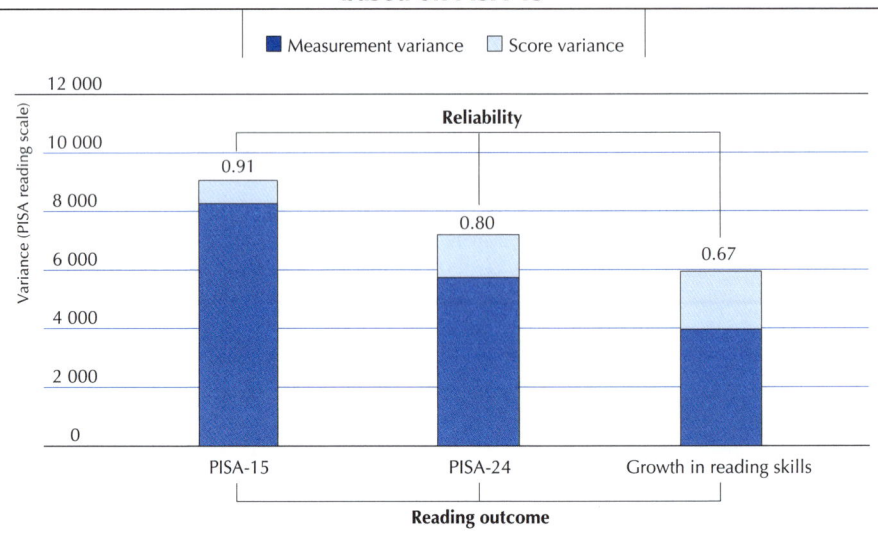

Source: Cartwright (2012).

Box A.1 provides details on the analytic implications of measurement error.

Box A.1 **The consequences of higher measurement error**

The practical consequence of the lower level of reliability is that observed relationships appear weaker than they truly are. The three charts in Figure A.2 illustrate simulated data corresponding to variables that are theoretically perfectly correlated, but where one variable is measured with error. Each chart corresponds to one of the reading outcomes described in this study. From left to right, as reliability decreases, the observable relationship between the two variables decreases, from a clear linear pattern when r=0.91 to a vague cloud of data points when r=0.67. Since lower reliability decreases the maximum observable correlation between two variables, any relationship observed in the presence of measurement error can be considered a 'lower bound' on the true magnitude of the relationship. The consequences for the current study are that many relationships are found by estimating relationships between other variables and these three reading outcomes. The numerical quantification of these relationships is mathematically certain to be underestimated, so traditional metrics of gauging substantive importance may not apply.[1]

■ Figure A.2 ■
Illustration of attenuation of correlation due to measurement error using simulated data based on perfectly correlated variables and reliabilities of reading outcomes

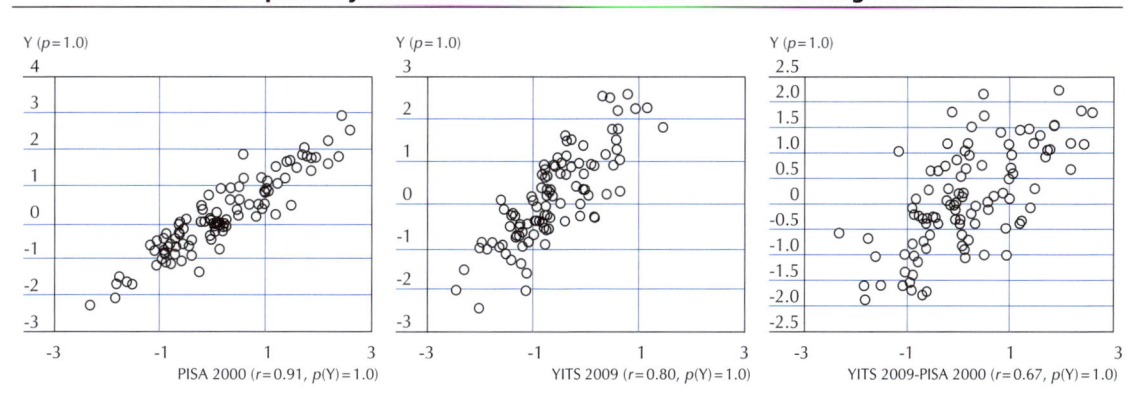

PISA 2000 (r=0.91, p(Y)=1.0)   YITS 2009 (r=0.80, p(Y)=1.0)   YITS 2009-PISA 2000 (r=0.67, p(Y)=1.0)

Source: Cartwright (2012).
StatLink http://dx.doi.org/10.1787/888932576871

---

1. Although there are known corrections for the attenuating effect of measurement error, they are only relevant when all measurement error is known and when the statistic is a product-moment correlation; for the analyses in this study, either the adjustments would be constant to all comparable analyses, no adjustment is possible, or the analyses would be missing reliability estimates for other variables. For simplicity, all estimates have been left unadjusted.

WHAT ARE THE CONSEQUENCES OF MEASUREMENT ERROR FOR A REPEAT ASSESSMENT?

Because measurement error is random, if an individual's proficiency is overestimated the first time it is measured, it will most likely be underestimated the second time. This implies that an individual who is far below or far above the average at the first point in time will tend to be closer to the average at the second point in time, a phenomenon known as "regression towards the mean". If there is a systematic change to the distribution between the two points in time, such as a global increase in scores, regression will be towards the new mean. The consequence of regression towards the mean is that measurement error in our estimate of proficiency growth is negatively correlated to PISA scores at age 15.

Because regression to the mean is a random phenomenon, it is not possible to determine how much any individual's estimated change in proficiency is a product of random variation versus true change. However, some expectations can be made at a group level. Using the initial results from the PISA-15 Canadian sample, regression to the mean for each proficiency level group is illustrated in Figure A.3 under two alternate assumptions: 1) no systematic change happens to the distribution; and 2) the distribution changes uniformly to match the mean and standard deviation of the PISA-24 sample. Under both assumptions, the group averages converge at the second test. Note that under the assumption of systematic uniform improvement, because all three groups are converging on a higher average, the improvement of the lowest group is artificially inflated, and the improvement of the highest group is deflated (in the absence of measurement error, all three groups would have the same growth trajectory). The reliability used to generate these random data is 0.67, the same as that for change in reading proficiency in this study.

Figure A.3
Expected regression to the mean for PISA proficiency levels for Canadian PISA-15 participants based on retest reliability of 0.67

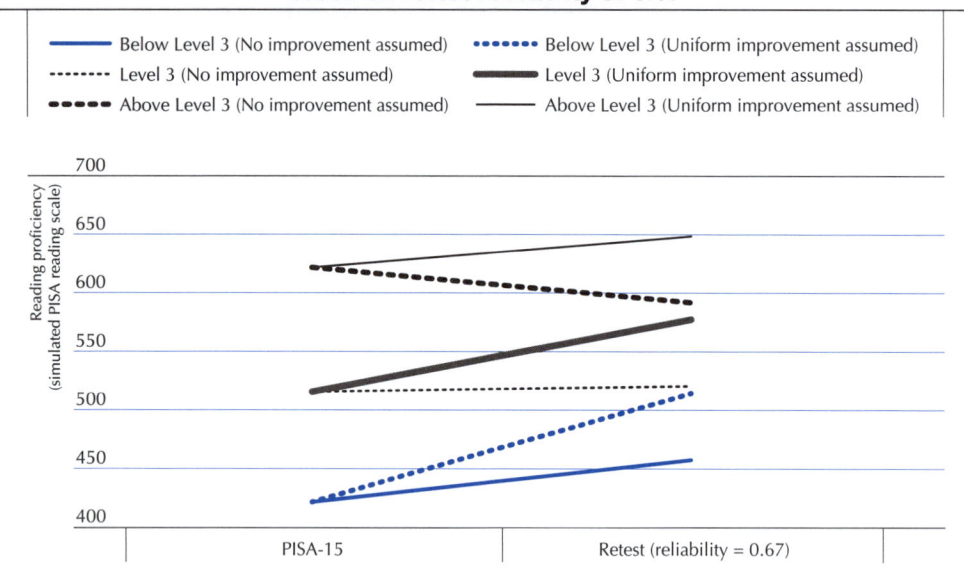

Source: Cartwright (2012).
StatLink http://dx.doi.org/10.1787/888932576871

The observed changes between PISA and PISA-24 are compared with the random simulated data from this example in Figure A.4. The simulated data are based on the specification that there is no relationship between initial status and the degree of change. Any observed relationships between initial status and degree of change are purely artefacts of regression to the mean. However, the magnitude of the group differences in the random scenario is almost identical to that in the observed data. When uniform improvement is assumed and the PISA-24 mean and standard deviation is applied, the average simulated change for each group appears to be of approximately the same magnitude as the average change observed in the actual data. Unequivocally, skills growth is occurring, but the data do not support the inference that skills acquisition is substantially greater or lesser for young people with higher or lower initial reading skill as measured by PISA-15.

Figure A.4
Expected regression to the mean for PISA proficiency levels under uniform change assumptions compared to observed differences for Canadian PISA-15 participants

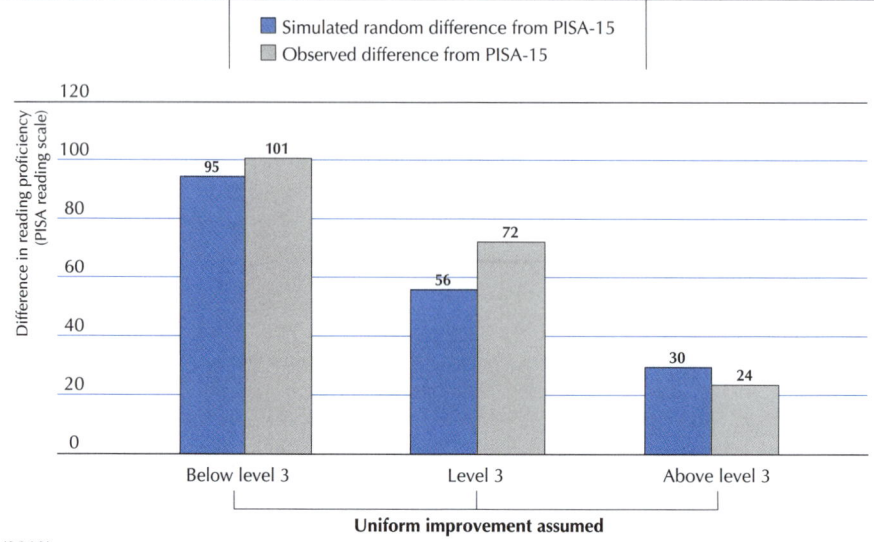

	Below level 3	Level 3	Above level 3
Simulated random difference from PISA-15	95	56	30
Observed difference from PISA-15	101	72	24

Uniform improvement assumed

Source: Cartwright (2012).
StatLink http://dx.doi.org/10.1787/888932576871

REGRESSION TO THE MEAN AND SKILLS CONVERGENCE

When interpreting these results, one should recall that randomness does not necessarily mean "noise" – rather it represents complexity that is not described in a statistical model. The pattern of regression in the results occurs because there is real and meaningful variation in the items used in assessing reading. There are different forms of reading, and since growth in reading skills is not the same on each of these forms, the measure of growth reflects this heterogeneity. However, without a greater number of items specific to each of these sub-components of reading, it is not possible to use more detailed sub-divisions of skills and still remain comparable to PISA-15.

So, what possibilities are left? Other than to provide caveats for interpretation and analysis of the PISA-24 results, how does awareness of this phenomenon inform the current analysis? The level of skills at age 15 remains one of the most important precursors to educational and career opportunities. One of the fundamental principles of PISA-15 is that the knowledge and skills at age 15 are key determinants of other choices made during a lifetime. Thus, it is critical that any analysis of downstream outcomes, particularly in early adulthood, considers the role of skills at age 15.

To resolve the conflict between the needs of analysis and the restrictions of the data, it is important to note that the phenomenon of regression to the mean is a random event. As a random event, it should decrease as the effect of measurement error decreases. The results of a single observation typically have more measurement error than the average results of several observations. In the educational context, school grades represent the aggregation of tens or hundreds of formal and informal observations of student proficiency. In the PISA data, several other measures of initial reading proficiency are available, describing the performance of students in their language class at school. While lacking the specificity and international comparability of the PISA test results, these reported grades provide triangulation for the effects of initial status on skills growth.

The relationships of the qualitative reports of grades in school language class to growth in reading skills are shown in Figure 5.2 and Figure 5.3. The percentage of students in each category is given in Table 5.1 in Annex B. Qualitative descriptions of marks relative to a passing standard, as well as grouped percentage scores, show consistent relationships with similar interpretations as the PISA proficiency-level grouping. In all cases, lower initial status is associated with greater improvements in reading proficiency.

For subsequent analyses requiring controls for skills at age 15, this study used school marks (low, medium and high, by percentages). Although this classification may not be as internationally comparable as PISA proficiency groupings are, it has the dual benefits of higher stability at the individual level and errors that are completely independent from measurement errors in the PISA scores. As shown in Figure 5.3, it has the weakest association with changes in reading skills, suggesting the smallest influence of regression to the mean. The similarity between group sizes also facilitates meaningful group comparisons.

SUMMARY AND CONCLUSIONS

The problem of measurement error, common to all assessments, is compounded in the case of a re-assessment – because estimates of proficiency growth include the error from both assessments, and because the phenomenon of regression to the mean overestimates growth for low-proficiency students and underestimates growth for high-proficiency students. There are two implications of regression to the mean for the questions posed in this report. The first is that it challenges whether or not the skills convergence observed among young people between the ages of 15 and 24 is a real occurrence. However, using students' language grades as a measure of initial reading proficiency shows that skills convergence is in fact happening; students with less proficiency have increased their skills level faster than students who are more highly proficient, no matter which measure of initial proficiency is used.

Second, initial proficiency is strongly correlated to both proficiency growth and to many of the behaviours and choices whose impact on skills growth analysed. For instance, one would like to know if certain behaviours that were associated with high PISA scores at age 15 are also associated with improvements in proficiency. However, without controlling for initial status it will not be clear if the behaviour in question is the cause of the observed improvement in proficiency or if initial proficiency is responsible. Therefore, in determining where students' initial skills level is important, analysis will be conducted for three groups of students defined by their reading proficiency, as measured by school grades in language classes.

DATA AVAILABILITY

For approved research proposals, access to the data file is possible through one of Statistics Canada's Research Data Centre. For more information on this process please contact *educationstats@statcan.gc.ca*.

For more information on the YITS cycle 5.5: Reading Skills Reassessment, please consult: *http://www.statcan.gc.ca/cgi-bin/imdb/p2SV.pl?Function=getSurvey&SurvId=4435&SurvVer=2&InstaId=17010&InstaVer=6&SDDS=4435&lang=en&db=imdb&adm=8&dis=2*.

Annex B
TABLES OF RESULTS

ANNEX B: TABLES OF RESULTS

Table 2.1 Item classification in the PISA reading framework, PISA-24 assessment questions and PISA-15 link items

Unit name	Unit item code	Item format (Question format)	Context (Situation)	Text type	Text format	Reading process (Aspect)	PISA reading level (Difficulty)
Drugged Spiders	R055Q01	Multiple Choice	Public	Expository	Continuous	Interpreting	2
	R055Q02	Open Constructed Response	Public	Expository	Continuous	Reflecting and evaluating	3
	R055Q03	Open Constructed Response	Public	Expository	Continuous	Interpreting	3
	R055Q05	Open Constructed Response	Public	Expository	Continuous	Interpreting	2
Aesop	R067Q01	Multiple Choice	Personal	Narrative	Continuous	Interpreting	1
	R067Q04	Open Constructed Response	Personal	Narrative	Continuous	Reflecting and evaluating	2 (code 1): 4 (code 2)
	R067Q05	Open Constructed Response	Personal	Narrative	Continuous	Reflecting and evaluating	2 (code 1): 3 (code 2)
Shirts	R102Q04A	Open Constructed Response	Personal	Expository	Continuous	Interpreting	4
	R102Q05	Closed Constructed Response	Personal	Table	Non-continuous	Interpreting	4
	R102Q07	Multiple Choice	Personal	Expository	Continuous	Interpreting	1
Telephone	R104Q01	Closed Constructed Response	Public	Table	Non-continuous	Retrieving information	1
	R104Q02	Closed Constructed Response	Public	Table	Non-continuous	Retrieving information	4
	R104Q05	Short Response	Public	Table	Non-continuous	Retrieving information	4 (code 1): 6 (code 2)
Exchange	R111Q01	Multiple Choice	Educational	Expository	Continuous	Interpreting	2
	R111Q02B	Open Constructed Response	Educational	Expository	Continuous	Reflecting and evaluating	3 (code 1): 5 (code 2)
	R111Q06B	Open Constructed Response	Educational	Expository	Continuous	Reflecting and evaluating	3 (code 1): 4 (code 2)
Employment	R219Q01T	Closed Constructed Response	Occupational	Form	Non-continuous	Retrieving information	3
	R219Q01E	Short Response	Occupational	Form	Non-continuous	Interpreting	2
	R219Q02	Open Constructed Response	Occupational	Form	Non-continuous	Reflecting and evaluating	1
South Pole	R220Q01	Short Response	Educational	Map	Non-continuous	Reflecting and evaluating	4
	R220Q02B	Multiple Choice	Educational	Chart/Graph	Non-continuous	Interpreting	3
	R220Q04	Multiple Choice	Educational	Expository	Continuous	Interpreting	3
	R220Q05	Multiple Choice	Educational	Expository	Continuous	Interpreting	1
	R220Q06	Multiple Choice	Educational	Expository	Continuous	Interpreting	2
Optician	R227Q01	Multiple Choice	Occupational	Descriptive	Continuous	Retrieving information	3
	R227Q02	Complex Multiple Choice	Occupational	Descriptive	Continuous	Retrieving information	2 (code 1): 4 (code 2)
	R227Q03	Open Constructed Response	Occupational	Descriptive	Continuous	Reflecting and evaluating	3
	R227Q06	Short Response	Occupational	Chart/Graph	Non-continuous	Retrieving information	2

Note: Code 1 refers to partial credit, while code 2 refers to full credit.
Source: YITS cycle 5.5: Reading Skills Reassessment.

Table 3.1 Distribution of reading skills, PISA-15 and PISA-24, Canadian participants age 15 in 2000

PISA reading scale	Reading skills in 2000, PISA-15 %	Cumulative	Reading skills in 2009, PISA-24 %	Cumulative
<225	0.0	0.0	0.0	0.0
225-249	0.0	0.0	0.1	0.1
250-274	0.1	0.1	0.1	0.2
275-299	0.5	0.7	0.1	0.3
300-324	1.1	1.7	0.2	0.4
325-349	1.1	2.9	0.2	0.7
350-374	1.5	4.4	0.5	1.2
375-399	2.7	7.1	0.8	2.0
400-424	3.7	10.8	1.2	3.2
425-449	4.6	15.5	1.5	4.7
450-474	6.0	21.4	2.1	6.8
475-499	7.3	28.7	3.5	10.3
500-524	8.7	37.4	5.0	15.2
525-549	9.3	46.7	6.2	21.5
550-574	9.1	55.8	8.6	30.0
575-599	9.5	65.3	11.7	41.8
600-624	9.9	75.2	13.4	55.2
625-649	8.6	83.8	12.3	67.5
650-674	6.3	90.1	10.2	77.7
675-699	4.5	94.6	8.4	86.1
700-724	2.9	97.5	6.1	92.2
725-749	1.4	98.9	3.6	95.9
750-774	0.6	99.5	1.9	97.8
775-799	0.3	99.8	1.1	98.9
800-824	0.1	99.9	0.6	99.5
825-849	0.0	100.0	0.2	99.7
>850	0.0	100.0	0.1	99.8

Notes: Estimates of percentage at each age group are smoothed averages. Differences in the highest cumulative totals from 100.0 are due to rounding error.
Source: YITS cycle 5.5: Reading Skills Reassessment.
StatLink http://dx.doi.org/10.1787/888932577308

Table 3.2 Comparison of reading performance at age 15 and age 24 by various demographic groups, Canadian participants age 15 in 2000

	Reading skills in 2000, PISA-15		Reading skills in 2009, PISA-24	
	Mean score	Standard error	Mean score	Standard error
All participants	541	(5.2)	598	(4.3)
Language				
Minority language speakers	528	(15.8)	597	(12.4)
Majority language speakers	545	(5.8)	600	(4.9)
Francophones	530	(7.9)	588	(6.6)
Anglophones	546	(6.6)	602	(5.5)
Gender				
Male	526	(8.2)	590	(6.7)
Female	558	(7.1)	608	(6.2)
Family background				
Low socio-economic background, age 15	506	(11.8)	568	(9.3)
High socio-economic background, age 15	572	(8.2)	618	(7.5)
In rural school, at age 15	523	(10.5)	590	(7.4)
In urban school, at age 15	546	(6.0)	600	(5.1)
Not born in Canada	524	(13.4)	601	(15.8)
Born in Canada	545	(5.8)	599	(4.7)

Source: YITS cycle 5.5: Reading Skills Reassessment.
StatLink http://dx.doi.org/10.1787/888932577308

Table 3.3 Distribution of reading skills by gender, PISA-15 and PISA-24, Canadian participants age 15 in 2000

	Reading skills in 2000, PISA-15				Reading skills in 2009, PISA-24			
	Boys		Girls		Men		Women	
PISA reading scale	%	Cumulative	%	Cumulative	%	Cumulative	%	Cumulative
<200	0.0	0.0	0.0	0.0	0.0	0.0	0.0	0.0
200-224	0.0	0.0	0.0	0.0	0.0	0.0	0.0	0.0
225-249	0.0	0.0	0.0	0.0	0.0	0.1	0.1	0.1
250-274	0.2	0.2	0.0	0.1	0.0	0.1	0.1	0.2
275-299	1.0	1.2	0.1	0.1	0.1	0.2	0.1	0.4
300-324	1.9	3.1	0.2	0.3	0.1	0.3	0.1	0.5
325-349	1.9	4.9	0.4	0.7	0.3	0.6	0.2	0.7
350-374	1.8	6.8	1.2	1.9	0.7	1.3	0.3	0.9
375-399	2.7	9.5	2.8	4.7	1.2	2.5	0.4	1.3
400-424	3.6	13.1	3.8	8.4	1.7	4.3	0.6	1.9
425-449	5.0	18.1	4.3	12.8	2.2	6.5	0.8	2.6
450-474	6.5	24.6	5.4	18.1	2.7	9.2	1.4	4.1
475-499	8.1	32.8	6.4	24.5	4.2	13.4	2.8	6.9
500-524	9.9	42.6	7.4	31.9	5.7	19.1	4.3	11.2
525-549	9.9	52.5	8.7	40.6	6.3	25.4	6.1	17.3
550-574	9.1	61.6	9.2	49.8	8.0	33.4	9.1	26.4
575-599	9.4	71.0	9.6	59.5	10.8	44.2	12.7	39.2
600-624	9.4	80.4	10.3	69.8	12.7	56.9	14.1	53.3
625-649	7.6	88.1	9.6	79.4	12.6	69.5	12.1	65.4
650-674	5.2	93.2	7.4	86.8	10.7	80.2	9.7	75.1
675-699	3.2	96.4	5.9	92.7	8.2	88.3	8.6	83.7
700-724	1.7	98.1	4.1	96.8	5.6	93.9	6.7	90.3
725-749	0.9	99.0	1.9	98.7	3.0	97.0	4.2	94.5
750-774	0.5	99.4	0.7	99.4	1.4	98.4	2.5	97.0
775-799	0.2	99.6	0.4	99.8	0.8	99.2	1.4	98.4
800-824	0.1	99.7	0.2	100.0	0.5	99.6	0.7	99.1
825-849	0.0	99.7	0.0	100.0	0.2	99.8	0.3	99.4
>850	0.0	99.7	0.0	100.0	0.0	99.8	0.0	99.4

Note: Estimates of percentage at each age group are smoothed averages. Differences in the highest cumulative totals from 100.0 are due to a rounding error.
Source: YITS cycle 5.5: Reading Skills Reassessment.
StatLink http://dx.doi.org/10.1787/888932577308

ANNEX B: TABLES OF RESULTS

Table 3.4 Distribution of reading skills by assessment language, PISA-15 and PISA-24, Canadian participants age 15 in 2000

PISA reading scale	Reading skills in 2000, PISA-15				Reading skills in 2009, PISA-24			
	English		French		English		French	
	%	Cumulative	%	Cumulative	%	Cumulative	%	Cumulative
<200	0.0	0.0	0.0	0.0	0.0	0.0	0.1	0.1
200-224	0.0	0.0	0.0	0.0	0.0	0.0	0.1	0.1
225-249	0.0	0.0	0.0	0.0	0.0	0.1	0.1	0.2
250-274	0.1	0.1	0.1	0.1	0.1	0.2	0.1	0.3
275-299	0.6	0.8	0.2	0.3	0.1	0.3	0.2	0.4
300-324	1.2	2.0	0.6	0.9	0.1	0.4	0.2	0.6
325-349	1.1	3.0	1.1	1.9	0.2	0.6	0.2	0.7
350-374	1.3	4.3	2.0	4.0	0.4	1.0	0.5	1.2
375-399	2.3	6.5	4.1	8.1	0.7	1.7	0.9	2.1
400-424	3.1	9.6	6.0	14.1	1.1	2.9	1.0	3.1
425-449	4.3	13.9	6.0	20.1	1.5	4.4	1.4	4.5
450-474	5.9	19.8	5.8	25.9	2.0	6.4	2.4	6.9
475-499	7.2	27.0	7.0	32.9	3.2	9.5	4.5	11.4
500-524	8.5	35.5	9.0	41.9	4.5	14.0	6.6	18.0
525-549	9.1	44.6	10.2	52.1	5.7	19.8	8.0	26.0
550-574	9.1	53.7	9.6	61.7	8.0	27.7	10.5	36.5
575-599	9.5	63.2	9.4	71.1	11.1	38.8	13.8	50.3
600-624	10.0	73.2	9.6	80.7	13.2	52.0	14.4	64.7
625-649	8.9	82.1	8.1	88.8	12.5	64.5	11.9	76.6
650-674	6.7	88.8	5.1	93.9	10.6	75.1	9.0	85.6
675-699	5.1	93.9	2.7	96.6	9.1	84.2	6.3	91.9
700-724	3.2	97.2	1.8	98.5	6.8	91.0	3.9	95.9
725-749	1.5	98.7	1.1	99.6	4.1	95.1	2.0	97.9
750-774	0.7	99.3	0.4	100.0	2.2	97.3	1.0	98.9
775-799	0.3	99.7	0.2	100.2	1.3	98.6	0.7	99.6
800-824	0.2	99.8	0.1	100.3	0.7	99.3	0.4	100.0
825-849	0.0	99.9	0.0	100.3	0.3	99.6	0.1	100.2
>850	0.0	99.9	0.0	100.3	0.1	99.7	0.0	100.2

Note: Estimates of percentage at each age group are smoothed averages. Differences in the highest cumulative totals from 100.0 are due to rounding error.
Source: YITS cycle 5.5: Reading Skills Reassessment.
StatLink http://dx.doi.org/10.1787/888932577308

Table 3.5 Comparison of reading performance at age 15 and age 24 by educational attainment, pathways and work experience at age 24, Canadian participants age 15 in 2000

	Reading skills in 2000, PISA-15		Reading skills in 2009, PISA-24	
	Mean score	Standard error	Mean score	Standard error
All participants	541	(5.2)	598	(4.3)
Educational pathways				
Continuous studies until completion	539	(2.4)	597	(2.2)
Gap in studies prior to completion	559	(3.7)	605	(3.1)
Educational attainment				
High school or lower	499	(11.5)	564	(8.2)
Post-secondary, non-university completion	533	(7.4)	584	(5.9)
University completion	596	(6.8)	652	(5.8)
Work experience				
Three or more years of work experience	529	(5.9)	585	(6.3)
Less than 3 years of work experience	549	(8.2)	606	(6.2)

Source: YITS cycle 5.5: Reading Skills Reassessment.
StatLink http://dx.doi.org/10.1787/888932577308

TABLES OF RESULTS: ANNEX B

Table 4.1 School grade and reading proficiency, Canadian participants age 15 in 2000

	Reading proficiency	
	Mean score	Standard error
PISA-15 (2000)		
3 years below modal grade	368	(19.7)
2 years below modal grade	427	(5.9)
1 year below modal grade	464	(2.9)
At modal grade	540	(1.4)
1 year above modal grade	576	(14.8)
Longitudinal Participants		
PISA-15 (2000)		
Below modal grade	472	(12.8)
At modal grade	543	(6.6)
Above modal grade	570	(33.6)
PISA-24 (2009)		
Below modal grade	549	(11.9)
At modal grade	599	(5.5)
Above modal grade	599	(31.0)

Note: The relative grade level is calculated by comparing the participant grade level to the modal grade level of participants living in the same province and born in the same month. Reading proficiency is adjusted to control for differences in proficiency related to the month of birth.
Source: YITS cycle 5.5: Reading Skills Reassessment.
StatLink http://dx.doi.org/10.1787/888932577308

Table 4.2 Item difficulty and average differences in item-correct scores between PISA-15 and PISA-24 by item type in the PISA reading framework, and individual characteristics at age 24, Canadian participants age 15 in 2000

Unit name	Unit item code	Estimated question difficulty in PISA-15[1]	Item-correct score difference[2] among all participants Mean	Standard error	Item-correct score difference[2] among self-perception of skill loss sample[3] No perceived skill loss Mean	Standard error	Perceived skill loss Mean	Standard error	Context (Situation)	Text type	Reading process (Aspect)
Drugged Spiders	R055Q01	-1.38	0.05	(0.03)	0.05	(0.03)	0.06	(0.05)	Public	Continuous	Interpreting
	R055Q02	0.50	0.07	(0.04)	0.07	(0.05)	0.02	(0.20)	Public	Continuous	Reflecting
	R055Q03	0.07	0.06	(0.04)	0.06	(0.04)	0.02	(0.05)	Public	Continuous	Interpreting
	R055Q05	-0.88	0.05	(0.03)	0.06	(0.03)	-0.19	(0.12)	Public	Continuous	Interpreting
Aesop	R067Q01	-1.73	**0.06**	(0.02)	**0.06**	(0.02)	0.16	(0.11)	Personal	Continuous	Interpreting
	R067Q04	0.52	**0.19**	(0.04)	**0.19**	(0.04)	**0.31**	(0.11)	Personal	Continuous	Reflecting
	R067Q05	0.18	**0.14**	(0.03)	**0.14**	(0.03)	0.05	(0.13)	Personal	Continuous	Reflecting
Shirts	R102Q04A	1.21	**0.22**	(0.06)	**0.23**	(0.05)	0.10	(0.48)	Personal	Continuous	Interpreting
	R102Q05	0.91	**0.22**	(0.06)	**0.20**	(0.06)	**0.60**	(0.24)	Personal	Non-continuous	Interpreting
	R102Q07	-1.57	0.02	(0.01)	0.03	(0.01)	0.00	(0.00)	Personal	Continuous	Interpreting
Telephone	R104Q01	-1.24	0.04	(0.02)	0.05	(0.02)	-0.04	(0.05)	Public	Non-continuous	Retrieving information
	R104Q02	1.11	**0.23**	(0.05)	**0.24**	(0.06)	0.11	(0.10)	Public	Non-continuous	Retrieving information
	R104Q05	1.88	**0.25**	(0.05)	**0.24**	(0.05)	0.34	(0.21)	Public	Non-continuous	Retrieving information
Exchange	R111Q01	-0.05	**0.14**	(0.03)	**0.13**	(0.03)	0.29	(0.21)	Educational	Continuous	Interpreting
	R111Q02B	1.37	**0.08**	(0.04)	**0.10**	(0.04)	-0.16	(0.13)	Educational	Continuous	Reflecting
	R111Q06B	0.81	**0.12**	(0.04)	**0.14**	(0.04)	-0.15	(0.27)	Educational	Continuous	Reflecting
Employment	R219Q01E	-0.55	**0.13**	(0.04)	**0.12**	(0.04)	0.25	(0.24)	Occupational	Non-continuous	Retrieving information
	R219Q01T	0.28	-0.02	(0.04)	-0.03	(0.04)	0.26	(0.15)	Occupational	Non-continuous	Interpreting
	R219Q02	-0.92	**0.09**	(0.03)	**0.09**	(0.03)	0.09	(0.19)	Occupational	Non-continuous	Reflecting
South Pole	R220Q01	0.79	-0.03	(0.05)	-0.04	(0.05)	0.07	(0.20)	Educational	Non-continuous	Retrieving information
	R220Q02B	-0.14	**0.14**	(0.05)	**0.14**	(0.05)	0.07	(0.07)	Educational	Non-continuous	Interpreting
	R220Q04	0.16	**0.18**	(0.05)	**0.19**	(0.05)	0.00	(0.03)	Educational	Continuous	Interpreting
	R220Q05	-1.60	-0.03	(0.03)	-0.03	(0.03)	0.03	(0.05)	Educational	Continuous	Interpreting
	R220Q06	-0.17	0.06	(0.04)	0.04	(0.04)	**0.52**	(0.27)	Educational	Continuous	Interpreting
Optician	R227Q01	0.20	0.09	(0.06)	0.11	(0.06)	-0.20	(0.35)	Occupational	Continuous	Interpreting
	R227Q02T	0.05	**0.18**	(0.03)	**0.19**	(0.03)	0.03	(0.03)	Occupational	Continuous	Retrieving information
	R227Q03	0.30	**0.13**	(0.04)	**0.14**	(0.04)	-0.09	(0.16)	Occupational	Continuous	Reflecting
	R227Q06	-0.92	-0.03	(0.04)	-0.04	(0.04)	0.06	(0.09)	Occupational	Non-continuous	Retrieving information

Note: Values in bold are statistically significant at the 95% confidence level.
1. Estimated question difficulty is defined for PISA-15, see Cartwright (2012).
2. Item score-correct difference is defined as the proportion of students who answered a question correctly. More precisely, since it is possible to earn partial credit on some items, the item-correct score is the total credit received for a particular question by all participants, divided by the total credit available to all participants. The scores are weighted by the student weights from PISA-24, but all questions are given an equal weight towards the overall average.
3. Self-perception of skill loss sample is based on the answer to a question in YITS about their perceived skill levels.
Source: YITS cycle 5.5: Reading Skills Reassessment.
StatLink http://dx.doi.org/10.1787/888932577308

ANNEX B: TABLES OF RESULTS

Table 5.1 Growth in reading skills by alternate measures of initial status, PISA-15 and PISA-24, Canadian participants age 15 in 2000

	Percentage of participants		Growth in reading skills	
	%	Standard error	Score difference	Standard error
Proficiency level PISA-15				
Below level 3 (less than 480.18 score points)	26.1	(2.4)	101	(8.4)
Level 3 (from 480.18 to less than 552.89 score points)	24.5	(1.9)	72	(7.0)
Above Level 3 (552.89 score points or above)	49.4	(2.2)	24	(5.2)
Qualitative grade in school language class				
Below the passing mark	9.3	(1.3)	82	(12.2)
At the passing mark	11.9	(1.7)	78	(15.4)
Above the passing mark	76.4	(2.2)	51	(4.0)
Percent grade in school language class				
Low: 0% to 69%	27.7	(2.1)	60	(8.8)
Medium: 70% to 79%	29.9	(2.2)	58	(7.9)
High: 80% to 100%	33.0	(2.2)	45	(6.6)

Note: Percent grades are based on student reports.
Source: YITS cycle 5.5: Reading Skills Reassessment.
StatLink http://dx.doi.org/10.1787/888932577308

Table 5.2 Relationship between correlations with PISA questionnaire indices and reading performance at ages 15 and 24, Canadian participants age 15 in 2000

	Low school marks in language: 0% to 69%				Medium school marks in language: 70% to 79%				High school marks in language: 80% to 100%			
	Phase 1: Reading skills in 2000, PISA-15		Phase 2: Growth in reading skills between 15 and 24 (PISA-24 minus PISA-15)		Phase 1: Reading skills in 2000, PISA-15		Phase 2: Growth in reading skills between 15 and 24 (PISA-24 minus PISA-15)		Phase 1: Reading skills in 2000, PISA-15		Phase 2: Growth in reading skills between 15 and 24 (PISA-24 minus PISA-15)	
	Correlation	Standard error	Correlation	Standard error	Correlation	Standard error	Correlation	Standard error	Correlation	Standard error	Correlation	Standard error
FAMILY CHARACTERISTICS AND INDIVIDUAL APPROACHES TO LEARNING												
Socio-economic status												
Highest parental education	0.12	(0.08)	-0.05	(0.08)	0.11	(0.06)	-0.02	(0.08)	**0.20**	(0.07)	-0.04	(0.07)
Highest parental occupational status	0.12	(0.12)	0.07	(0.12)	**0.22**	(0.11)	-0.10	(0.09)	**0.24**	(0.08)	-0.02	(0.07)
Family support of learning												
Family educational support	0.10	(0.10)	-0.05	(0.11)	-0.14	(0.09)	0.07	(0.08)	-0.09	(0.08)	0.04	(0.08)
Parental cultural communication	**0.16**	(0.08)	0.02	(0.08)	**0.29**	(0.11)	-0.11	(0.12)	**0.18**	(0.09)	-0.04	(0.10)
Individual approaches to learning												
Sense of mastery[1]	-0.03	(0.08)	0.06	(0.10)	-0.30	(0.20)	0.12	(0.16)	-0.03	(0.08)	0.04	(0.07)
Student perception of school environment												
Student-teacher relations	0.03	(0.08)	-0.04	(0.08)	0.14	(0.09)	-0.13	(0.10)	0.09	(0.08)	0.05	(0.08)
School achievement pressure	-0.16	(0.10)	0.11	(0.12)	-0.20	(0.15)	0.09	(0.12)	**-0.13**	(0.07)	0.11	(0.07)
SCHOOL LEARNING ENVIRONMENT												
School characteristics												
Average school socio-economic background	**0.29**	(0.06)	-0.10	(0.08)	**0.32**	(0.10)	-0.09	(0.11)	**0.26**	(0.08)	-0.03	(0.08)
School size	**0.23**	(0.09)	-0.13	(0.10)	0.10	(0.08)	-0.02	(0.11)	**0.17**	(0.08)	-0.13	(0.09)
School resources												
School education resources	-0.08	(0.08)	0.05	(0.10)	-0.02	(0.09)	0.03	(0.08)	-0.08	(0.08)	0.06	(0.07)
School material resources	-0.05	(0.09)	0.01	(0.10)	0.08	(0.10)	0.00	(0.10)	0.01	(0.08)	-0.02	(0.08)
Teacher characteristics and engagement												
Student-teacher ratio	0.02	(0.09)	0.07	(0.11)	**0.25**	(0.07)	**-0.19**	(0.08)	0.14	(0.07)	-0.05	(0.12)
Teacher shortage	**-0.19**	(0.08)	0.11	(0.11)	0.02	(0.10)	-0.02	(0.11)	-0.02	(0.08)	-0.02	(0.09)
Proportion of specialised reading teachers	**0.26**	(0.08)	**-0.18**	(0.08)	-0.05	(0.12)	0.10	(0.11)	**0.14**	(0.06)	-0.06	(0.07)
Teacher morale	0.07	(0.10)	0.08	(0.12)	-0.06	(0.09)	0.07	(0.10)	0.04	(0.06)	-0.04	(0.07)
Teacher participation in decision making	0.15	(0.11)	-0.13	(0.10)	-0.13	(0.08)	0.09	(0.10)	0.05	(0.08)	0.11	(0.08)
School use of resources												
Total instructional hours	0.04	(0.10)	-0.03	(0.10)	-0.06	(0.07)	0.01	(0.13)	0.05	(0.10)	0.12	(0.10)
School governance												
School autonomy	0.02	(0.10)	0.02	(0.10)	**0.23**	(0.07)	-0.10	(0.08)	0.05	(0.07)	0.08	(0.07)
School climate												
Supportive school environment	0.17	(0.09)	-0.10	(0.09)	0.14	(0.09)	-0.08	(0.08)	0.08	(0.06)	0.03	(0.07)
Student behaviours	-0.11	(0.08)	0.02	(0.09)	0.02	(0.09)	-0.11	(0.08)	-0.06	(0.07)	-0.02	(0.08)
Teacher behaviours	-0.07	(0.07)	0.01	(0.08)	0.06	(0.11)	-0.14	(0.09)	-0.03	(0.06)	0.02	(0.08)

Note: Values in bold are statistically significant at the 95% confidence level.
1. Sense of mastery is a variable collected only in Canada through the PISA-24 survey implemented along with PISA-15.
Source: YITS cycle 5.5: Reading Skills Reassessment.
StatLink http://dx.doi.org/10.1787/888932577308

TABLES OF RESULTS: ANNEX B

Table 5.3 Standardised multiple regression coefficients of factors associated with reading performance at ages 15 and 24, Canadian participants age 15 in 2000

Factors associated with reading performance	Phase 1: Reading skills in 2000, PISA-15				Phase 2: Growth in reading skills between 15 and 24 (PISA-24 minus PISA-15)			
	Regression coefficient	Standard error	Beta coefficient[1]	Standard error	Regression coefficient	Standard error	Beta coefficient[1]	Standard error
All participants								
Intercept	8.23	(115.54)			**274.85**	(90.07)		
School achievement pressure	**-16.56**	(4.47)	**-0.16**	(0.05)	**10.76**	(4.80)	**0.13**	(0.06)
Family educational support	**-12.36**	(5.27)	**-0.12**	(0.05)	5.36	(4.24)	0.06	(0.05)
Family socio-economic background	**1.73**	(0.31)	**0.29**	(0.04)	-0.32	(0.24)	-0.07	(0.05)
Supportive school environment	**0.84**	(0.21)	**0.18**	(0.04)	**-0.38**	(0.17)	**-0.10**	(0.04)
Sense of mastery	**-7.18**	(2.27)	**-0.20**	(0.07)	3.40	(1.70)	0.12	(0.06)
Low school language marks (0% to 69%)								
Intercept	87.68	(171.32)			**335.69**	(169.20)		
School achievement pressure	**-14.23**	(6.37)	**-0.17**	(0.08)	6.97	(9.28)	0.08	(0.11)
Family educational support	-0.59	(8.96)	-0.01	(0.09)	-3.52	(8.05)	-0.04	(0.08)
Family socio-economic background	0.60	(0.59)	0.12	(0.12)	0.32	(0.49)	0.06	(0.09)
Supportive school environment	**0.73**	(0.30)	**0.18**	(0.07)	-0.55	(0.31)	-0.13	(0.07)
Sense of mastery	-1.93	(3.65)	-0.04	(0.06)	3.37	(4.25)	0.06	(0.07)
Medium school language marks (70% to 79%)								
Intercept	149.68	(199.62)			**314.19**	(144.37)		
School achievement pressure	-7.68	(7.06)	-0.09	(0.08)	5.12	(6.78)	0.06	(0.08)
Family educational support	-11.74	(7.08)	-0.12	(0.07)	**13.10**	(5.71)	**0.16**	(0.07)
Family socio-economic background	**1.79**	(0.39)	**0.30**	(0.07)	**-0.90**	(0.41)	**-0.17**	(0.08)
Supportive school environment	0.58	(0.37)	0.13	(0.08)	-0.40	(0.26)	-0.10	(0.07)
Sense of mastery	-6.96	(6.83)	-0.21	(0.18)	2.79	(4.13)	0.10	(0.11)
High school language marks (80% to 100%)								
Intercept	334.74	(120.47)			32.28	(117.46)		
School achievement pressure	**-14.73**	(5.96)	**-0.16**	(0.06)	**14.18**	(5.63)	**0.17**	(0.06)
Family educational support	**-17.10**	(6.11)	**-0.20**	(0.08)	6.23	(4.98)	0.08	(0.06)
Family socio-economic background	**1.40**	(0.38)	**0.27**	(0.07)	-0.12	(0.24)	-0.03	(0.05)
Supportive school environment	0.33	(0.22)	0.08	(0.06)	0.03	(0.21)	0.01	(0.06)
Sense of mastery	-2.06	(5.06)	-0.04	(0.08)	4.52	(3.62)	0.08	(0.06)

Note: Values in bold are statistically significant at the 95% confidence level.
1. Beta coefficient refers to a regression where all factors have been standardised to have a zero mean and a standard deviation of one within the sample.
Source: YITS cycle 5.5: Reading Skills Reassessment.
StatLink http://dx.doi.org/10.1787/888932577308

Table 5.4 **Reading skills at ages 15 and 24 and skills growth, by individual factors at age 15, Canadian participants age 15 in 2000**

	Reading skills in 2000 (PISA-15)		Reading skills in 2009 (PISA-24)		Growth in reading skills between 15 and 24 (PISA-24 minus PISA-15)	
	Mean score	Standard error	Mean score	Standard error	Score difference	Standard error
Sense of mastery						
Bottom third	530	(7.7)	586	(6.9)	55	(7.65)
Top third	537	(12.7)	596	(9.1)	60	(7.43)
School achievement pressure						
Bottom third	557	(6.9)	607	(6.9)	51	(6.63)
Top third	527	(8.4)	593	(9.8)	66	(8.29)
Family educational support						
Bottom third	551	(8.7)	606	(8.4)	55	(9.04)
Top third	529	(11.9)	591	(8.3)	62	(6.99)
Supportive school environment						
Bottom third	517	(13.1)	580	(9.3)	63	(8.36)
Top third	559	(5.5)	612	(6.0)	54	(5.24)
Parental cultural communication						
Bottom third	515	(10.7)	575	(8.9)	60	(9.06)
Top third	572	(6.9)	621	(6.2)	49	(6.30)
Family socio-economic background						
Bottom third	506	(11.8)	568	(9.3)	62	(7.83)
Top third	572	(8.2)	618	(7.5)	46	(6.57)
Highest parental education						
ISCED2	470	(14.1)	571	(34.5)	101	(34.51)
ISCED3	500	(14.7)	563	(10.7)	63	(10.65)
ISCED5	535	(9.1)	594	(9.9)	59	(9.93)
ISCED6	551	(7.5)	606	(5.1)	54	(5.09)

Source: YITS cycle 5.5: Reading Skills Reassessment.
StatLink http://dx.doi.org/10.1787/888932577308

Table 6.1 **Development of reading skills by educational attainment and education-to-work pathways at ages 15 and 24, Canadian participants age 15 in 2000**

	Percentage of participants		Reading skills in 2000 (PISA-15)		Reading skills in 2009 (PISA-24)		Growth in reading skills between 2000 and 2009 (PISA-24 minus PISA-15)	
	%	Standard error	Mean score	Standard error	Mean score	Standard error	Score difference	Standard error
Attainment								
High school or lower	29.8	(2.2)	499	(11.5)	564	(8.2)	65	(7.2)
Post-secondary non-university	40.7	(2.5)	533	(7.4)	584	(5.9)	51	(6.4)
University	29.0	(2.0)	596	(6.8)	652	(5.8)	56	(8.0)
Pathway								
High school or lower (no gap[1])	29.1	(2.2)	498	(11.8)	563	(8.4)	65	(7.4)
High school or lower (gap)	0.9	(0.3)	527	(22.9)	600	(18.2)	73	(20.9)
Post-secondary non-university (gap)	6.2	(1.3)	552	(17.4)	593	(11.2)	40	(16.0)
Post-secondary non-university (no gap)	34.7	(2.6)	529	(8.2)	582	(6.6)	53	(6.9)
University (no gap)	14.8	(1.8)	590	(9.6)	654	(10.2)	64	(14.0)
Early university completion (before age 20)	13.2	(1.4)	601	(9.9)	648	(8.7)	47	(9.5)
University (gap)	1.2	(0.5)	604	(23.6)	663	(21.5)	60	(25.9)
Work experience								
High school or lower (no work experience)	13.2	(1.9)	488	(22.3)	551	(15.2)	63	(12.9)
High school or lower (work experience)	16.7	(1.7)	508	(9.7)	574	(8.6)	66	(8.7)
Post-secondary non-university (no work experience)	22.4	(2.1)	530	(11.0)	586	(7.8)	57	(8.6)
Post-secondary non-university (work experience)	18.5	(2.0)	536	(8.7)	581	(9.5)	45	(10.5)
University (no work experience)	25.2	(1.9)	598	(7.8)	653	(6.4)	56	(9.1)
University (work experience)	4.0	(0.8)	583	(16.6)	643	(13.1)	60	(15.9)

1. A gap refers to students who experienced at least one year during which they were not enrolled as full-time students, after which they returned to full-time studies before completing their education.
Source: YITS cycle 5.5: Reading Skills Reassessment.
StatLink http://dx.doi.org/10.1787/888932577308

Table 6.2 Development of reading skills by educational attainment and time spent in formal education, PISA-15 and PISA-24, Canadian participants age 15 in 2000

Total years spent in education until age 24	Growth in reading skills between 2000 and 2009	
	Score difference	Standard error
High school or lower		
1	41	(9.0)
2	63	(13.2)
3	68	(13.6)
4	73	(13.7)
5+	76	(24.2)
Post-secondary non-university		
1	33	(12.9)
2	38	(15.8)
3	51	(13.2)
4	54	(11.6)
5+	74	(12.6)
University		
1	32	(23.3)
2	55	(15.0)
3	45	(13.3)
4	60	(12.4)
5+	67	(21.6)

Source: YITS cycle 5.5: Reading Skills Reassessment.
StatLink http://dx.doi.org/10.1787/888932577308

Table 6.3 Skills growth regressions, joint model

Dependent variable = Growth in reading skills (difference in score PISA-24-PISA-15)

Independent variables	Model 1				Model 2				Model 3			
	Coefficient	Standard error	Standardised coefficient	Standard error	Coefficient	Standard error	Standardised coefficient	Standard error	Coefficient	Standard error	Standardised coefficient	Standard error
Years in post-secondary education by age 24	**7.1**	(3.2)	**0.1**	(0.05)	–	–	–	–	**6.7**	(3.2)	**0.1**	(0.05)
Post-secondary education completion by age 24	–	–	–	–	13.7	(7.4)	0.1	(0.04)	11.2	(7.2)	0.1	(0.04)
Performance PISA-15	**1.1**	(0.2)	**1.3**	(0.20)	**1.0**	(0.2)	**1.1**	(0.23)	**1.1**	(0.2)	**1.2**	(0.21)
Performance PISA-15 squared	0.0	(0.0)	-0.7	(0.18)	0.0	(0.0)	-0.6	(0.21)	0.0	(0.0)	-0.6	(0.19)
Family socio-economic background	**2.7**	(1.1)	**0.5**	(0.21)	**2.7**	(1.2)	**0.5**	(0.22)	**2.6**	(1.1)	**0.5**	(0.21)
Family socio-economic background squared	0.0	(0.0)	-0.4	(0.20)	0.0	(0.0)	-0.4	(0.21)	0.0	(0.0)	-0.4	(0.20)
Female	-1.0	(6.9)	0.0	(0.04)	-3.1	(7.3)	0.0	(0.04)	-3.1	(7.0)	0.0	(0.04)
Immigrant	10.1	(13.1)	0.0	(0.05)	12.0	(14.1)	0.0	(0.05)	8.6	(13.1)	0.0	(0.05)
Enjoyment of reading at age 15	1.9	(3.4)	0.0	(0.04)	2.5	(3.5)	0.0	(0.04)	2.0	(3.4)	0.0	(0.04)
(Constant)	66.3	(81.5)	–	–	110.5	(94.5)	–	–	79.2	(83.8)	–	–

Note: Post-secondary education here includes university and non-university. Family socio-economic background refers to the highest parental socio-economic status (HISEI). In bold, statistically significant values at 95% of confidence. "–" means the variable was not included in the model. Standardised coefficients refers to a model where all variables have been standardised to have a zero mean and standard deviation one in the sample.
Source: YITS cycle 5.5: Reading Skills Reassessment.
StatLink http://dx.doi.org/10.1787/888932577308

Table 6.4 Development of reading skills by rural/urban mobility status, PISA-15 and PISA-24, Canadian participants age 15 in 2000

	Percentage of participants		Reading skills in 2000 (PISA-15)		Reading skills in 2009 (PISA-24)		Growth in reading skills between 2000 and 2009 (PISA-24 minus PISA-15)	
	%	Standard error	Mean score	Standard error	Mean score	Standard error	Score difference	Standard error
Always urban	74.1	(2.8)	552	(3.6)	605	(4.0)	53	(3.1)
Always rural	14.2	(2.3)	518	(7.8)	586	(9.2)	68	(8.3)
Rural to urban	4.4	(1.6)	446	(57.6)	509	(24.0)	63	(33.0)
Urban to rural	7.3	(1.0)	534	(8.6)	598	(9.0)	64	(8.9)

Source: YITS cycle 5.5: Reading Skills Reassessment.
StatLink http://dx.doi.org/10.1787/888932577308

ANNEX B: TABLES OF RESULTS

Table 6.5 Development of reading skills by initial language proficiency and later living arrangements, PISA-15 and PISA-24, Canadian participants age 15 in 2000

	Percentage of participants %	Standard error	Reading skills in 2000 (PISA-15) Mean score	Standard error	Reading skills in 2009 (PISA-24) Mean score	Standard error	Growth in reading skills between 15 and 24 (PISA-24 minus PISA-15) Score difference	Standard error
INDEPENDENCE								
Living with parents								
School language marks: 0% to 69%	33	(11.5)	506	(7.4)	563	(10.6)	57	(8.9)
School language marks: 70% to 79%	32	(11.0)	543	(10.2)	605	(10.6)	61	(11.1)
School language marks: 80% to 100%	35	(11.3)	587	(9.5)	635	(9.8)	48	(10.4)
Independent								
School language marks: 0% to 69%	29	(11.0)	501	(13.8)	564	(9.4)	63	(15.5)
School language marks: 70% to 79%	34	(11.9)	548	(15.1)	603	(9.9)	55	(10.4)
School language marks: 80% to 100%	38	(11.3)	599	(6.8)	641	(9.0)	43	(7.7)
RELATIONSHIP STATUS								
Single								
School language marks: 0% to 69%	30	(9.1)	501	(9.0)	560	(9.2)	59	(11.2)
School language marks: 70% to 79%	32	(9.1)	553	(8.0)	609	(8.1)	56	(9.0)
School language marks: 80% to 100%	38	(9.4)	591	(6.6)	640	(7.8)	49	(7.4)
Other relationship								
School language marks: 0% to 69%	32	(16.5)	509	(15.4)	572	(10.4)	63	(15.3)
School language marks: 70% to 79%	36	(16.1)	527	(22.9)	592	(12.8)	64	(15.2)
School language marks: 80% to 100%	32	(12.6)	599	(11.4)	633	(10.6)	35	(11.0)

Source: YITS cycle 5.5: Reading Skills Reassessment.
StatLink http://dx.doi.org/10.1787/888932577308

Table 6.6 Development of reading skills by living arrangements and educational attainment, PISA-15 and PISA-24, Canadian participants age 15 in 2000

	Percentage of participants %	Standard error	Reading skills in 2000 (PISA-15) Mean score	Standard error	Reading skills in 2009 (PISA-24) Mean score	Standard error	Growth in reading skills between 15 and 24 (PISA-24 minus PISA-15) Score difference	Standard error
INDEPENDENCE								
Living with parents								
High school or lower	33	(11.5)	482	(19.3)	545	(12.6)	63	(12.0)
Post-secondary non-university	32	(11.0)	528	(7.4)	580	(9.3)	53	(8.4)
University	35	(11.3)	587	(9.4)	650	(7.6)	63	(11.4)
Independent								
High school or lower	29	(11.0)	516	(10.9)	583	(8.3)	67	(8.7)
Post-secondary non-university	34	(11.9)	537	(11.2)	587	(8.4)	50	(9.9)
University	38	(11.3)	610	(9.1)	655	(9.1)	45	(9.6)
RELATIONSHIP STATUS								
Single								
High school or lower	29	(8.5)	496	(15.0)	558	(10.3)	61	(9.6)
Post-secondary non-university	37	(9.7)	533	(6.7)	585	(7.6)	51	(7.8)
University	34	(8.5)	592	(7.4)	651	(6.3)	59	(8.5)
Other relationship								
High school or lower	32	(12.7)	506	(14.5)	580	(9.9)	74	(10.7)
Post-secondary non-university	52	(14.6)	531	(15.8)	582	(9.3)	51	(11.8)
University	16	(8.6)	615	(15.7)	658	(12.5)	43	(16.2)

Source: YITS cycle 5.5: Reading Skills Reassessment.
StatLink http://dx.doi.org/10.1787/888932577308

ORGANISATION FOR ECONOMIC CO-OPERATION AND DEVELOPMENT

The OECD is a unique forum where governments work together to address the economic, social and environmental challenges of globalisation. The OECD is also at the forefront of efforts to understand and to help governments respond to new developments and concerns, such as corporate governance, the information economy and the challenges of an ageing population. The Organisation provides a setting where governments can compare policy experiences, seek answers to common problems, identify good practice and work to co-ordinate domestic and international policies.

The OECD member countries are: Australia, Austria, Belgium, Canada, Chile, the Czech Republic, Denmark, Estonia, Finland, France, Germany, Greece, Hungary, Iceland, Ireland, Israel, Italy, Japan, Korea, Luxembourg, Mexico, the Netherlands, New Zealand, Norway, Poland, Portugal, the Slovak Republic, Slovenia, Spain, Sweden, Switzerland, Turkey, the United Kingdom and the United States. The European Commission takes part in the work of the OECD.

OECD Publishing disseminates widely the results of the Organisation's statistics gathering and research on economic, social and environmental issues, as well as the conventions, guidelines and standards agreed by its members.